More Praise for
Discovering the Soul of Service

"Another Len Berry classic that every service company executive should read. This book definitely will be on the reading list for the Chapters team."

> —Lawrence N. Stevenson, President and Chief Executive Officer, Chapters, Inc.

"Len Berry gets it. Customers count. Insightful lessons from a real student of business."

> —L. Daniel Jorndt, Chief Executive Officer, Walgreen Company

"A road map for overcoming the maladies of complacency, overconfidence, and arrogance that often accompany success. In addition, it's a great read."

> —James L. Heskett, UPS Foundation Professor of Business Administration Emeritus, Harvard Business School

"This well-written book demonstrates Berry's passion for service excellence. I've closely followed his pioneering work, and this is his best book!"

> —Stephen W. Brown, Edward M. Carson Chair in Services Marketing, Arizona State University

"Demonstrates compellingly that the nine drivers of excellence can be implemented across a wide variety of businesses."

> —Philip S. Orsino, President and Chief Executive Officer, Premdor, Inc.

"A refreshing and insightful view of service, particularly the emphasis on humane values and their vital importance to achieving excellence in service companies."

> —Denise Ilitch, Vice Chairwoman, Little Caesar Enterprises, Inc.

OTHER BOOKS BY LEONARD L. BERRY

ON GREAT SERVICE:
A FRAMEWORK FOR ACTION

MARKETING SERVICES:
COMPETING THROUGH QUALITY

DELIVERING QUALITY SERVICE:
BALANCING CUSTOMER PERCEPTIONS AND EXPECTATIONS

SERVICE QUALITY:
A PROFIT STRATEGY FOR FINANCIAL INSTITUTIONS

BANKERS WHO SELL:
IMPROVING SELLING EFFECTIVENESS IN BANKING

MARKETING FINANCIAL SERVICES:
A STRATEGIC VISION

BANKING TOMORROW:
MANAGING MARKETS THROUGH PLANNING

MARKETING FOR BANKERS

Discovering the
Soul of Service

THE NINE DRIVERS OF
SUSTAINABLE BUSINESS SUCCESS

LEONARD L. BERRY

THE FREE PRESS

fP

THE FREE PRESS
A Division of Simon & Schuster Inc.
1230 Avenue of the Americas
New York, NY 10020

Designed by Carla Bolte

Manufactured in the United States of America

20 19 18 17 16 15 14 13 12 11

Library of Congress Cataloging-in-Publication Data

Berry, Leonard L., 1942–
    Discovering the soul of service : the nine drivers of
sustainable business success / Leonard L. Berry.
        p. cm.
    Includes bibliographical references and index.
    1. Customer services—Management.   2. Customer services
—Management—Case studies. 3. Service industries. I. Title.
HF5415.5.B478   1999
658.8'12—dc21   98-37393
                                                                    CIP

ISBN 0–684–84511–3

This book is dedicated with love to my wife, Nancy;

to my sons, Matthew and Jonathan;

to my mother, Mae Berry;

and to the memory of my father, Abe Berry.

CONTENTS

ACKNOWLEDGMENTS

Researching and writing this book has been an inspiring journey. I am a career-long student of services management and marketing, and this book afforded me the opportunity to closely study 14 of the best service companies in the world. Visiting and conducting interviews at these companies, gathering and studying considerable background material, observing and using their services whenever possible, developing a conceptual framework for the book from the field research, and weaving together lessons from the companies with secondary research and my own base of knowledge was a powerful experience. I've learned more from this project than any other in a 30-year professional career, and today I feel blessed by the opportunity and grateful to the many people who have helped me.

Only time will tell whether this book makes the difference in the practice of management that I hope it will make. I am certain, however, that it is my best work, and this is an immensely satisfying feeling.

I am eternally grateful to the leaders of the 14 companies featured in this book for their cooperation, their assistance, and, most of all, their trust. These companies allowed me to speak with whom I wanted to speak, to see what I wanted to see, to go where I wanted to go. They cooperated with numerous follow-up requests for information and additional interviews after the field research. They not only allowed me inside their doors, they allowed me inside their cultures.

I am indebted to the more than 250 individuals listed in the appendix who participated in interviews and candidly shared their ideas and experiences. The pages that follow are filled with their stories and quotes. At each company, a few people went to great lengths to support my research, and I acknowledge them here:

- Dick Bergstrom, John Bergstrom, and Steve Tyink—Bergstrom Corporation
- David Pottruck, Mark Thompson, and Nancy Mitchell—The Charles Schwab Corporation
- Dan Cathy, Steve Robinson, and Linda McEntire—Chick-fil-A
- Garrett Boone, Kip Tindell, Sharon Tindell, Barbara Anderson, Nancy Donley, and Melissa Reiff—The Container Store
- Judy Corson and Jeff Pope—Custom Research Inc.
- Ed Shultz and Bruce Mullkoff—Dana Commercial Credit
- Napoleon Barragan and Jennifer Grassano—Dial-A-Mattress
- Andy Taylor, Dick Janicki, Joanne Peratis-Weber, and Christy Conrad—Enterprise Rent-A-Car
- Tim Hoeksema, Tamara McClelland, and Brenda Skelton— Midwest Express Airlines
- Bix Norman and Gary Van Spronsen—Miller SQA
- Sven-Olof Lindblad, Margaret Hart, and Tom O'Brien—Special Expeditions
- Mike Veeck and Jody Beaulieu—St. Paul Saints
- Bob Ukrop and Bob Kelley—Ukrop's Super Markets, Inc.
- Bill Cooney, Paul Ringenbach, and John Walmsley—USAA

It really is quite amazing how much effort goes into producing a product as small as a book. To create this product, I was ably assisted by members of the book team:

- Sandi Scamardo, a marketing doctoral student at Texas A&M University, who has participated in every phase of the project, including assisting with the field and secondary research and preparing exhibits and tables. Sandi has added interview note-taking wizardry, a keen eye for detail, library research acumen, and mastery of Adobe Illustrator software to the efforts of the team.
- Shirley Bovey, communications coordinator at the Center for Retailing Studies, who moonlighted to provide skillful, sensitive editorial assistance. This is my third book on which Shirley has assisted.
- Glenda Bessler, my administrative assistant of more than 12 years

whose wonderfully active life will calm just a bit with the book's completion. Glenda helped immeasurably in arranging the company visits, typing the manuscript, and chasing down details. This is the fifth book Glenda has helped me prepare for publication.

- A. "Parsu" Parasuraman, a chaired marketing professor at The University of Miami and my best friend, closest professional colleague, and research collaborator of many years, who read drafts of each chapter and provided many helpful suggestions.
- Kathleen Seiders, an assistant professor of marketing at Babson College, my former doctoral student, and a very close friend, who also read chapter drafts and provided constructive comments.
- Robert Wallace, senior editor at The Free Press, who is a strong supporter of my work and a sage advisor. With a long record of publishing achievement, Bob Wallace is known as one of the best business book editors in America. This is my fourth book under his watchful eye.

I also wish to thank my colleagues at the Center for Retailing Studies for their support and encouragement: Lucy Morgan, Cindy Billington, Holly Clark, Shirley Bovey, and Dave Szymanski. P. Varadarajan, the head of the marketing department at Texas A&M, is a wonderful friend and colleague who did everything possible to protect my time so I could complete the book on schedule. Dino Battista, vice president, director of professional and academic marketing at Simon & Schuster, is a creative marketing force and an author's friend. I appreciate his efforts on my behalf as I do the assistance of other talented Free Press executives and professional staff, including Paula Duffy, Suzanne Donahue, Jaime Ariza, Maria Arteta, Maureen Kelly, Paul O'Halloran, Caryn-Amy King, Iris Cohen, Edith Lewis, and Tom Stvan. Special thanks go also to freelance copyeditor Linnea Johnson, who worked on my prior two books and whom I specifically requested for this book.

Finally, I thank my wife, Nancy, and my sons, Matthew and Jonathan, for their love and their unwavering support of my quest to write the best book I am capable of writing.

Today marks approximately one and a half years since I first proposed this book to Bob Wallace. I had been thinking about a book on services success but was unsure that I wanted to embark on still another arduous two-year project followed by a year of post-publication marketing activity. I was inspired to write the book after reading an article by Peter Drucker in which he describes seven influential personal experiences in his life. One is hearing the opera *Falstaff*, the last opera written by the nineteenth-century Italian composer, Giuseppe Verdi. Drucker describes how he was overwhelmed by the experience. He later learned that Verdi wrote this opera when he was 80. To Drucker, Verdi's undertaking of such a demanding project at that age was incredible. Drucker then read Verdi's explanation of why he did it: "All my life as a musician, I have striven for perfection. It has always eluded me. I surely had an obligation to make one more try." Drucker resolved that Verdi's words would be his lodestar.

Drucker's story about Verdi had a tremendous impact on me. I picked up the phone to call my editor. I, too, wanted to keep trying to get it right.

Leonard L. Berry
College Station, Texas
July 8, 1998

AUTHOR'S NOTE

A number of individuals provided original material for this book by participating in interviews. Individuals who are quoted without an accompanying citation provided material expressly for use in this book.

1

SUSTAINING SUCCESS IN SERVICE COMPANIES

A customer, recovering from knee surgery and walking with a cane, was Christmas shopping. When the customer asked for an item in most stores, the salesperson would point and say disinterestedly, "Over there." However, the customer's experience was different at The Container Store. After determining the product the customer wanted, the salesperson replied, "It's in the back of the store. I'll go get it for you." Before the salesperson returned, two other salespeople cheerfully asked the customer if they could be of service.

Another customer of The Container Store completed her purchase of multiple items and headed for her car, children in tow. She placed her package on the ground as she put the children in the car—and then drove off forgetting the package. Realizing her mistake just a few minutes later, she returned to the parking lot, but the package was gone. She reentered the store hoping that someone had turned in her package, but no one had. Salesperson James Castleberry remembered the customer and asked her what she had bought. He then proceeded to gather up the products, handed them to the customer without charge, and said: "Your day will get better." And it did, starting at that moment.

Amy Carovillano, vice president of inventory control and distribution at The Container Store, was at the airport waiting for her flight to

Houston. She noticed a woman animatedly talking to the airline's gate agents. Considerable head shaking suggested that the woman was not receiving the response she was seeking. She was obviously displeased when she left the counter.

She began looking around as if she were searching for someone. More than 100 people were in the area at the time. Then the woman headed for Amy, passing at least 50 people closer to her. She asked Amy if she were flying to Houston. When Amy replied yes, she asked for a favor. The woman's husband had flown to Houston on an earlier flight but was stranded at the airport's rental car counter. He had left his wallet home and could not rent a car without his driver's license. The woman had come to the airport hoping that one of the airline's crew would carry the wallet to Houston on the next flight. No one was willing to do so, which brought the woman to Amy.

Amy was glad to help but did have one question: Why did the woman single her out? The woman said it was because Amy was wearing a Container Store tee-shirt. She assumed Amy was an employee. The woman added that she was a loyal customer and knew how nice and willing to help all the employees were. Amy met the woman's husband when she deplaned in Houston and handed him his wallet.

The Container Store is one of America's most successful retail chains because it has employees who delight in helping customers solve problems—and who possess the freedom and confidence to do so. The Container Store sells storage and organization products—boxes, bottles, jars, trunks, trays, racks, baskets, buckets, hooks, shelving systems, hangers, garment bags, drawer organizers, and much more—about 12,000 different products. The company is the largest retailer of elfa® storage systems and Skandia shelving systems in the United States, even though, by design, it is not a large chain with only 19 stores at year-end 1997. From its founding in 1978 with two employees, the company has achieved average annual sales growth of 25 percent without incurring debt. Two-thirds of the revenue growth comes from existing stores, one-third from the one or two new stores opened each year. The company's owners, Garrett Boone, Kip Tindell, Sharon Tindell, and John Mullen, all actively involved in running the company today, continually say "no" to suitors wanting to fund rapid expansion through venture capital, franchising, or a public offering. Becoming big was never the dream; creating the perfect retail store in which employees would earnestly, enthusiastically, and creatively work together to serve customers and improve operations and products was always the dream. As Garrett Boone states: "We are a company that understands our business is helping customers. We have a willingness to continually reexamine what we do and ask if we can do it better."

The Container Store has been notably successful in attracting exceptional employees who share the strong customer-focused values of the owners. More than 1,500 employees strong now, The Container Store's values-driven execution of the business is difficult for imitators to match. The company patiently practices its craft of selling excellent boxes excellently. It waits until it finds just the right employee, just the right store location, just the right vendor. Elizabeth Barrett, vice president of operations, admits: "I still have the reputation for holding a store position open for six weeks to look for the right person."

The quest for excellence pays off in human terms as well as financial terms. Employees love working in this company that celebrates excellence, and customers love the experience of shopping in the stores. Once a minister announced from his pulpit that for his birthday his family was taking him to The Container Store. The whole congregation applauded. Messages from a departing part-time employee, a ninth-grade student, and a frantic customer reflect the human dividends contributed by corporate excellence.

Dear Kip:

I am a part-time employee working in the Virginia store. I work full-time for CNN.

When I was hired last June, I wanted to gain knowledge about opening a business. What I learned was more important. I learned customer service. Our extensive training was exceptional. The people sent to train us were incredible. Jane Dunnington is one of the best managers I have worked under in my career! She disseminates information and is fair. Chris Hix and Lori Stuardi have gone out of their way to keep me informed and enthused.

I enjoy the "team atmosphere" at the store and will miss it very much. Other projects in television are demanding more of my time. I am forced to resign my part-time position.

I leave with a more demanding attitude about customer service, a better organizer of closets, a contributor to a million dollar sales month, feeling valued and appreciated. If I didn't love television so much I would be tempted to come aboard full-time.

Thank you for creating a positive environment, and I hope to contribute that attitude wherever I go.

Dear Container Store,

In late April I came to your store to purchase some packaging materials. I needed these materials to ship my ninth-grade science project to Tucson, Arizona, where I would be attending the International Science and Engineering Fair in early May. I had been searching in many places for these materials, and finally found them at The Container Store, thanks to an employee named Amy Robertson. As soon as I walked into the store, she found the materials that I needed to pack my oversize project. Amy not only found the materials but spent an additional two hours and helped me pack the project in the store. She brought out tape, scissors, and screwdrivers and finished within hours what would have taken me days. The project arrived in Tucson in beautiful condition. At the Science Fair, I was awarded third place in the world in the category of microbiology. I would like to sincerely thank Amy Robertson and all of The Container Store employees who helped me on Thursday, April 25. My gratitude cannot be expressed.

Dear Container Store,

I am writing to praise Chris Grey, one of your employees. On September 11, 1996, I spent 40 minutes with her on the phone as she "coached me and encouraged me" as I put the metro system together. The following day I came to the store to thank her in person. I was in the middle of a move and frantic. She helped me tremendously. When I met her I cried, I was so grateful to her.

I hope this letter will go into her employee file.

STUDYING SUSTAINABLE SUCCESS

The Container Store is a mature, service-intensive company that continues to improve its operations; its financial performance is stellar, its human dividends rich. Growth has not dulled its enthusiasm, success has not moderated its work ethic, praise has not slowed its efforts to improve. This company, and 13 other service companies I studied for this book, model *sustainable success*. The companies in my study range from local to worldwide operations. Although operating different businesses, they create value for customers through labor-intensive service operations. All are highly successful by any measure. The average age of these companies as of 1999 is 31 years.

My purpose in this book is to identify, describe, and illustrate the underlying drivers of sustainable success in service businesses. Creating a successful service operation is unquestionably a difficult task. However, sustaining success can be even more difficult. Services are performances, and the challenge of sustaining the performers' energy, commitment, skills, and knowledge day after day, week after week, month after month, year after year—especially as the organization grows and becomes more complex—is daunting. The greater the involvement of people in creating value for customers, the greater the challenge. This is a book on the lessons 14 outstanding service companies teach about sustainable success. And the lessons they teach are clear indeed. Although the sample companies differ on the *outside*—the nature, size, and structure of their businesses—to a remarkable degree they are the same on the *inside*, sharing the drivers of their ongoing success.

The companies selected for the sample met several tests. The primary consideration was the achievement of sustained customer acceptance and financial success. I also sought a balanced sample—companies in different businesses and of varying sizes. Firms representing fresh case studies for readers also was an important criterion.

Selecting companies with a high labor component in their services was purposeful. Labor-intensive service companies should provide the best test of a services success sustainability model. If a model could fit companies that were absolutely dependent upon the actions, creativ-

TABLE 1–1
Profile of Sample Companies

Company	Headquarters	Principal Business	Revenue ($ millions)[a]	Scope of Operations	Number of Employees	Ownership	Years in Business[b]	Profitable Years in Business[b]
Bergstrom Hotels	Appleton, WI	Hotels	25	Regional	840	Private	21	21
The Charles Schwab Corporation	San Francisco, CA	Securities Brokerage and Other Financial Services	2,299	International	12,000	Public	26	26
Chick-fil-A, Inc.	Atlanta, GA	Quick Service Restaurants	672	International	40,000 300 at HQ	Private	52	52
The Container Store	Dallas, TX	Specialty Retailer	150	National	1,500	Private	19	19
Custom Research Inc.	Minneapolis, MN	Marketing Research	26	National	120	Private	23	23
Dana Commercial Credit	Toledo, OH	Leasing	2,000 (in assets)	International	750	Public	18	18
Dial-A-Mattress	Long Island City, NY	Bedding Retailer	70	National	250	Private	21	21
Enterprise Rent-A-Car	St. Louis, MO	Car Rental	3,680	International	35,000	Private	40	40
Midwest Express Airlines	Oak Creek, WI	Airline	345	National	2,300	Public	13	11
Miller SQA	Holland, MI	Office Furniture Manufacturer	198	National	720	Public	15	14
Special Expeditions	New York, NY	Expedition Travel	52	International	167	Private	18	16
St. Paul Saints	St. Paul, MN	Professional Baseball Team	5	Local	10	Private	5	5
Ukrop's Super Markets, Inc.	Richmond, VA	Food Retailer	Not Available	Local	5,500	Private	60	60
USAA	San Antonio, TX	Insurance and Financial Services	7,454	International	18,500	Private	76	76

[a]All data as of year-end 1997.
[b]Several sample companies have undergone name or ownership changes in their history. The Years in Business column reflects the year in which the original company started.

ity, and commitment of service providers to survive, then it would fit to some extent all companies. All companies after all are service companies to the degree that they create customer value through performances.

I visited each sample company, interviewing senior and middle managers and frontline service providers. I also followed up with numerous telephone interviews. In all, I interviewed more than 250 people from the 14 companies. In addition, I observed and directly experienced service delivery at the sample firms, collected a small mountain of documentation from them, and conducted secondary research on service management. My career-long specialization in services marketing and management provides a vital backdrop for this research, the most ambitious project I have undertaken.

The sample companies readers will meet in this book are profiled in Table 1–1. In addition to The Container Store, they are:

➤ *Bergstrom Hotels*, a group of three full-service hotels in northeastern Wisconsin: The Paper Valley Hotel, The Pioneer Inn, and The Valley Inn.* The hotels have built strong relationships with employees, customers, and their communities through attention to detail, caring, and a big corporate heart. The company was awarded the 1996 Wisconsin Service Business of the Year Grand Award.

➤ *The Charles Schwab Corporation*, a securities brokerage and investment company that passionately and innovatively champions the investors' cause. Schwab's energy for continuous improvement, technological leadership, and profitable growth is remarkable.

➤ *Chick-fil-A*, one of the world's best quick-service restaurant chains with an unwavering commitment to excellent food, respectful customer service, store operator success, and teamwork. At Chick-fil-A, there is a free lunch—in the employee cafeteria at the home office in Atlanta.

➤ *Custom Research Inc.*, a highly progressive marketing research com-

---

*The three hotels were sold by Bergstrom Corporation to Montclair Hotel Investors in January 1998. Because Bergstrom Hotels owned and operated the properties when the research was conducted, its name appears here and elsewhere as appropriate. Reasons for the sale are discussed in Chapter 3.

pany that has built a strong business with *Fortune* 500 clients through team service delivery, innovative practices, competence, and an emphasis on continuous improvement. Custom Research won the 1996 Malcolm Baldrige National Quality Award.

➤ *Dana Commercial Credit*, an indirect wholly owned subsidiary of Dana Corporation providing lease financing services with integrity, quality, and creativity. Notable for investing in its people's success, Dana Commercial Credit won the 1996 Malcolm Baldrige National Quality Award. The company also won the 1995 Michigan Quality Leadership Award.

➤ *Dial-A-Mattress*, a company that sells bedding over the telephone 24 hours a day, seven days a week, and delivers orders as soon as customers want them—within two hours if desired. For years it was nearly impossible to live in New York City and be unfamiliar with the company's advertising theme: "Dial 1-800-MATTRES and leave the last 's' off for savings." The company's founder, president and CEO Napoleon Barragan, probably is the nation's most passionate believer in the marketing power of toll-free 1-800 numbers.

➤ *Enterprise Rent-A-Car*, the fastest-growing rental car company in America, which attracts talented, entrepreneurial-minded people to the organization and allows them to run their businesses. In recent years, Enterprise has been hiring more college graduates than any other company in America.

➤ *Midwest Express Airlines*, a jewel of an airline that began service in 1984 as part of Kimberly-Clark Corporation. Now an independent, public company, Midwest Express takes great pride in offering "the best care in the air." In Zagat's 1997 survey of 60 of the world's largest airlines on comfort, service, timeliness, and food, Midwest Express ranked first in the United States and was the only U.S. airline to place in the world's top 10.

➤ *Miller SQA*, a highly successful division of Herman Miller that is reinventing office furniture manufacturing and marketing by focusing on the process rather than the product. Miller SQA lives the initials in its name—"simple, quick, and affordable."

➤ *Special Expeditions,* an environmentally conscious travel company that uses small ships and Zodiac landing craft to expose travelers to dramatic geology, wildlife, and native culture in remote places in the world. Travelers are active participants in an expedition led by a staff of naturalists. The company was rated among the top 10 cruise lines in the world in the 1996 Condé Nast Traveler Reader's Choice Awards.

➤ *St. Paul Saints,* a minor-league baseball team in St. Paul, Minnesota, that sells out every home game and has a season-ticket waiting list of more than 1,000 people. Operating on the principle that "fun is good," the Saints offer a strong entertainment value for families and have earned the affection and loyalty of the entire community.

➤ *Ukrop's Super Markets,* a family-owned chain in Richmond, Virginia, that in 1997 held an astonishing 37.6 percent[1] share of the local grocery market. A leader in ready-to-eat meals, a pioneer in relationship marketing, a generous and active corporate citizen, Ukrop's has forged an unshakable bond of trust with its customers, associates, and community.

➤ *USAA,* headquartered in San Antonio, Texas, a worldwide insurance and diversified financial services association that primarily serves members of the U.S. military and their families through toll-free telephone calls, fax, and mail. Aggressive investment in technology, customer feedback systems, employee training, and the quality of work life contribute to superlative service and an insurance customer retention figure of about 97 percent. USAA was included in the book *The 100 Best Companies to Work for in America.*[2]

These 14 sample companies provide the book's foundation. Their lessons not only teach but also stretch us to imagine, to ask "what if" questions about our own companies; they inspire. Lessons from the sample firms are infused into every chapter, and readers will be intimately acquainted with all 14 companies upon completion of the book. These truly are great service companies, companies that demonstrate the grand possibilities accompanying leadership with heart, companies that show the way to sustainable success.

THREE CHALLENGES IN SUSTAINING SERVICE SUCCESS

Three specific challenges in sustaining success are accentuated in enterprises that create value for customers primarily through services. The more labor-intensive the services, the greater the challenges of:

- operating effectively while growing rapidly
- operating effectively when competing on price
- retaining the initial entrepreneurial spirit of the younger, smaller company

Execution Versus Growth

Balancing the need for growth with the requirements for execution is one of the most difficult challenges managers face. In the early 1990s, computer marketer CompUSA was the fastest-growing retail company in America. However, by 1994 the company's survival was threatened as a result of weak financial controls, undisciplined merchandising practices, and poor in-store operations. Rapid growth had outstripped the small-company infrastructure and systems in place at the time. The chief executive was ousted and the new CEO, Jim Halpin, halted the expansion. Most senior managers were replaced. The company centralized merchandising, revamped store operating practices, and strengthened the balance sheet. Only then did it cautiously ramp up new store expansion. CompUSA has become a strong performer under Halpin, and the lesson of out-of-control growth still reverberates in the company's boardroom to this day.

During periods of rapid growth, adhering to original operating standards becomes problematic. Relaxing standards is common when fast-growing companies select, orient, train, and educate many new managers and employees. Maintaining effective internal company communications, reinforcing the company's vision and culture, and delivering consistently high quality service—essential success factors—are challenged by expansion. Not allowing the pressures of growth to undermine the effectiveness of labor-intensive value creation requires a higher level of leadership and discipline than exists in many companies.

No matter how brilliant a company's strategy, it still must be executed. Otherwise, the strategy is simply being advertised for competitors to imitate, execute better, and win away the market. Service companies create value through performances. "Product quality" is a function of performance quality, which, in turn, is a function of the ability and motivation of the performers. Performance suffers when growth weakens organizational practices that promote employee ability and motivation.

ValuJet was a fast-growing, profitable—yet deeply troubled—airline well before its tragic May 11, 1996 crash of Flight 592 in the Florida Everglades that killed 110 people. Yes, it was a moneymaker, but its profits came to a sudden halt on the day of the accident. Lax controls, the outsourcing of all maintenance and training, and a weak culture undermined by a lack of attention to nonfinancial goals paved the way for ValuJet's undoing. Six days after the crash, ValuJet cut its daily schedule of 320 flights by about half in an attempt to maintain reliable operations during an FAA evaluation. The airline was forced to refund more than $4 million to passengers who were reluctant to fly ValuJet or whose flights were canceled. On June 17, 1996, ValuJet became the largest airline ever to be grounded by the FAA. The company resumed flights three months later but was unable to regain profitability. The negative brand equity associated with ValuJet became a liability that could not be overcome. In 1997, ValuJet assumed the name of an acquisition and renamed itself Air Tran Airlines.

Service companies sell a promise. Passengers who board an airliner have no technical basis for judging the competence of the crew or the airworthiness of the airplane. All they can do is trust, and their willingness to do so is a function of their prior experiences and the company's reputation. The customer's confidence is the most precious asset for any company that sells promises for a living. Superb execution of the service day after day after day is a cornerstone of confidence building. Strengthening the customers' confidence isn't about making promises but about keeping them. When a service company loses its customers' confidence, it loses everything. This is what happened to ValuJet. ValuJet made $20.7 million in profits in 1994—its first full year of operations. Southwest Airlines earned as much only after its first eight years. Yet Southwest Airlines became America's most consistently profitable airline with a strong reputation for value, reliability, safety, and fun; ValuJet had to change its name to, in effect, disguise who it is and to begin building a new reputation.

Execution Versus Price

The lack of physical differentiation among competing services encourages managers to overuse price as a marketing tool. Whereas the fit and feel of a pair of trousers or the styling of an automobile can give customers nonprice reasons for favoring one brand over another, services managers often are limited to nonphysical means of differentiation. They frequently choose price cutting, which may lead to cost cutting and may weaken execution. Although managers could strive to differentiate their services with higher quality rather than lower price, price cutting is a favored path because it can be implemented quickly and may be deemed more salient with targeted markets.

One of the biggest mistakes managers make is assuming that value and price mean the same thing to customers. They do not. Price is part of value but not its equivalent. To customers, value is the benefits received for the burdens experienced; it is what customers receive in exchange for what they must endure to receive it. Burdens have both a monetary component (price) and a nonmonetary component (for example, unknowledgeable service providers, inconvenient service locations or hours of operation, busy telephone lines).

Price is price; value is the total experience. Companies that sacrifice the customers' satisfactory experience for lower costs to support lower prices may decrease rather than increase customer value. Preparing for deregulation and expected price competition, local telephone service providers began eliminating thousands of workers from their payrolls in the mid-1990s. The layoffs occurred as demand for services escalated because customers were requesting additional telephone and fax lines. More demand combined with less capacity undermined adequate service delivery, resulting in rising consumer complaints and regulator activism. In 1996, for example, New York's Public Service Commission ordered NYNEX to rebate $50 million to five million consumers because of slow repair and installation services; Wisconsin's Public Service Commission filed a civil suit against Ameritech for slow, unreliable service; and Idaho levied fines on US West for taking too long to fix telephone outages.[3] By equating price and value, decision makers in these companies took the wrong path.

Preparing for intensified competition requires strengthening execution, not weakening it. The tougher the price competition in a market, the more important quality of service is to sustainable success. Why? Because without differentiated quality, without a superior total experience to offer customers, a company has few, if any, nonpricing options when key competitors cut their prices.

Entrepreneurship Versus Maturity

Maintaining an entrepreneurial culture that celebrates continuous improvement and discovery is challenged by organizational maturity and growth. Innovative entrepreneurship comes from conditions more typical of newer, smaller organizations than mature, larger ones: the dream of building a great business and the fear of failure.

Inspired service providers are most likely to invest the personal energy and endure the risks of improvement seeking. They are most likely to identify better ways to perform their service and to speak up when they see their company going in a wrong direction. Yet, inspiration is jeopardized as the business grows and adds employees, locations, and more formalized operating policies and systems. Rules replace the informality that nurtures personal interaction throughout the organization. Turfism replaces teamwork. Memos replace face-to-face communications. Supervisory layers replace impromptu visits with the owner. The power of the dream, the sense of mission, can easily fade as a company not only becomes more successful but also bigger, more complex, spread-out, and bureaucratic.

Most service positions involve significant discretionary effort, which is the difference between the maximum amount of energy an individual employee can bring to the service role and the minimum necessary to avoid penalty. The difference between the maximum and minimum energy investment is discretionary to the individual employee. Personal entrepreneurship is a discretionary act; the individual service provider decides whether to try something new, whether to risk helping a customer with an unusual or difficult request, whether to assume the mantle of leadership in solving a company problem. One of the principal differences between outstanding and mediocre service companies is that the former receive far more discretionary effort from employees. Personal entrepreneurship—a discretionary act—is jeopardized as firms grow, age, become more complex, and change leadership. And yet sustained success requires continual innovation and improvement.

Holiday Inn was a feisty, innovative company in its youth. Founder Kemmons Wilson envisioned creating a chain of clean, comfortable, consistent, and economical way stations for families traveling by automobile. In the 1960s, Holiday Inn emerged as the undisputed winner in the U.S. hospitality market. By the 1980s, however, the chain's fortunes and reputation had begun to decline. The market was changing—more segmented hotel concepts, more price discounting, more business travelers supplanting families as the primary customer—and Holiday Inn was losing its leadership position. Strategic innovation in the company was centered more on new concepts such as launching Embassy Suites and entering into the gaming industry than on the core Holiday Inn business.

Holiday Inn was built on consistency of presentation but was allowed to become inconsistent with a highly variable mix of properties operating under the brand name. Many Holiday Inn properties became tired and worn. The negative images evoked by the brand became sufficiently strong and so widespread that management removed the Holiday Inn name from the company's more upscale Crowne Plaza properties. By 1997, with the company belatedly but vigorously replacing or renovating older, run-down Holiday Inn properties, the company found it necessary to air television advertising portraying hotel housekeepers with chainsaws destroying a sleeping room and then completely refurbishing it. In effect, Holiday Inn was admitting that many of its hotels were worn out—and was asking for a chance to restore the confidence of travelers. A famous brand name became tarnished because the service it represented lost its currency. In its evolution as a company, the founder's vision and entrepreneurial spirit faded away. An innovative company ceased to be very innovative. It happens in many companies.

Execution versus growth. Execution versus price. Entrepreneurship versus maturity. These perils may simultaneously contribute to a company's decline. Companies frequently become less effective strategically *and* executionally because strategy affects execution and vice versa and because both are a function of the quality of leadership in the company. A weak strategy drains the commitment of the service providers who are supposed to implement it. It is difficult for employees to be excited about a strategy that doesn't excite customers. Conversely, poor execution undercuts even the most brilliant strategy. Customers cannot receive the full benefits of a company's service strategy if the performers do not perform it well. Eventually, the strategy loses its luster because it is not producing the expected results.

SUSTAINING SUCCESS IN SERVICES

Sustaining the skilled actions, personal innovation, and emotional commitment of people in service businesses as time passes and the organizations change is a tall order. The quality of machine-produced products is far less dependent on the actions, creativity, and commitment of individual employees—perhaps hundreds or thousands of them—than the quality of people-produced products. In services performed directly for customers, such as in retailing, education, health care, and transportation, the service is inseparable from the people performing it. An inept salesperson is an inept store; a nurse's personality may send patients in search of a new doctor.

In 1983, Royal Dutch Shell commissioned a study on corporate longevity. The purpose of the research was to identify the success drivers of firms older than Shell, which was then 100 years old. The study focused on 27 companies in North America, Europe, and Japan that ranged in age from 100 to 700 years. The findings from the research, discussed in a 1997 book, *The Living Company*, are fascinating.[4] The book's author, Arie de Geus, makes a strong point when he argues that most companies are underachievers and do not come close to realizing their full potential. In an article on his findings, de Geus writes:

The high corporate mortality rate seems unnatural. No living species suffers from such a discrepancy between its maximum life expectancy and the average span it realizes. And few other types of institutions— churches, armies, or universities—have the abysmal record of the corporation.

Why do so many companies die young? Mounting evidence suggests that corporations fail because their policies and practices are based too heavily on the thinking and the language of economics. Put another way, companies die because their managers focus exclusively on producing goods and services and forget that the organization is a community of human beings that is in business—any business—to stay alive. Managers concern themselves with land, labor, and capital, and overlook the fact that *labor* means real people.[5]

Companies need not die young. I was inspired to research and write this book to learn, distill, and share the success sustainability lessons of great service companies. Despite the perils posed by time, growth, and success, some service companies keep getting better. How do the Charles Schwabs, Enterprise Rent-A-Cars, and Chick-fil-A's do it? I anticipated that these long-time achieving companies would share certain traits in common but also would differ in certain respects, if only because the particulars of their businesses were different. I sought to identify and understand the underlying success sustainers in service businesses that transcended the particulars of any one type of business. What came from intensive study of truly outstanding service companies is the most exciting discovery of my research career to date: *the drivers of sustainable success in labor-intensive service businesses are common across the different businesses*. The portraits of success sustainability for 14 distinct companies ranging from a supermarket chain to an airline to a furniture manufacturer to a baseball team are virtually identical.

I need not draw multiple success models for different types of service companies; if a company creates customer value through labor-intensive performances, I need draw only the one picture shown as Exhibit 1–1. This exhibit is a comprehensive, accurate portrait of each sample company I studied. This is what a world-class service company with sustained success looks like.

Each chapter of the book develops one part of the success sustainability model. Exhibit 1–1 is a picture of the book. Just as there are no shortcuts in implementing this sustainable success model, there are no shortcuts in understanding it. Readers are encouraged to read every chapter in sequence as each chapter builds on previous ones. I found nine drivers of excellence in my study of the sample companies. The

EXHIBIT 1–1

Drivers of Sustainable Success in Service Businesses

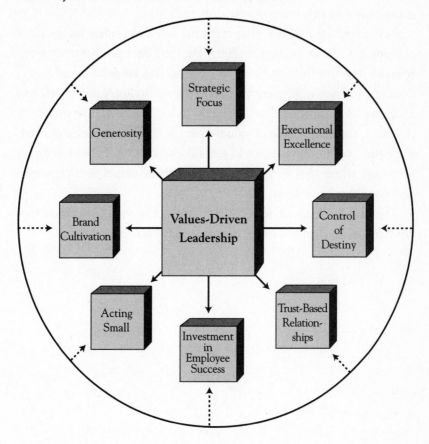

central driver of excellence, values-driven leadership, gives root to the other eight. The bold arrows in the model depict the primary relationships. The dotted-line arrows from the circle indicate the interrelationships among the success drivers; each success driver in the model nourishes others.

The book is about the overriding importance of humane values in building a lasting service business. Great service companies build a *humane* community (the organization and its partners) that *humanely* serves customers and the broader communities in which they live. Everyone benefits from the existence of a great company—customers, employees, suppliers, investors, cities, nations. Strong institutional values enabling human beings at work to realize their full potential as individuals and as members of a community contribute to the creation of compelling value inside and outside the company. The company survives as a success because it is more fully alive.

Restaurant owner Drew Nieporent has not had a single failure since opening his first restaurant in 1985. By 1997 he was operating seven restaurants—five in New York City, one in San Francisco, and one in London. He has won every major restaurant industry award. By any measure, he is successful in a difficult, fickle business. Nieporent understands the central role of values-based leadership in creating a lasting business. "Restaurants are like children," he says. "They need your attention when they're young. You give them values and principles and hope they grow up strong."[6]

This is a book about lessons learned from service companies that have grown up strong. These companies have much to teach us.

2

SUCCESS-SUSTAINING VALUES

Mike Rabbitt, a pilot for Midwest Express, had flown for several other airlines prior to joining Midwest. He tells a story of his teenage children's reaction to his decision to join Midwest Express:

> My children had flown many other airlines before. Kids can be brutal. My son was very status conscious and was asking, "Who is Midwest Express?" I took them on a flight and afterwards, they said, "This is COOL!" They became psyched about the airline. This gives me great satisfaction. Midwest Express won my kids over on one flight, and I have been trying to do this all of their lives.

Midwest Express has won the hearts of many demanding customers over the years. Flight attendant Beverly Donaldson recalls an incident during a winter storm when a flight from Newark could not land in Milwaukee. A customer loudly proclaimed her disbelief that the problem was weather-related: "Other customers heard what this customer told me and they took up for Midwest Express. They would not let the customer give me a hard time. Our loyal customers came to my rescue."

Midwest Express wins the loyalty of passengers by coupling competence with caring. A passenger needed reassurance that her dog was on the flight. Michael Desmond, working in the ramp area, retrieved the dog cage from the hold and held it up so the passenger could see her dog through the window. A delayed passenger waiting in the airport needed a diaper for her baby, and a Midwest Express employee went to his truck to get one for her. Customer Service Representative Denise Dembosky took care of a child who was traveling alone and had a three-and-a-half-hour layover. She kept the child at her side as she performed her job: "I got a phone call from her father and he told me that I had made a best friend." Midwest Express lost the suitcase of a passenger who had an important meeting the next day. A customer service representative went home, got one of his own suits, and took it to the passenger's hotel. The suit was delivered to the passenger's room with this note: "I noticed that we are the same size; I know all of the stores are closed, so here's one of my suits. Just return it when you are done."

Why did these employees decide to help the customers in personal ways? Midwest Express and the other 13 companies featured in this book use the power of values-driven leadership to sustain their success. The leaders of these companies recognize that every employee makes countless decisions each day that directly or indirectly affect customers and strengthen or weaken the company's reputation. How to guide the decisions individual employees make, often in split-second time frames with customers facing them or on the other end of a phone line, is a pivotal question in service companies. Midwest Express has rules, of course, but not about holding up a dog cage to reassure a passenger or loaning a passenger a suit of clothes. What distinguishes Midwest Express from competitors, what makes it a special company that attracts special employees, what sustains commitment to service, harmony, and improvement is a strong and clear set of values that include service excellence, mutual respect, honesty, and integrity.

These core values start with Timothy Hoeksema, Midwest Express chairman, president, and CEO. Hoeksema's values-driven leadership is his service to Midwest—teaching the values through deeds and words, spreading them throughout the organization, reinforcing them at every turn. The values of the senior leader have resulted in an organization of decision makers with similar values, including pilots, flight attendants, customer service representatives, station managers, reservation agents, and baggage handlers.

Although demographically and experientially diverse, Midwest Express employees share common values. They are attracted to the company and the company is attracted to them because of values compatibility. Once they are on the job, the values are continuously reinforced. Midwest Express's value system is its secret weapon.

VALUES: A COMPANY'S TREASURE

What's in the company vault? Like the money in a bank's vault, values are the company's treasure. Values reflect what the leader holds worthy, what the organization assigns worth. They are the ideals, principles, and philosophy at the center of the enterprise. They are protected and revered. They reveal the company's heart and soul. They energize the covenant.

Unlike stacks of $100 bills or gold ingots, these valuables are intangible. From them, however, flows the company's life. Their force and spirit permeate the company at every level, and they become palpable in decisions and behavior. What's in the company vault at Midwest Express explains an employee spontaneously showing a passenger her dog from the loading ramp, another loaning a stranger a business suit, and yet another watching over a vulnerable child traveler.

The stronger the fit between the values of senior managers and employees, the stronger the guiding and motivating influence of organizational values. Kouzes and Posner make the point well:

> When individual, group, and organizational values are in synch, tremendous energy is generated. Commitment, enthusiasm, and drive are intensified: people have a reason for caring about their work. . . . Shared values are the internal compasses that enable people to act independently and interdependently.[1]

The sample companies studied for this book are remarkably dynamic, original, and energetic in their business approaches. Yet their dynamism is coherent, their originality channeled, their energy focused. Clear organizational values that tap into the employees' deepest values offer the stability in what are otherwise high-motion enterprises.[2] As Southwest Airlines founder and chairman Herb Kelleher writes:

I have seen brilliant entrepreneurial strategies falter as an organization grows and matures. Obviously, you manage a $25 billion company differently than you do a $25 million company. But you change your *practices*, not your *principles*.[3]

Great service companies have a soul that underlies their strategies and day-to-day operations. Strategies and tactics change; the company's value system—its soul—is stable. And from these values come all of the success sustainers modeled in Exhibit 1–1 and developed in this book. The winning strategies, the transforming decisions made during crises, the big-dollar investments in distant payoffs, the commitments to developing human potential and vitalizing the larger community—all are rooted in clear, compelling core values. Strong values-driven leadership enables organizations to achieve what John Gardner calls wholeness incorporating diversity. Speaking to a Stanford University graduating class, Gardner told them their goal was "not to achieve wholeness by suppressing diversity, not to make wholeness impossible by enthroning diversity, but to preserve both."[4]

COMMON CORE VALUES

The vaults of the sample companies safeguard seven commonly held core values: excellence, innovation, joy, teamwork, respect, integrity, and social profit. They are interrelated, organic to the defining culture that transforms a corporation on paper into an achieving community in practice. Exhibit 2–1 shows no interior lines because these values meld, reflecting pictures of the same body from different vantage points.

As a group, these core values generate benefits for *all* company stakeholders—customers, employees, vendors, partners, communities, nations. Customers, employees, and other stakeholders are not separate entities but rather integral to the whole value system.

Excellence

Although the sample companies are strong profit performers, profit itself is not a defining value; rather it is an outcome. The pursuit of ex-

EXHIBIT 2–1
Core Values That Sustain Service Performance

CORE VALUES

Excellence

Joy

INNOVATION

Respect

Teamwork

SOCIAL
PROFIT

INTEGRITY

cellence, however, is a defining value. The word *good* is rarely used in the sample companies. *Good* isn't good enough. The pride of achievement comes from striving for excellence.

Sustainable success stems from insisting on exceptionally high standards in operating the business. What is acceptable to most companies is unacceptable to the sample firms. Chick-fil-A products must demonstrate significant taste superiority over competitive products to be marketed by the company. In 1997, after two years of testing and refinement, Chick-fil-A stopped testing a chicken pot pie product.

The product sold well in 15 test market stores, but it didn't score significantly above the competition on taste tests. States Dan Cathy, executive vice president of Chick-fil-A, "Every decision on what is on the menu either adds strength to our brand or dilutes it."

Midwest Express spends significantly more on food per passenger than its competitors. The company is noted for serving full meals on china plates with silverware and linen napkins accompanied by free wine or champagne. Its legendary chocolate chip cookies are baked on board. "Back in the early 1990s, when airlines were bleeding money," notes Tim Hoeksema, "we could have saved millions cutting back on food, but we would have lost our reputation."[5] Between 1990 and 1994, among the worst years in airline industry history, only Midwest Express and Southwest Airlines were profitable every year.

Excellence as a core value is beautifully captured by Peter Drucker, who writes about seven life-changing experiences. One of the experiences concerned the Greek sculptor, Phidias:

> I read a story that conveyed to me what *perfection* means. It is a story of the greatest sculptor of ancient Greece, Phidias. He was commissioned around 440 B.C. to make the statues that to this day stand on the roof of the Parthenon, in Athens. They are considered among the greatest sculptures of the Western tradition, but when Phidias submitted his bill, the city accountant of Athens refused to pay it. "These statues," the accountant said, "stand on the roof of the temple, and on the highest hill in Athens. Nobody can see anything but their fronts. Yet you have charged us for sculpting them in the round—that is, for doing their back sides, which nobody can see." "You are wrong," Phidias retorted. "The gods can see them."[6]

The quest for excellence creates economic value, but it is valuable in its own right for it uplifts the human spirit and burnishes the joy of personal achievement. Excellence is worthwhile even if only the gods can see it, and this is its true meaning.

Innovation

The values of innovation and excellence are inextricably linked. Innovation—changing what exists into something better—is the primary tool of excellence. Great service companies revel in *leading* change; they hear the beat of their own drums rather than competitive drums, they invent rather than imitate.

Gary Hoover, an entrepreneur who created three innovative businesses (BookStop, Hoover's Handbooks, and TravelFest) claims that customers always get what they want. It is just a matter of who gives it to them and when. One of the ways excellent companies sustain success is by finding new ways to create value for customers. In a videotaped message to Charles Schwab employees, company founder and chairman Charles "Chuck" Schwab discussed what he hopes will be written about the company in history books: first, that the company encouraged every American to invest and participate in the ownership process; and second, that a little company was able to transform Wall Street by instigating watershed changes in how investment firms handled their partnerships with investors. The spirit of innovation is deep religion at Charles Schwab.

Leading change is deep religion at Custom Research Inc., too. Listen for the value expressions embedded in these comments:

- "We have tried to lead the market, to stay ahead of our clients, to respond not only to what they ask for but to lead them."—Jeff Pope, co-founder
- "You have to keep reinventing yourself. Keep the core, the enduring, but keep looking for new opportunities."—Judy Corson, co-founder
- "We are successful because we never are satisfied. At every level of the company, we always are looking for input for how we can do something better. Our whole culture revolves around always getting better."—Diane Kokal, executive vice president
- "Continuous improvement is so embedded in our culture at all levels. It starts with the Steering Committee, but if the Steering Committee went down in a plane, we would still do the same thing."—Lisa Gudding, account manager

High performers pursue innovation at two levels: strategic innovation and operational innovation. They seek to improve strategically (doing the right things) and operationally (doing things right). Miller SQA values both types of innovation. Miller SQA's success is due primarily to its willingness to reinvent the office furniture manufacturing business. Instead of focusing on making better and fancier furniture in infinite variety, Miller SQA developed a system to deliver well-made, reliable furniture to customers at an economical price and in days instead of the weeks characteristic of the industry. Says Bix Norman, who led Miller SQA before becoming Herman Miller's chief information officer in 1998: "The industry was a system designed to fail. We set out to reinvent the industry. Everything we did, we said let's change it by tenfold. We focused on the process, not the product. The industry was focused on the product, a cooler looking panel or chair."

Central to Miller SQA's new approach is unique software that enables field sales representatives to use a laptop computer to quickly and efficiently perform all selling steps from accessing the product catalog to designing an office suite with the customer's participation to transmitting the order. States Gary Van Spronsen, Miller SQA's president: "In the laptop, you have the capabilities of the company."

Joy

Profits are only part of the success equation; uplifting the human spirit, bringing human potential to full flower, celebrating achievement—this also is part of being successful. A company's financial success that detracts from the quality of life of customers, employees, or other stakeholders is a hollow success. Sustainably successful service companies achieve their consistency by investing in that which brings satisfaction, pride, and joy to the service performers who, in turn, are more likely to bring satisfaction and pleasure to their customers.

The sample companies are remarkably joyful places. These companies recruit employees whose personal values match the organization's. Thus, employees work in conditions of strong values alignment. The company's values are their values; their values are the company's. Employees don't face daily ethical conflicts, they don't have to tolerate a double standard for bosses and workers, they don't have to abide mediocrity when they believe in excellence. Instead, they take pride in the company's emphasis on excellence, its success, and its strong reputation with customers and in the community. They revel in their own development and growth in a high-achievement company culture. They enjoy being part of something special, being on a successful team, an achieving team; they enjoy feeling connected, feeling like an owner.

The humaneness imbedded in the value systems of great service companies is in large measure what makes them great.

When asked why employees like working at Custom Research Inc., Executive Vice President of Sales and Marketing Jan Elsesser answers: "The quality of work we do is a tremendous source of pride." Eileen Taylor, senior vice president of human resources, adds:

> The integrity in the organization. We feel good about how we are treated and how clients are treated. Each employee is part of what goes out to the client and has a real impact on the company. There is a feeling of involvement and ownership in the company. We have fun and celebrate at the drop of a hat.

Once a year, Custom Research staff bring their pets to work on "Pet Day." A pet parade occurs during the day with each pet winning an award. The company hosts an indoor golf tournament in its own building each winter; every department or team creates one of the holes complete with hazards. "Good news" days occur on the third Thursday of the month. With the West and East Coast offices linked by telephone, company and personal good news is shared and awards are presented. Says research staffer Carolyn MacLeod, "It would be really hard to work anywhere else because I know I would be disappointed."

Professional baseball returned to St. Paul, Minnesota, in 1993 after a two-decade absence. Mike Veeck was instrumental in bringing baseball back to the area as part-owner and president of the St. Paul Saints. Veeck is the son of the late Bill Veeck, a Hall of Fame baseball team owner known for his creative flair and keen marketing sense. Having fun at the ballpark is a lesson Mike Veeck learned early in life.

The dominant value of the St. Paul Saints is "Fun Is Good." This slogan begins the company's short- and long-term marketing plans. It is written on the tops of the dugouts. It is the ethos of this minor league baseball team that sells out every home game and has been profitable from its first year. Asks Mike Veeck: "When did ballparks become no-laughter zones? My dad taught me: 'If it makes you laugh, and if it makes the people you care about laugh, do it.' We don't laugh enough in our society; a Saints game is a three-and-a-half-hour monument to humanity."

At Saints' home games, a band plays as fans enter the ballpark. A machine at the front gate sprays fans with bubbles. "I get asked 'why do you have bubble machines at the entrance?'" comments Mike Veeck. "When people ask why, that is a good sign we are doing something worthwhile."

A pig is the team's mascot. It carries water and new baseballs to the umpire between innings, wearing different costumes throughout the game. Once it served as ringbearer for an on-field wedding held before a game.

Events are staged on the field between innings—a sumo wrestling match, a young fan racing a giant sandwich around the bases, two fans bending over and touching their foreheads to bat handles, circling wildly for 30 seconds, then running to third base and back—that is, if they can keep from falling down due to dizziness. In the third inning, G-Men come out on the field in their trench coats and toss little boxes of General Mills cereal into the stands. In the seventh inning, press box personnel throw bags of peanuts into the stands (a local lumber yard sponsors the peanuts).

Nuns circulate in the stands to give neck massages to fans. Fans can get a haircut while they watch the game from a barber chair behind the third-base dugout. Players hold a pre-game autograph session on the field.

Each home game features an overall promotional theme. For example, on Jerry Garcia night in 1997 players wore tie-dyed jerseys; the loudspeaker system played Grateful Dead music; they held a Jerry Garcia look-alike contest; lava lamps lined the ballpark; fans came to the game dressed for the occasion.

Serving customers well, bringing them satisfaction and pleasure, is rewarding work. Creating fun for St. Paul Saints fans is fun for the staff. Pete Orme, former director of group sales and promotions, explains:

> We were given free rein to make this what we want. We were given leeway in selling tickets, the promotions, advertising, game-day operations. All of these decisions come from the group. We built this. We all have a

sense of ownership. I take it personally if a writer criticizes us, or a fan is not happy.

Adds Jody Beaulieu, community relations director: "We all love our jobs and it shows through to the fans. We are a fan-oriented team."

Teamwork

"Teamwork," says The Container Store president Kip Tindell, "is one of the most beautiful experiences in life." Teamwork—individuals collaboratively pooling their resources in pursuit of a common purpose—is a core value of the sample companies and a primary way they enrich employees' quality of work life.

Being a member of a team that is tested and challenged, that overcomes and experiences victory, that makes a difference in people's lives, is as energizing in work life as it is in sports. The reality of teamwork lifts the human spirit and generates energy for the next day, as the comments below suggest:

- "Everyone pitches in. It's a total team effort from top to bottom." —Mary Ellen Scieszinski, room attendant, Pioneer Inn
- "We give each other on our team a lot of encouragement; we stand behind each other."—Jeanne Wichterman, senior vice president and team leader, White Team, Custom Research Inc.
- "On the stressful days, it's the teamwork. Your fellow co-workers are willing to give you a helping hand."—Denise Dembosky, customer service representative, Midwest Express
- "I feel a part of a team. This is very important. Many people do not feel like they are a part of a team. They feel that they are just a number."—Jim Blackwell, managing director retail operations, Ukrop's

How do the sample companies nurture teamwork as a value? They do it by recruiting people most likely to be team players, by modeling teamwork in senior management, by establishing such high performance standards that attainment requires teamwork, by celebrating group effort and achievement and minimizing any type of "star system," and by giving employees a strong sense of belonging to the company as a whole through information sharing, company gatherings, and job rotation assignments.

New distribution center employees of The Container Store spend the third day of their orientation program at a store to see the distribution process from the store employees' perspective. Within a year, each distribution center employee spends another day at a store, unloading products from the truck, working at the cash register, and watching products leave the store. Conversely, store employees spend time working in the distribution center. States distribution center executive Mike Hoover:

> We put a tremendous amount of emphasis on delivering on time. We have a crew of maybe 17 people at a store at 5:00 A.M. waiting to unload the truck and put the merchandise on shelves before the store opens at 9:00 A.M. The store needs to be perfect when it opens and if the driver is 30 minutes late, it may not be perfect. The stores are our customers. We treat our stores the same way they treat their customers.

The photos and names of employees in each store are mounted on a wall within The Container Store headquarters; each store has a photo board for all headquarters personnel. Amy Carovillano, vice president of inventory control and distribution, remarks: "No one takes the blame and no one takes the credit in our culture; it is a group effort."

Respect

Fundamental respect is another core value in all the sample companies. Respect for the customer. Respect for the employee. Respect for suppliers and other business partners. Respect for the community.

Great service companies compete through respect. On the surface, respect seems too elementary and nebulous to forge competitive advantage. But it is a powerful influence. Respectfulness dignifies transactions for both customer and server; it invests esteem into the proceedings of business; it underscores worthwhileness.

Based on years of service quality research, I attempted to succinctly capture customers' most common service complaints. I derived the 10 categories shown in Table 2–1 and was struck by the pervasiveness of basic disrespect. From the first, "True Lies" (cheating customers), to the tenth, "Misplaced Priorities" (ignoring customers), each category is associated with customer disrespect. Companies that offer respect as part of their service significantly strengthen their service overall.

One of Ritz-Carlton's core values, taught to employees from their first day on the job, is: "We are ladies and gentlemen serving ladies and gentlemen." It is an extremely powerful values statement because of the dignity it invests in the act of serving. At Ritz-Carlton hotels, bellhops, drivers, room attendants, telephone operators, maintenance

TABLE 2–1
Common Customer Service Complaints

1. *True Lies.* Blatant dishonesty or unfairness, such as service providers selling un-needed services or purposely quoting fake, "lowball" cost estimates.

2. *Red Alert.* Providers who assume customers are stupid or dishonest and treat them harshly or disrespectfully.

3. *Broken Promises.* Service providers who do not show up as promised. Careless, mistake-prone service.

4. *I Just Work Here.* Powerless employees who lack the authority—or the desire—to solve basic customer problems.

5. *The Big Wait.* Waiting in a line made long because some of the checkout lanes or service counters are closed.

6. *Automatic Pilot.* Impersonal, emotionless, no-eye-contact, going-through-the motions nonservice.

7. *Suffering in Silence.* Employees who don't bother to communicate with customers who are anxious to hear how a service problem will be resolved.

8. *Don't Ask.* Employees unwilling to make any extra effort to help customers, or who seem put out by requests for assistance.

9. *Lights On, No One Home.* Clueless employees who do not know (i.e., will not take the time to learn) the answers to customers' common questions.

10. *Misplaced Priorities.* Employees who visit with each other or conduct personal business while the customer waits. Those who refuse to assist a customer because they're off duty or on a break.

workers, and front-desk personnel experience what many employees in other companies do not and that is the feeling of being respected.

Respect as a core value consists of trust, sensitivity, and listening, characteristics illustrated by USAA and the St. Paul Saints. Respect is embedded in the heritage of both companies. USAA was started in 1922 by 25 army officers who could not find adequate automobile insurance because most insurers deemed military personnel poor insurance risks. Meeting in a San Antonio hotel on June 20, 1922, the 25 assembled military officers organized themselves into an association through which they pledged to share one another's financial risks. The group had little knowledge of automobile insurance, no capital, and no business office. What they did have was a belief in an idea and trust in one another. They could not imagine then that their "association" (originally named the United States Army Automobile Association) would eventually serve the insurance and financial needs of more than three million people.[7]

USAA attracts, motivates, and retains exceptional employees with an exceptional array of employee services and benefits, a sophisticated listening system, and loyalty. USAA, which never has had a layoff, is loyal to its employees who in turn are expected to be loyal to the members (customers). Wilson "Bill" Cooney, deputy CEO for USAA's Property and Casualty Insurance operations, calls this the "loyalty chain." He states:

> If you don't take care of the employees, they can't take care of the customers. We give employees all they need to be happy and absolutely enthralled to be here. If they are unhappy, we will not have satisfied customers in the long run. . . . We must have a passion for customers. If we don't, we are in the wrong business. Our members have served our country, and we want to serve them. We take them seriously. We always ask, "What is the impact on our members?"

During an era when major league baseball has been widely criticized for its *lack* of respect for fans, the St. Paul Saints—a minor league team—can teach the big leagues a lesson in customer respect. What Mike Veeck learned from his parents has clearly shaped his approach to the business of baseball:

I grew up as the son of a barnstormer; he spoke 300 times a year for free to any group. He would always thank those in the audience for letting him come to speak. Whether it was a group of 25 people or a hundred people, they were prospective customers. Why wouldn't you want to take the opportunity to speak to them?

My mom was the first female publicist for Ice Capades. I watched my mom and dad and saw what it meant for people to see them at a public appearance. My mom taught me: "You cannot pretend, you must be."

Many people compare my dad with P.T. Barnum, but that always makes a Veeck bristle. P.T. Barnum believed there was always a sucker out there. My dad didn't think of people as "suckers." My dad *was* the people. People are smart and know if you are sincere. People could sense my dad's enthusiasm and generosity.

The Saints provide strong entertainment value for an entire family. Ticket and other prices are kept low. In 1997, general admission seats were $4, bleacher reserved $5, and reserved seats $7. Parking was $3. Through its first five seasons, the Saints had not raised concession prices. When asked what he was most proud of, Mike Veeck replied: "Holding concession prices for five years because it speaks of a commitment to the fans who keep coming to our games in record numbers. I would love to raise prices, but I think it is important not to."

Midway Stadium, the Saints ballpark, is painted with murals. Poetry is in the game program. The Saints were the first baseball team to include a braille page in the game program. Management take tickets at the turnstiles and sit in the stands during games to hear what fans have to say. The club does an annual fan survey and has a "Suggestion Pig" at the ballpark.

With every home game a sellout, the St. Paul mayor wanted to build the Saints a new stadium. In characteristic fashion, Veeck put the issue to a vote of the fans. Veeck explains: "The mayor wants to build us a new stadium. I went to the fans and asked them. They didn't want it; 2,500 voted against it, 200 in favor. They said 'Mike, you came to us and said you were going to play ball in this crooked stadium and we believed you.' The fans were against the new stadium, so we declined."

Integrity

Charles Schwab Corporation's vision is to "provide customers with the most useful and ethical financial services in the world." Dana Commercial Credit distributes an ethics card with 10 "Dos and Don'ts" to every employee on their first day. A three-hour discussion of the ethics card and Dana's values ensues. Charles Schwab, Dana Commercial Credit, and the other 12 sample companies compete with integrity. These companies value honesty and fair play not only as the right way to compete but as the best way to compete. Integrity with stakeholders, it is believed, wins the day. And in industries such as securities brokerage and leasing that do not have the strongest reputations for ethical practices, demonstrated fair play can become a huge competitive advantage.

The intangibility of services heightens customers' sensitivity to fairness. As performances, services are difficult for customers to evaluate prior to purchase. Customers cannot try on services for fit and feel; there are no tires to kick or test drives to take. Customers typically must buy the service to actually experience it. Thus, they must trust a service company to deliver on its promise and conduct itself honorably.

Some services are difficult for customers to judge fully even after they have been performed, and therefore trust plays an even bigger role. These "black box" services usually are technical in nature or performed away from the customer's presence. As important as fairness is for services in general, it is even more important for black box services because customers are more vulnerable.[8]

Leasing and other financial services clearly fit the black box definition. Dana Commercial Credit Chairman and CEO Ed Shultz made several key decisions in 1990 that proved crucial in transforming the company into an industry leader and Baldrige winner. One decision was to do business with ethical companies. Shultz states: "We decided we were not going to do business with anybody but the top customers. No longer would we deal with companies who make promises that can't be met and don't offer the best quality and service."

Another key decision was to promote from within and promote

those whose behavior reflected the highest ethical practice. Shultz explains: "If I were to die tomorrow and the person who settled my estate—knowing no one would ever know—acted ethically and responsibly, then he or she is the person for our senior management. This is the level of trustworthiness I seek. Getting the mercenaries out of the corporation was one of my best decisions." Adds Executive Vice President and Chief Financial Officer Rod Filcek, "The leasing industry has not always had the best reputation. Our culture and reputation have given us an advantage. We have a level of trust with clients that they haven't experienced before."

Charles Schwab's remarkable growth is a direct result of its core value of providing a level playing field for investors. Chuck Schwab's vision created a securities company that is on the customer's side, that provides a safe haven from account churning practices and from aggressively sold, high-risk investments. It has earned the trust of millions of investors. Investor trust has become Charles Schwab's number one marketing weapon. "The passion for the investor is at the heart of our ethos," says Mark Thompson, senior vice president of consumer education.

Contrary to industry practice, Schwab does not pay sales commissions. Sales representatives earn bonuses based on their customer service performance and the assets they attract to the firm. Temptations to churn accounts or sell particular investment vehicles do not exist. States Schwab account executive Eric Salz: "I feel like I can really help somebody. I didn't feel that way as a full-commission broker. I can now tell my clients that my role is that of an educator. You don't feel like you need to push products."

Similarly, the extensive network of financial advisors partnering with Schwab throughout the country are fee-compensated rather than paid on commission. A fundamental tenet at Schwab is that anyone who provides service should be noncommissioned to remove conflict of interest.

Social Profit

The first value of The Container Store is: "Fill the other person's basket to the brim and making money becomes an easy proposition." The "other person" is anyone who comes in contact with the company or is affected in any way by the company's actions. The Container Store values giving, not just getting; it believes in enriching—economically or otherwise—all of its stakeholders.

Creating economic profit is too narrow a goal for The Container Store, Special Expeditions, Ukrop's, and the other sample companies. These companies intensely value the creation of social profit. Companies create social profit when their actions produce net benefits to society beyond the marketing of goods and services and the creation of employment opportunities, the necessary instruments of economic profits. The spirit of social profit is investing financial and nonfinancial wealth (such as knowledge) possessed by the organizational community in the larger societal community. Social profit is analogous to profit sharing, except the profits are not limited to financial profits, and the sharing is not confined to the organization.

Although businesses commonly are involved in charitable activities and community support programs, the centrality of social profit creation to the sample companies' "reason for being" is highly unusual. Creating social profit is part of the companies' mission; it is a core value that guides and motivates behavior in the daily life of the organizations.

One of the most important findings of the research, developed in Chapter 11, is that good works are not just a result of economic profit but a producer of economic profit. Valuing the creation of social profits is one reason the sample companies succeed economically.

Special Expeditions is a devoutly conservationist company. It practices "responsible tourism," devoting considerable funds, time, and other resources to protecting—and in some cases repairing—the places in the world where it takes customers. The company seeks to inspire travelers to become more aware and informed about environmental issues, not by propagandizing but by taking them to precious places worldwide and educating them about their experiences. Founder, owner, and president Sven-Olof Lindblad explains:

> Our concept is to give people a sense of wonder about their world and secondly to get them involved in the issues associated with these places. Much damage has been done to the world, and we need to repair what we

can. Part of our company functions almost like a foundation. We want to be a platform for people to become aware of issues. If you open someone's eyes to the beauty and wonder of an area, it naturally follows that they will become interested in preserving that area.

Special Expeditions' commitment to environmental preservation has a strong impact on the morale and motivation of employees and the pride they take in the company. It is a key factor in the company's ability to recruit and retain the high caliber of naturalists, historians, and cultural experts who lead the expeditions. As Peter Butz, vice president of operations, puts it: "Our involvement with conservation translates into a sense of mission to which employees gravitate. This involvement inspires our employees to go the extra mile. They want to do it."

Ukrop's is as committed to improving its hometown community of Richmond, Virginia, as Special Expeditions is to conserving the world's natural environment. Playing a leadership role in the economic development of Richmond, providing financial support to numerous charities, and investing in the quality of family life are important matters at Ukrop's. Ukrop's policy to close on Sundays so associates may be with their families costs the company money and probably has encouraged some competitors to enter the market. But making money, which Ukrop's does well, is not really the company's heart and soul. As Bob Ukrop, president and chief executive officer, states: "We enjoy what we do. It's not about the money. It's about life."

Like the other sample firms, Ukrop's is adept at identifying opportunities that benefit the community and the company. It hires older, retired people to work as courtesy clerks while younger workers are in school. In 1997, Ukrop's donated $500,000 to the local J. Sargeant Reynolds Community College to establish a Culinary Institute to teach students (including current and prospective employees) the art and science of food preparation. Ukrop's customers can designate a specific charity to receive a percentage of their expenditures through the "Golden Gift" program. At this writing, Ukrop's has donated $7 million to more than 5,000 organizations. Debbye Mahan, who manages human resources for Ukrop's Support Center, says: "Jim and

Bobby [James Ukrop, company chairman and brother Bob Ukrop] truly want to make this a better community. They are so sincere and not driven by money. They do so many things that the public does not know. They truly want life to be better." Adds Bob Ukrop: "The selfish part of it is that if we help the community, it helps us. The unselfish part is we grew up that way."

A set of core values permeates the high-performance service companies studied for this book. These values are remarkably consistent among the companies. The values of excellence, innovation, joy, teamwork, respect, integrity, and social profit underlie the ongoing success of the sample firms. Unchanging, these core ideals, principles, and philosophies define the very soul of these dynamic companies.

Chapter 4 argues the contribution of focused strategy to sustained success. Focused strategy, however, is insufficient when an organization must depend on people to directly implement it for the benefit of customers. Sustained performance of quality service depends on organizational values that truly guide and inspire employees. And how does an organization get such values? It gets them from its leaders who view the infusion and cultivation of values within the organization as a primary responsibility.

3

LEADING WITH VALUES

Craig Hall depends on the work ethic, skills, and judgment of young people in their teens and early twenties for his livelihood. Hall is the operator of Chick-fil-A restaurants in Bryan and College Station, Texas, and 80 percent of his employees work part-time while attending high school or college. The managers of his two restaurants both are in their twenties. Despite the staff's youth, Hall's restaurants are very successful. The food quality is consistently excellent, the service friendlier than in many more expensive restaurants, the atmosphere casual and comfortable, the facilities immaculate.

Hall is the consummate one-on-one teacher, starting with the job interview. He looks for the common ground between his goals and the prospective employee's. If the individual wants the job to be able to make car payments, Hall explains that practicing the Golden Rule and becoming invaluable to the team will result in more hours and more money for the car payments. He tries to spend two or three hours with new employees soon after they are hired, encouraging their confidence and commitment: "I tell them to never diminish their self-worth, that each individual can make a difference. I want them to use their talent to its fullest."

Hall backs up his words. If he sees a table that needs to be cleaned, he cleans it. If he spots customers needing service, he serves them. Hall's idea of leadership is to lead by example: "I could stand here all day long and say that we want to deliver great customer service but never lift a finger. That won't get it done. I want an employee to go home and say, 'You know, mom, the owner wiped tables with me today.'"

ROLES OF VALUES-DRIVEN LEADERS

Values-driven leaders infuse their values into the fabric of the organization. They lead not with commands, not with a thick rulebook, but with a set of core values—what the firm represents and aspires to be. The more these values tap into employees' own core values, the more they guide individual decision making and inspire personal achievement.

The most effective values-driven leaders mobilize emotional and spiritual resources that so often lie dormant in other organizations. People at work often have more of themselves to give than they actually give. Core values' compatibility energizes an organization. People at work don't just have a job; they have a cause.

Studying leaders from the sample companies reveals a common set of critical roles they perform to drive values into the organization. Leaders also perform other important roles, but here the focus is on how they lead with values.

Articulating the Dream

Values-driven leaders articulate the company's "reason for being." They convey the company's fundamental aspirations and why they are important. The company's reason for being—the dream—is the strategic manifestation of its core values. Miller SQA manifests Bix Norman's dream to reinvent office furniture manufacturing and distribution and reflects his impatience with tradition-bound mediocrity in the industry. Norman explains: "The system made it almost impossible to get it right. Handoffs from the supplier to the manufacturer to the distributor to the customer created many opportunities for errors. The cycle time was eight to 10 weeks. Buying office furniture was a pain in the ass. We needed a fundamentally different approach. We set out to make buying office furniture a delight."

Norman is a maverick, a champion of innovation, a true believer that one can always find a way to accomplish something truly worthwhile. With the strength of a big dream and an ability to survive in the Herman Miller organization as a maverick, Norman built Miller SQA into an organization that today is full of true believers. He did it by recruiting talented executives to the company who shared his enthusiasm for change. He did it by finding metaphorical ways to convey that Miller SQA wasn't just quick furniture but a fundamentally new concept, a new process. He did it with unwavering commitment to the dream, including bet-the-company investments in technology. He did it by creating a demanding yet positive and reinforcing organizational climate. He did it through voracious reading and continually floating new ideas by the management team. Most of all, Norman did it by genuinely involving others in pursuit of the cause.

Gary Van Spronsen captures the essence of Norman's leadership. Van Spronsen started with Miller SQA in 1992 as vice president of product and service, was promoted to general manager in 1997 and to president in 1998 when Norman was elevated to the chief information officer position at Herman Miller. Van Spronsen states: "I came to serve Bix in accomplishing his dream. Over time it became as much my dream as his because I got to live it, add to it, invest my stuff in it. Bix had the right idea, attracted others who wanted to participate, and let them participate." Adds Norman: "I contributed to a gene pool."

Defining Organizational Success

Values-driven leaders continually convey by their words and actions the meaning of success. They not only make palpable the dream (where we are going, why we are going there), they define the indicators of progress (how we know we are getting there). A key factor in sustaining success is combining a compelling dream that inspires commitment with a success definition that is *reinforcing* rather than *contradicting*.

Special Expeditions' primary success measure is happy travelers. Inspiring adventurous travelers by exposing them to nature at its best is the company dream. The ship officers and expedition staff in charge of each voyage know and believe in both the dream and the definition of a successful voyage. They know what to do and relish the freedom to do it.

Bud Lehnhausen is an expedition leader for Special Expeditions. He is responsible for the passengers' day-to-day itinerary on a voyage, working closely with the naturalist staff on board and with the ship's captain. Lehnhausen has been with the company since 1983, starting as a naturalist. He comments: "The success of the company is the success of the trips. Whatever it takes to make passengers happy, we do it. We don't call the office to ask permission. We have complete autonomy to change an itinerary."

Lehnhausen can recall only one time when he called headquarters to ask for guidance. In 1993, the ship was five days into a two-week voyage up the Amazon River when it could go no farther because the river was unexpectedly low. Lehnhausen and his staff felt they could still make it a good trip by going back down the river and stopping at places they had never had time to visit on previous trips. Lehnhausen contacted company owner Sven-Olof Lindblad who told him to do whatever he needed to do and not to worry about costs. Passengers were given the option to leave the ship and fly home with a full refund or to go back down the river. Seven of 80 passengers went home; the others stayed and visited a variety of inland areas, sometimes transported by trucks. When the ship stopped at Manaus, a Flamenco opera was playing and Special Expeditions bought tickets for everyone. During the following two weeks, Special Expeditions repeated the Amazon River trip for a Stanford University alumni group that elected to go ahead with the river-land combination rather than cancel. For this second group, Special Expeditions had some planning time and rented the opera house in Manaus. "The people on these trips loved them," recalls Lehnhausen. "These were the most fulfilling trips ever for me because of the challenge of making the trip work for the passengers. All of us on the staff felt like we really accomplished something."

With Special Expeditions and the other sample companies, important success measures are stepping-stones to realizing the companies' dream. And if situations arise that test commitment to the dream, such as when serving customers well requires unanticipated expense, the dream prevails. Values-driven leaders derive measures of progress directly from their intrinsic leadership values.

Living the Values

The primary way values-driven leaders articulate the dream and define organizational success is through their own behavior. They live out the values in their daily behavior. Through their actions large and small, leaders demonstrate core values. Through their words, they reinforce what they model. Words alone are insufficient, however. And words contradicted by behavior are worse than insufficient. They ring hollow and destroy trust.

Values-driven leaders are visible, authentic leaders. They devote considerable time and effort to personally communicating the company's values in the workplace. They stay connected. They do not write many memos. They do not remain closeted in their offices. They do not send surrogates to do their job. Through visiting work sites, leading meetings, participating in company rallies and forums, and teaching in company educational programs, values-driven leaders become real and credible to the people they lead. As Kouzes and Posner write:

> Leaders go first. They set an example and build commitment through simple, daily acts that create progress and momentum. Leaders model the way through personal example and dedicated execution.[1]

Garrett Boone, CEO of The Container Store, epitomizes the visibility and authenticity consistently demonstrated by the leaders of the sample companies. Boone's first priority is staying in touch with people in the stores. He explains:

> I feel like my presence in the company is important. When I go to a store, I spend the whole day there and have breakfast, lunch, and dinner with small groups of employees to brainstorm. My purpose is not to examine the store but to talk to everyone in the store.

Boone sends handwritten notes to the stores every month to recognize employees' performance and reinforce the company's values. He also forwards customer letters received in headquarters and typically adds a personal note.

Leaders cannot lead without first gaining the trust of the organization. Trust is a leader's most powerful tool; with it, a leader can build an achieving, lasting community; without it, the leader cannot build anything exceptional or lasting. By personally living the values, a leader gains the trust needed to lead. As Peter Drucker writes in a seminal essay: "The final requirement of effective leadership is to earn trust. Otherwise there won't be any followers—and the only definition of a leader is someone who has followers."[2]

The Container Store employees were asked why the company is so successful. Their comments reveal the inherent role of trust in values-driven leadership:

- "Success hasn't changed management; the belief system is so strong."
- "Kip and Garrett have as much enthusiasm as we do."
- "Trust in the company. I've never seen top management cheat anyone and they won't cheat me."
- "Kip and Garrett never change."
- "Our management is for real."

Cultivating Leadership

A critical role of values-driven leaders is cultivating the leadership qualities of others in the organization. Leadership is not the exclusive province of senior managers. In labor-intensive service companies, inspired leadership at the point of service delivery is especially important.

Embedded in the language of business is the phrase "middle managers." A distinguishing characteristic of excellent service companies, however, is the existence of "middle leaders" who bring to their responsibilities the leadership qualities that sustain success. Leadership that comes *only* from the top of the organization cannot sustain the core values required to perpetuate success.

Service work often is demanding, exhausting, and repetitive. Customer-contact personnel are always "on stage." Time to recharge, to regroup, to regain composure after a difficult customer may be nonexistent. The show goes on, ready or not. Managers at the scene must assume the mantle of leadership; they must be the ones to coach, teach, and inspire hour after hour, day after day, week after week. Values-driven leaders cultivate leadership at the point of service delivery by putting the right people in charge in the first place and by teaching them how to realize their full potential as leaders.

Few senior manager decisions are more important than choosing the middle managers. Who is in charge of the stores, hotels, branch offices, restaurants, ships, stations, sales forces, and other points of service delivery primarily determines how well the services will be delivered. A sure way to nurture values-driven leadership in an organization is to identify candidates for promotion who cherish the core values of the company *and* who have demonstrated leadership qualities through past performance. Four good things happen when the company promotes individuals who meet both of these tests. First, they further develop their leadership capabilities because of their expanded role. Second, through their new role they have a greater opportunity to help the firm succeed. Third, other employees see individuals who are living the company's values moving up in the organization. Fourth, and most importantly, putting values-driven leaders in charge gives others a role model from whom to learn. Promoting people with the most potential for values-driven leadership helps transform followers into leaders.[3]

The sample companies adhere to a policy of promoting from within. Three factors underlie this policy and each cultivates values-driven leadership. Promoting from within enables employees who brought the company to its present level of performance to benefit from the fruits of their labors. Rewarding deserving members of a community rather than outsiders strengthens the community. Promoting from within also gives those promoted the opportunity to further develop their leadership capabilities as just noted. Finally, promoting from within means promoting someone whose values already are known in the company. The sample companies practice a simple but powerful formula: hire entry-level people who share the company's values and, based on performance and leadership potential, promote them into positions of greater responsibility. Occasionally, these companies hire executives from the outside, usually for specialized staff positions, but such hires are rare. Much has been written about companies needing "fresh blood" and clearly many companies require just that. However, this research shows that excellent service companies grow their own leaders. Staying in-house is a way they perpetuate the values that key their success.

Promoting the right people into leadership positions is one piece of the puzzle; teaching them more about leadership is another. Professor Noel Tichy has devoted more than 25 years to studying the differences between high-performance companies and mediocre performers. He believes a defining characteristic of high performers is leaders who are developing at all levels of the organization. Tichy writes:

> If long-term success requires more leaders at more levels than your competitors, then teaching, coaching, and cultivating others becomes a strategic imperative for senior executives. . . . leaders need to build not just a learning organization but a *teaching* organization—one with the capacity to build leaders—into the fabric of the organization. They need to create an environment where leaders are teaching leaders.[4]

Dan Cathy, executive vice president of Chick-fil-A, personally teaches a vision and values day for new store operators and staff on their first day. Cathy does this six or seven times each year. The day begins in Atlanta at 8:00 A.M. and ends around 10:00 P.M. Participants learn about the company's history, tradition, and values—but not in a classroom. Instead, they get in a van and make multiple stops during the day. Between stops, Cathy tells company stories from the front of the van. Stops include the Dwarf House® (Truett Cathy's first restaurant), the Southlake Mall Chick-fil-A, the Clayton Fixture Company (makers of Chick-fil-A counters), Pro Source (distributors of Chick-fil-A supplies), and the home-office headquarters. At headquarters, participants each share one impression they never want to forget from their experiences during the day. Then they travel on to Dan Cathy's home for a dinner he prepares.

Chick-fil-A carefully chooses operators for the 80 or so new stores it opens each year. With only 5 to 6 percent annual turnover of store operators, the company selects the best of the best from the approximately 9,000 applications it receives each year. Still, the company invests in leadership teaching from the very first day. "My responsibility at Chick-fil-A is to carry on the values of the business," explains

Dan Cathy. "This has focused me on the history of the company. I didn't want to delegate Vision and Values Day to anyone else."

Asserting Values in Tough Times

Values-driven leaders rely on their values to navigate their companies through difficult periods. They remind others in the organization about the guiding power of the company's core values and occasionally they remind themselves.

Many of the senior leaders interviewed for this book discussed their handling of a crisis, or series of crises, as key turning points for their companies. In every case, they turned to core values for guidance. Robert Tillman, chairman, president, and CEO of Lowe's Companies, Inc., uses an apt expression to set the context: "Companies are like tea bags. You can't tell how strong they are until they are in hot water."[5] Values-driven leaders assert and affirm their intrinsic values during crisis periods to mobilize the essential strengths of their companies.

In 1987 Special Expeditions was a young, capital-poor company. Its ship *Polaris* had a technical problem on its inaugural voyage and hit a concrete pier, putting a hole in the bow. Three months later, the ship arrived in the United States and was cited by the U.S. Coast Guard for inadequate fire protection. Later, a terrible storm at sea damaged the ship. The company lost $2.2 million that year and could not pay all its bills. Company founder Sven-Olof Lindblad was reminded during this turbulent year that what makes Special Expeditions "special" is inspired people—those who serve the travelers, the travelers themselves (some of whom floated loans to the company), and company suppliers, including the craftsman who prepared the ship to meet the Coast Guard's fire standards and who said, "Pay me when you can." Core values of teamwork, respect, and integrity figure into the story, which Lindblad takes from here:

> I learned so much that year about the resilience of the people we had and the intense loyalty that existed among passengers who were exposed to those events. At the end of the day, I learned the importance of a dedicated, talented team of people. My dad [famed expedition travel pioneer Lars-Eric Lindblad] was an incredible man but he was like an "island" on

a different level than the others. I learned from 1987 that I had to have a strong team of people around me.

I also learned about how powerful the truth is even when it is negative. We owed a lot of money that we didn't have. I decided to tell creditors what was happening, explain the problem, and ask for their help in creating a plan to keep the whole thing going. Everyone worked with me. The truth is the most underrated and powerful tool that exists.

Values also guided Dana Commercial Credit through a difficult period. The year was 1991 and the company faced a crossroad. Business was not particularly good and morale was down. The company held a three-day, closed-door meeting of its top managers to assess the situation and determine a course of action. It was an emotional meeting with much discussion of the company's core values. Michael Gannon, executive vice president and manager of the Dealer Products Group, recalls the time: "We had 14 people sitting in the room and reached a unanimous decision on where we had to take this company." The company abandoned its generalist structure for selling, refocused on national accounts, established an education group to intensify training, implemented a strategic planning process, and embarked on improving its service quality.

Like Special Expeditions, Dana Commercial Credit was guided by values in dealing with difficult issues. Chairman and CEO Ed Shultz remembers the 1991 period well:

> We had become unrigorous about our values. We decided to get serious about our values, do strategic planning, focus on what we were good at, and begin the quality effort. We went through a two-year period where I couldn't call someone in the company who wasn't in a strategic planning or quality meeting or in an education course.
>
> Then, boom, in about two years morale was up. We began to get successes from strategic planning and the quality initiative and started to get buy-in to the process. You are not going to be successful until you have the strategic plan and quality training, and it takes a long time and is real painful.

All companies are seriously tested at certain points in their history. How they handle these challenges can produce lessons so strong that it's as though they were forged in steel. This is what happened at Special Expeditions, Dana Commercial Credit, and most of the other companies studied. Values already in place were strengthened by how the companies confronted serious problems. Severe challenges exposed the benefit of rigorously attending to core values.

Challenging the Status Quo

Values-driven leaders not only assert core values during crises but also during periods of relative normalcy. The values of excellence and innovation do not permit organizations possessing them to rest. A primary role of values-driven leaders is to keep the organization awake, striving to improve, searching for ways to enhance competitiveness. On the surface, all might seem well in hand, but the leader fears complacency or senses trouble and stirs the pot.

Midwest Express's Tim Hoeksema did just this when he initiated a major improvement effort in 1996. The initiative is known in the company as CHIP, named for the chocolate chip cookies the airline bakes on board its flights and four business principles linked to its core values:

Customer focus
Highly involved employees
Information-based decision making
Process improvement

The CHIP initiative involves seven specific objectives to enable Midwest Express to achieve its vision, all of which are based on the four CHIP principles. What is most instructive about this comprehensive improvement effort is not that the company undertook it, but that it undertook it while performing so well—at least by most people's standards. But it wasn't performing well enough for Tim Hoeksema:

> The real impetus of this change initiative came from my gut feeling that we were becoming complacent. Even though we were highly successful and received many complimentary letters, I saw little signs that there was room for improvement. This initiative identifies our need for more effective processes, tracking, and measurement. We must get people more in-

volved and become more innovative. It's an important renaissance to help ensure that we do not become complacent.

From its humble beginnings as a St. Louis car leasing firm in 1957, Enterprise Rent-A-Car had grown into a big company by the early 1990s on founder Jack Taylor's simple but powerful ethos: "Treat customers well, treat employees as partners, and profits will follow." Jack Taylor's son, Andy, who became the CEO in 1991, felt the company needed a new focus on customer satisfaction. The company was growing very rapidly, the bottom line was excellent, and on the surface nothing appeared amiss. Yet Andy Taylor felt the company's core values were in jeopardy, and he instigated change by challenging field managers to address the issue. The managers broke the existing car rental system into pieces and then put it back together as a refined, improved process called "the cycle of service." They implemented a customer satisfaction measurement system and customer satisfaction scores became an essential factor in being promoted. Andy Taylor explains:

> The issue was not solving the problem; when we agree on a problem, it is crushed. The issue was getting people to understand the problem. We had a good bottom line. It didn't look broken. We were at a crossroad on the customer satisfaction issue. I insisted this was a priority.

One company whose pot always is stirring is Charles Schwab. Indeed, at Charles Schwab the senior leadership challenges the status quo so much that there is no status quo; perpetual innovation is the company's routine. David Pottruck, who was promoted to co-CEO in 1997, discusses the leadership role of challenging the status quo in its purest form:

> Success creates corporate arrogance. I am a great subscriber to paranoia. We don't have copyrights, patents, secret formulas. I try to stimulate the sense of the competition—we are not in a protected place. We have to perform. We have nothing here except our human talent. Once upon a time I would have said technology, but it is changing so fast, that advantage is going away. We are down to brand and talent pool as our competitive advantage. Build a corporate sense of whatever you are, you are not good enough; we spend little time celebrating success. We are always in meetings asking what's next. Ten percent of our budget each

year is reinvested in nonmandatory project spending. We manage this budget very carefully.

Encouraging the Heart

By living and teaching values that tap into the most human of employees' own values, values-driven leaders encourage the heart. "Encouraging the heart" is a fundamental practice Kouzes and Posner have found in leaders when they are at their personal best. With caring and encouragement, leaders uplift the spirits and kindle the energy of people at work who may be wearing down. As Kouzes and Posner write, "Leaders encourage the heart of their constituents to carry on."[6]

Each of the seven core values discussed earlier and shown in Exhibit 2–1 encourages service performers to "carry on" because they bring a sense of achievement, collaboration, civility, purpose, and contribution to the employee. Hard work is much harder without these qualities, much easier with them. Hard work is not what defeats most people on the job. What defeats them is work without personal growth, without teammates, without kindness, without meaning. Service companies that care only about making money are destined for mediocrity, if not outright failure, because sustaining service performance requires encouraging employees' hearts; a goal of making money in and of itself is not heartening.

Napoleon Barragan, the founder and chief executive of Dial-A-Mattress, encourages employees' hearts through involvement and participation. "Nap keeps us all involved," states Maureen Renneberg, assistant director of sales. "We are part of the team. In all the other companies I've worked for, I had no idea what was happening in another part of the business; here I know everything." Adds Joe Vicens, executive vice president and general manager of the national division, "Nap shares the vision with the group and the vision is what excites us." Jennifer Grassano, a bedding consultant who both sells and coaches other bedding consultants, comments: "Nap treats everyone the same way. He lets everyone have a voice regardless of position in the company, and he takes their advice."

Mike Veeck encourages the heart by giving people a chance to show what they can do. In 1997, he signed a female relief pitcher, Ila Borders, and told the team's manager simply to give her a chance. The St. Paul Saints' commentator for radio broadcasts, Don Wardlow, is blind. Wardlow is a knowledgeable baseball man and listeners would not know from the broadcast that he can't actually see the game. Mike Veeck explains: "The fact that I hired a blind color commentator was not that I specifically wanted to hire a blind person but was about growing up with a father with one leg. I saw him overcome barriers and prejudices."

Ukrop's encourages the hearts of its more than 5,000 associates by saying thank you in personalized ways. For their birthdays, full-time associates get the day off and receive a birthday card signed by James and Bob Ukrop. The card includes a $50 check. Many associates say, "The check is nice, but what I really like is the signed birthday card." The company also sends associates wedding and baby gifts. Part-time employees can assign up to $100 of their pay each quarter to a college fund and the company will match the sum dollar for dollar.

SUSTAINING SUCCESS WITH STABLE LEADERSHIP

Leading with values is difficult if the leader keeps changing. The sample companies as a group are notable in their senior management stability, a key contributor to their sustained success. Infusing values throughout an organization is a delicate process. Humane values are especially vulnerable for they require trust in the organization. It takes time for leaders to earn this trust. It takes time for leaders to establish the authenticity of values such as excellence, joy, and integrity. It takes time for leaders to assert themselves in the leadership roles described in this chapter. And the work is never done. Values-based leadership is an ongoing process; it is a journey.

Table 3–1 documents the leadership stability of the sample companies. Only three of the 14 companies have had more than two CEOs in their history. The majority of the companies still have their original chief executives as of this writing.

In 1997 David Pottruck was promoted to co-CEO of Charles Schwab Corporation, sharing the title with founder Charles Schwab, the company's sole CEO until that time. Charles Schwab remains as chairman. Pottruck joined Schwab in 1984, was named president of

TABLE 3–1

Leadership Stability in Sample Companies

Company	Year Company Started in Business	Number of CEOs in Company History[a]
Bergstrom Hotels	1976	2[b]
The Charles Schwab Corporation	1971	2[c]
Chick-fil-A, Inc.	1946	1
The Container Store	1978	1
Custom Research Inc.	1974	2[d]
Dana Commercial Credit	1980	1
Dial-A-Mattress	1976	1
Enterprise Rent-A-Car	1957	2
Midwest Express Airlines	1984	1
Miller SQA	1982	3[e]
Special Expeditions	1979	1
St. Paul Saints	1992	1
Ukrop's Super Markets, Inc.	1937	3
USAA	1922	8[f]

[a] All data as of August 1998.

[b] Bergstrom Hotels had only one chief executive, Richard Bergstrom, until it was sold in 1998 to Montclair Investors, Inc.

[c] Includes David Pottruck appointed co-CEO with Charles Schwab in 1997.

[d] Custom Research Inc. has been jointly led since its inception by partners Judith Corson and Jeffrey Pope.

[e] Includes the chief executive of the predecessor companies, Tradex and Phoenix Designs, Dwight Hoover.

[f] USAA first used the title of CEO in 1991. Since 1922, eight individuals have served in the senior leadership role at USAA under the title general manager, president, or CEO.

the brokerage unit in 1988, and president and chief operating officer and a board member of the corporation in 1994. Enterprise Rent-A-Car has had two CEOs in its history, company founder Jack Taylor and his son Andy. Bix Norman started as president of Phoenix Designs (later renamed Miller SQA) in 1989. The Herman Miller subsidiary's primary function at the time was reconditioning and selling used office furniture, a business Norman felt had little growth potential. Norman went to work reinventing the business, working in close partnership with Gary Van Spronsen and other managers he recruited. When Norman was promoted in 1998 to become chief information officer of Herman Miller, Van Spronsen replaced him as president. Ukrop's, in business for more than 60 years, is run by James and Bob Ukrop, the sons of the founder. All the CEOs in USAA's history have been retired military officers. General Robert Herres became chairman and CEO in 1993, replacing General Robert McDermott who retired from USAA after heading the company from 1968.

Bergstrom Hotels changed not only its leadership but also its ownership. In January 1998, John and Richard (Dick) Bergstrom, owners of Bergstrom Corporation, sold the Paper Valley Hotel, Pioneer Inn, and Valley Inn (Bergstrom Hotels) to Montclair Hotel Investors. Bergstrom Hotels was selected for the sample and studied prior to the transaction. Several years may be required to determine if the core values so strongly cultivated in the hotels by John and Dick Bergstrom and their management team can live through new owners. The Bergstrom Hotel Company I studied prior to the ownership change was a superb company. The prospects for sustaining the hotels' excellence remain high because the Bergstroms cultivated the development of "middle leaders" and the company adopted many progressive practices that are likely to be continued.

The Bergstroms' story is instructive. John Bergstrom sold automobiles and Dick worked in a bank when they joined forces and converted a former post office into a nightclub in 1974. They opened a second nightclub in 1975 and operated both while maintaining their day jobs. In 1976, the brothers bought the Valley Inn in Neenah, Wisconsin, in a bankruptcy sale; two years later they purchased another hotel, the Pioneer Inn and Marina in Oshkosh, that was muddling along with absentee ownership. With no background in the hotel business but a strong customer service ethic, the Bergstroms turned both properties into profitable businesses. They sold the nightclubs. John and Dick both recall the period when they first became hoteliers. John says, "In the beginning, we needed customers. We did not have the benefit of time. Whatever it took, we did and figured out later how to make money." As Dick remembers, "We found that in the nightclub business you can work hard on Friday and Saturday and make $2,000 a month, and in the hotel business you can work just as hard and make $10,000 a month if you do it right—and that was back in the 1970s."[7]

In 1981, the Bergstroms decided to build the Paper Valley Hotel in downtown Appleton, which opened in June 1982. The Paper Valley also became very successful, but not before the Bergstroms experienced a serious financial crisis. Budgeted to cost $10 million, the hotel wound up costing $13.6 million. Dick Bergstrom remembers the time vividly: "It was terrible. Business was good from the start, but we spent too much money. Having never built a hotel before, we got in over our heads. Fortunately, the banks stuck with us and we made it through." In 1985 and again in 1993, the Paper Valley Hotel added 100 rooms, expanding to its present capacity of 400 guest rooms. The Paper Valley is the largest of the three hotels and in 1997 was the only hotel in Wisconsin with a AAA Four Diamond designation for both lodging and dining.

While operating their hotels, the Bergstroms also were building the largest automotive business in Wisconsin, which in 1998 consisted of 22 car dealerships. The brothers found the car business profitable and less risky than the hotel business. "In the hotel business you have fixed debt, but in the automobile business you can manage your inventory up or down depending upon demand cycles," explains Dick Bergstrom. "We were in two profitable businesses and enjoyed them both but decided to devote our time and energy to the one with less risk. It was a business decision."

Business considerations aside, the Bergstroms probably would still own the hotels had they not found a buyer who shared their values. The brothers had not only invested their money in the hotels, they had invested themselves. Dick (whose primary role had been to run the hotels) visited each hotel daily. John also was a regular visitor. They referred to the visits as "making rounds." The brothers frequently sent handwritten notes to employees to recognize their contribution to the company. They lent money at no interest to employees in need and made sure employees with a serious illness received the proper medical care. The brothers operate with an "employees come first" philosophy, believing that if they take care of their employees the employees will take care of the customers. Finding the right buyer was crucial, as Dick Bergstrom explains:

> We were not willing to sell to someone who wasn't going to take care of the hotels and employees. This is our hometown. Our friends are here. This is where our family has been for 150 years. In Montclair Hotel Investors, we found a small company that is growing. The principals seem a lot like us. They are personable, down-to-earth people and not too fancy. I was prepared to insist that they retain all the employees, but it wasn't an issue. They said at the get-go, 'we want all of your people. We are not moving even one person in.'

REINFORCING VALUES

Values are intangible. Leaders cannot hold values in their hands to show an orientation class of new employees. What is most dear to the company, what more than anything else must be preserved, is invisible. For this reason, leaders often devise teaching aids to symbolize core values or make them more tangible. These aids can be especially helpful in the acculturation of newer employees.

Committing the values to written form is a common approach. In 1988, 10 years after The Container Store opened its first store, president and co-founder Kip Tindell was preparing to address the employees of the new Houston store prior to its opening. Over the years, Tindell had mentally processed the values guiding the company, but on this occasion he wrote them down. Tindell didn't really intend to write a formal values statement, but, rather, wanted the new employees to understand what their company stood for and how it differed from other retail stores. Tindell's words became known as the "foundation principles," and they have played an important role in codifying, teaching, and reinforcing the company's beliefs.

Every employee in the company is expected not only to know and practice the foundation principles but also to teach them to other employees. A primary role of all managers is to reinforce these principles. Barbara Anderson's primary role in the company is to help preserve the company culture. She says: "One of my greatest responsibilities is taking our six foundation principles to the stores and making sure everyone understands. I look for the principles being practiced." Anderson adds: "I believe a company can grow and still retain its values. We have found 1,500 people who share our values."

Although the foundation principles are written down in several employee handbooks, Anderson and others teach them primarily through oral story telling, mentoring, and role modeling. One of the six principles is "astonish our customers by helping them in the true sense of the word." The story always used to teach this principle is the "man in the desert." A man lost in the desert is parched and dry and cannot speak. He desperately wants water. What the principle teaches, however, is that giving the man water is but the starting point to truly helping him. "This man is so parched he can't say a word," Barbara Anderson tells an orientation class. "How will you use all of your abilities to help this man beyond giving him water? What else are you going to do to really help him?"

The foundation principles provide the guidance that corporate policy manuals are supposed to give but often don't and the motivational power that is beyond the reach of policy manuals. Store employee Karla Marie explains: "Our foundation principles are very specific in a flexible way. We don't have a procedures manual, but we do have a very specific philosophy. The principles allow plenty of room to do what is needed. I like the foundation principles a lot." Adds store colleague Melani Meyer: "What do we do in this situation? We go back to what the foundation principles say."

In different ways, other sample companies codify their values and/or ways to implement them. Charles Schwab Corporation periodically publishes a vision and values booklet and disseminates it to all employees. Ukrop's gives each employee a card on which its vision, mission, and shared values are printed. Ukrop's also gives Values Champion pins to employees who can recite the company's values—a useful approach in a company that relies on many young people working part-time while attending school. At Dial-A-Mattress, the vision statement is posted on the walls throughout its building: "The first and finest global tele-retailer of bedding committed to world class customer service."

Miller SQA's Street

Miller SQA reinforces its values through its building which functions both as an office facility and a factory in Holland, Michigan. Opened in 1995, the building represents core values such as innovation, joy, teamwork, and respect. A long, skylighted indoor walkway called the *Street* bridges the production and office areas and encourages interaction between office and factory workers. Plantings, street lamps, and natural lighting from the skylights give the Street an authentic feel. Employees enter the building through the Street; workers from both sides of the building use adjacent bathrooms.

The building has few walls or doors. A wellness center that includes a basketball court is available for all employees and their families to use. With 66 skylights in the building, employees can enjoy a sunny day while they work. The manufacturing floor is kept impeccable. The air in the building is completely replenished every hour. The hallways, byways, nooks, and niches are filled with colorful wood carvings of different animals symbolizing joy, playfulness, and the diversity of the work force. Every employee has a mail slot in the mail room. Outside the building is an all-natural environment of indigenous plants and grasses; water from the site forms ponds for wildlife. The Miller SQA facility won the *Business Week/Architectural Record* Award in 1997 for successful translation of specific business goals into architectural solutions. The building was cited for its use of natural light and its creation of areas for communication.[8]

The Container Store's "Gumby®"

The Container Store has a cartoon-character mascot known as Gumby®. From the six-foot-tall wooden Gumby® standing near the front door at company headquarters to the six-inch rubber Gumby® that stands on a desk or counter, the ever-present mascot symbolizes teamwork and flexibility. When employees hear the phrase, "We have to be Gumby®-like," they know it refers to doing whatever needs to be done to serve a customer, help a teammate, or complete a task. Gumby® is a tangible antidote combating the attitude, "It's not my job." The largest conference room at company headquarters is referred to as "The Gumby® Room." Why? Because it can be configured in various ways and is the building's most flexible room.

Dial-A-Mattress "Bedding Consultants"

Dial-A-Mattress refers to its salespeople as "bedding consultants" to reinforce the educational foundation undergirding the company's strategy and integrity. The terminology is a reminder to the salespeople *and* the customers. A company that aspires to make a living selling bedding over the telephone must be good at educating customers about bedding and at helping them make good choices.

Dial-A-Mattress, like a number of the sample companies, uses specific language to reinforce values and strategies. A word or phrase connoting a specific cherished value that is commonly emphasized within the company but rarely used outside of it can be powerfully symbolic. The language becomes company-specific and helps employees visualize what makes their company different. The frequent use of such language continually communicates the company's ethos.

Special Expeditions staff do not use the word *cruise*. They say *expedition* and *voyage* to reinforce the educational, experiential, and participatory nature of their service and to convey their respect for the places they visit.

Ukrop's calls its headquarters the *Support Center* to symbolize management's primary role of supporting associates and to connote teamwork. The company's commitment to innovation is reflected in language such as *solution shopping*, *meal idea centers*, and *service self-service*.

At The Container Store part-time employees are *prime-timers*. These employees work when the stores are busiest and the prime-timer phrase conveys the excellent performance expected of them, the respect due them, and their full membership on the team. The company couples the word *sales* with various job functions, for example, *visual sales* instead of *stock and display* and *register sales* instead of *cashier*. Kip Tindell explains: "We deliberately use the word *selling*.

There is no difference between selling and customer service; they are the same thing."

Businesses that depend on people to serve customers effectively require the sustaining power of values-driven leadership. Keeping performers performing at a high level month after month, year after year, despite myriad service gremlins ranging from task repetitiousness to emotional burnout is a task too tall for numerous companies. Many service companies never perform at a high level; many others excel initially but lose their effectiveness over time. A smaller group of companies has been able to sustain high levels of service performance and continue to improve. What they hold in common is a strong set of values that tap into employees' own core values, and a strong set of leaders who teach, model, and cultivate the values. Values-driven leadership sustains the high discretionary efforts of human beings to individually and collaboratively achieve and *gives root* to the eight other success drivers discussed in the remainder of this book.

4

STRATEGIC FOCUS

Napoleon Barragan started Dial-A-Mattress in 1976 as a sideline to his primary business, a small furniture store in the Queens borough of New York City. By 1998, Dial-A-Mattress was generating more than $70 million in annual sales and the store in Queens was a memory.

Barragan immigrated to New York City in 1968 from Ecuador. He had a wife and child and about $10 in his pocket. He had been a teacher in Colombia and had even run a school there, but he had no license to teach in New York. His poor command of English was another obstacle. He worked in small factories for a few years and then in 1973 began working as a salesman in a furniture store and soon became sales manager. The next year he opened his own furniture store in an area attracting many Hispanic immigrants. Because Spanish was Barragan's first language and he was an immigrant himself, he felt comfortable setting up shop in a multicultural community.

Barragan eked out a living but was frustrated because he could not attract customers who lived outside the borough or serve those who wanted to shop during off-hours. Barragan's idea for Dial-A-Mattress took root in September 1976 when he spotted a small advertisement in *The New York Post* for Dial-A-Steak, a company that would deliver ready-to-eat steaks to people's homes in about 40 minutes. Barragan thought this was an incredible idea, and in a few days he was advertising mattresses that could be ordered over the telephone and delivered to customers' residences. The offer included removing the customer's old mattress at no additional cost. The phone started ringing and a new business was born.[1]

As the years passed, Barragan refined the strategy to include a toll-free telephone number (1-800-MATTRES*); 24-hours-a-day, seven-days-a-week ordering; and same-day delivery (within two hours if needed). Through franchised distributors, coverage was expanded to include East Coast markets including New England, Maryland, and Florida. Dial-A-Mattress also has been opening showrooms in alliances with store retailers to accommodate customers who need to see and touch a mattress before buying. By 1998, the Dial-A-Mattress "Network of Retailers" had grown to more than 20 companies nationwide. In addition to providing showroom space, these retailers advertise the Dial-A-Mattress 1-800 number. Dial-A-Mattress makes the sale, the local retailer delivers and installs the bedding, and the two companies share the revenue. Barragan is extending his retailer network to other countries.

Dial-A-Mattress is a dynamic company, always searching for ways to improve the business. Unchanged, however, is the basic strategy of making it easy for consumers to buy a product that is notoriously difficult to buy. Most consumers are inexperienced bedding buyers and some are easy prey for mattress retailers who use bait-and-switch tactics and misrepresentation in selling. Barragan has built a business that turns its inventory 60 times a year (the industry average is 10 turns) by stressing ethical selling through customer education, by offering customers the convenience of buying day or night over the telephone toll-free, by delivering the bedding to customers' homes when they want it—day or night—and by investing in customers' satisfaction through a 30-day trial period. Sometimes Dial-A-Mattress sends two mattresses to the customer's home, and the truck brings back the one the customer doesn't want. Thirty percent of the company's new buyers are referred by satisfied customers.

Bedding consultant Louise Siracusano comments: "Customers are

---

*The missing "s" in Mattress is not a typographical error. This is the original 1-800 number. However, Dial-A-Mattress also controls a variety of related numbers to accommodate caller mistakes. All the numbers ring in the company's call center. For example, the 7 to 8 percent of callers who misspell mattress with one "t" still reach the call center.

surprised that they can get the mattress today and that we are really here to help them and not just get in their pocket. A lot of callers start laughing, saying that they never have bought a bed on the telephone before." Napoleon Barragan adds: "Buying a mattress is not a pleasurable experience; it's a chore. If you can make it easy for consumers, if you give them what they want, the way they want it, and when they want it, you can do business."

Dial-A-Mattress illustrates a success-sustaining characteristic found in every sample company: strategic focus. Once Napoleon Barragan sensed the power of telemarketing to make mattress buying easier and more satisfying for customers, he diligently pursued this course, transforming it into a clear, compelling mission. He continues to refine and improve the strategy, through changes such as adding showrooms for customers reluctant to buy bedding sight unseen, but he has not strayed from the fundamental idea of making mattress buying easy and comfortable for consumers. The first rule Barragan learned as a store retailer was "location, location, location." After seeing the Dial-A-Steak advertisement and experimenting with selling mattresses over the telephone, Barragan learned an even more powerful lesson: location doesn't matter when customers use a 1-800 telephone number.

The sample companies define their business in strikingly clear terms. They know how they want to create value for customers and devoutly pursue this basic concept of the business. They do not drift from the central strategy that defines the company's "reason for being." These companies know what they want to do—and what they do *not* want to do. They are dynamic, innovative companies, but their dynamism and innovation are channeled in service of a central mission. These firms have a constancy of purpose that rarely is penetrated by distraction.

A CONSTANCY OF PURPOSE

Just as the sample firms benefit from a clear set of values, so do they benefit from a clear strategy. In a very real sense, the strategy stems from and is sustained by the values. It is doubtful that Dial-A-Mattress could have made a business out of selling mattresses over the telephone without the guiding force of values such as respect and integrity;

it probably wouldn't have tried were it not for Napoleon Barragan's passion for innovation. The crucial relationship among core values, strategy, and execution is portrayed in Exhibit 4–1. The openings in the rings indicate the interplay among values, strategy, and execution. Values guide and motivate strategy and execution; they, in turn, strengthen the values. This chapter discusses the two strategy rings; Chapter 5 covers the execution ring.

Sustainable success in service businesses requires a core strategy that galvanizes the human spirit and transforms potential into performance. This core strategy is the *definition* of the business, and it changes rarely, if at all. Supporting the core strategy is an integrated system of substrategies that turn a basic idea (the core strategy) into the service or service plus tangible product combination that is marketed—the market offer. The substrategies constitute a system of activities that collectively represent the *design* of the business. Business design changes occur frequently as the company adds or drops activities to more effectively implement the core strategy.

Execution refers to the performance of individual substrategies. Executional change is continuous in excellent companies as senior and

EXHIBIT 4–1
Strategy Connections

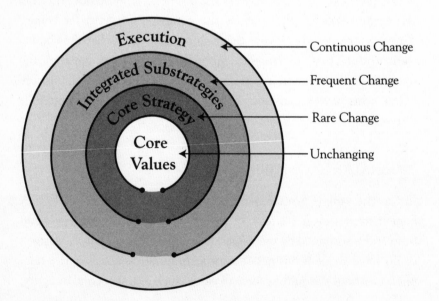

middle leaders challenge the status quo and seek performance improvement. Collins and Porras conclude that excellent companies have a special ability to manage continuity and change.[2] This certainly is true for the sample companies. Their values are unshakable and their core strategies clear, strong, and stable. Their substrategies and executional efforts, on the other hand, are in motion—just as values such as excellence and innovation require.

Core Strategy

On the surface, the core strategies of the sample companies are quite different. Closer analysis reveals common traits. First, the companies' core strategies focus on *serving a specific market need rather than on marketing a specific product for that need*. By defining their businesses in terms of fundamental customer needs rather than currently popular ways to satisfy those needs (customer wants), the sample firms have identified enduring paths to follow. The substrategy mix changes as customer wants change, but the underlying mission remains the same.

Defining the business in terms of the market instead of the product is an old idea, first proposed by Theodore Levitt in 1960 in his classic article, "Marketing Myopia."[3] Levitt argued that the real business of railroads was not railroads but transportation. Rail travel was the product, transportation was the need. Products change, needs endure.

A common reason companies find it necessary to redefine their business is that part or all of the original definition was product-focused. Charles Schwab Corporation is a good example. In 1995, the company changed its 20-year-old core strategy from "to provide investors with the most useful and ethical brokerage services in America" to "to provide customers with the most useful and ethical financial services in the world." The first part of Schwab's original business definition is need-focused ("useful and ethical"), but the second part is product-focused ("brokerage services"). Chuck Schwab's vision of encouraging and enabling people to become investors through efficiently delivered and ethically sold services endures. What has changed is the scope of the business—broadening from brokerage to financial services, from not advising investors to advising them, and from the U.S. market to the world market.

Some readers might argue that even "financial services" is too limiting for a company like Charles Schwab, that it too is "product-focused." This is not correct, however. For a core strategy to provide a focused path, definition of scope is necessary. The key is distinguishing between a changeable want and an unchanging need. At some level of generality, a product becomes a need. Investors' wants for specific financial instruments change, but they continue to need financial services.

Second, the sample companies focus on *serving underserved market needs*. Without exception, these companies are doing something that needs doing. They found openings in the market and built successful businesses by providing customers something valuable that they weren't getting before. Charles Schwab Corporation gave investors who knew what stocks they wanted to buy or sell the opportunity to do so without paying full commissions for "advice" they didn't use. Enterprise Rent-A-Car focused on serving local people whose personal cars were temporarily unavailable to them and built a business in "the replacement market." While Hertz, Avis, and National Car Rental emphasized airport locations to target travelers, Enterprise targeted people whose cars were in the shop and quietly built a rental fleet bigger than any other rental car company. USAA focused on a market group that other automobile insurers did not want—members of the military who move often. Starting as an automobile insurer, USAA evolved into a one-stop financial services provider for the military market, today serving more than three million customers.

Third, the companies focus on *serving their chosen markets in a superior manner*. A principal reason for the sustained success of these companies to date is the customer-perceived superiority of their market offers. They not only are doing something that needs doing, they are doing it exceptionally well—which is a good thing since success inevitably attracts many imitators that want a piece of the action. Chick-fil-A's food is unusually tasty for quick-service food, generally rating at least one scale point higher than competitive entries on taste tests using five-point scales. Ukrop's faces more competitors in the Richmond market than at any time in its history, yet the company commands by far the largest market share with products, customer service, and stores that are demonstrably better than the competition's.

The Container Store's success encouraged many startup retailers specializing in storage and organization products. A number of these companies eventually failed because The Container Store is difficult to imitate. Most of these retailers, for example, have been unwilling or unable to sell complex products like component, modular storage systems because they require highly trained salespeople. The Container Store sells two-thirds of the elfa® storage system product line in the United States. As President Kip Tindell states: "Our niche is to sell the hard stuff."

A willingness to defy conventional wisdom frequently opens the way to a superior offer. It is hard to be demonstrably better when adhering to conventional practice. Opportunity more often is found outside the boundaries of convention. Midwest Express is an unusually successful airline because they treat commercial airline passengers flying coach as though they were flying first class. No passengers sit in middle seats because there are no middle seats. The seats are larger than normal, leather, and comfortable; they look like first-class seats. The airline serves full meals on china, even at nonmeal times. They serve complimentary wine or champagne and chocolate chip cookies freshly baked on board. And the flight attendants are invariably friendly. Midwest Express has been true to its core strategy of the "best care in the air" and has achieved competitive differentiation as a result. In a commodity-like industry, Midwest Express is a noncommodity player.

A fourth trait, *focusing on the core strategy*, facilitates its superior presentation to customers. Strategic focus involves purposely erecting strategic boundaries and then competing within those boundaries for maximum effectiveness. In a strategic sense, less is more. These companies have chosen a core strategy, and they pursue it with unrestrained exuberance. In so doing, priorities are clear in designing a substrategy system, employees who must execute the strategy know and understand it, and a consistent image of what the company is about is presented to stakeholders.[4]

Genuine commitment to a core strategy eludes many companies because, as Michael Porter cogently argues in a seminal article entitled "What Is Strategy?" tradeoffs and limits have the appearance of constraining growth. Serving one group of customers and excluding other groups, for example, places a real or perceived restraint on growth. Thus, executives are continually tempted to broaden the strategy by extending product lines, seeking new market segments, adding new businesses. Unfortunately, this often results in a blurred core strategy, as Porter explains: "Attempts to compete in several ways at once create confusion and undermine organizational motivation and focus. . . . Strategy is making tradeoffs in competing. The essence of strategy is choosing what *not* to do."[5]

Custom Research's core strategy is to help clients make better business decisions through customized marketing research information. The company tailors a common set of processes to the specific requirements of each client and each study. As Executive Vice President Diane Kokal explains, "We are a custom business with a common backbone. Each project is different. We do 450 unique projects every year." In 1988, Custom Research made one of its most critical decisions: to accept business only from larger clients needing multiple research studies during a year. To provide the level of customized service it wished to provide, it made sense to focus staff attention on clients with whom an ongoing relationship already existed or could be built. This decision meant giving up half of the client list. Yet management decided to take this step when it compared Custom Research to an advertising agency. Just as advertising agencies wouldn't create only one advertisement for a client, it didn't make sense for Custom Research to serve one-study clients. Thus, Custom Research stopped soliciting the business of smaller companies.

The staff learned how to turn down clients. It proved to be a great decision. In 1988, the company's revenue from 138 clients was $10.9 million; 1997 revenue was $26 million from 80 clients. The efficiencies associated with doing more business with fewer clients boosted profits considerably. "It was a wonderful decision. It also was a scary decision at the time we made it," says company co-founder Jeff Pope.

Enterprise Rent-A-Car also illustrates the power of core strategy commitment. Focusing on the replacement market for rental cars has enabled Enterprise to develop a finely tuned system of substrategies to serve it. If Enterprise knows how to rent cars, one might ask, why don't they also rent them at airports and significantly expand their business? The answer is that renting cars to travelers is a different business from renting to people needing replacement vehicles. The replacement market requires a different type of marketing and service delivery system. The customers' needs differ, as Enterprise CEO Andy Taylor explains:

> Our business is more complicated than the airport rental business. The airport renter plans the trip and makes a reservation for the car. Our customer wakes up in the morning not planning on having a car accident and needing a rental car. We not only have the driver as a customer but also the body shop or insurance agency.
>
> Yes, it's a problem not being at the airport. Customers like us and when they travel they want to use us and we are not there. We do have locations near the top 100 airports, but it's a "friends and family" type of service. My position is to stay focused on the home city market and do it better than anyone else. The market is growing nicely.

For Enterprise Rent-A-Car, one of America's fastest growing service companies, less clearly is more. Its focus on the replacement market has given it clarity of purpose, experience and credibility in this specific business, and a big head start.

Integrated Substrategies

The Container Store's core strategy is the same today as when the company started in 1978: "To better customers' lives by giving them more time and space." From this fundamental idea has evolved one of America's best retail chains—a company revered by its customers, employees, and vendors and incessantly copied by hopeful competitors. The power of this basic idea is quite remarkable. It captures a fundamental, enduring need of human beings to do something with possessions they are not currently holding in their hands—to not only put things away but to put things away in their proper places.

The idea of giving customers more time and space is sufficiently narrow to provide strategic guidance and sufficiently broad to allow infinite creativity. Co-owner and Vice President of Merchandising Sharon Tindell elaborates: "You are not born an organized or disorganized person. It's a conditioned state. Organization is on a continuum. For example, some people may keep all of their belts in a box, whereas others may separate all of their belts by style and color. Even after 20 years, there is so much left to explore with our focus."

The Container Store's business definition has each of the traits discussed in the last section. It reflects a market need that is underserved. It lends itself to inspired application and provides the opportunity for performance-based differentiation. It involves "bettering peoples' lives," a path worthy of focused commitment. The Container Store's core strategy is powerful—but a powerful idea is not enough. The business graveyard is home to many failed businesses that were premised on powerful ideas.

For a business to become and remain successful, the core strategy still must be implemented through an effective business design (the substrategies) and effective execution. The execution of the business design is the market offer. The market offer, in turn, directly influences the total product—the gestalt of the customers' experience with the company's mix of services, goods, service quality, and facilities. The market offer is what the company puts on the market; the total product is what the customer experiences. Exhibit 4–2 portrays these relationships.

An idea in and of itself cannot solve customers' problems; only an

EXHIBIT 4–2

From Core Strategy to Total Product

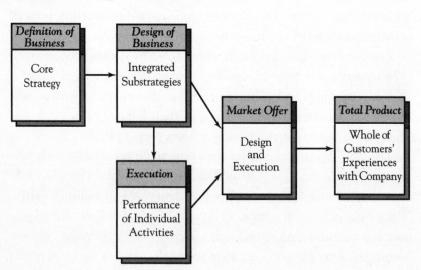

Definition of Business	Design of Business		Market Offer	Total Product
Core Strategy	Integrated Substrategies		Design and Execution	Whole of Customers' Experiences with Company
	Execution			
	Performance of Individual Activities			

idea transformed into actual goods and services has that power. Strategy has two essential parts: a need-fulfilling idea and a system of activities that turns the idea into a valuable market offer. Integrating these activities to reinforce and complement one another is critical. Competitive advantage and sustainable success come from the entire system of activities; it is more difficult for competitors to imitate an entire system of activities than it is to imitate individual activities.[6] The sustained success of The Container Store and other sample companies stems not only from their focused core strategies but also from their focused substrategies.

One vendor has tried more than once to convince The Container Store to carry lamps. The answer always is "no." The Container Store does not stray from selling multipurpose storage and organization products that are expected to meet three criteria:

- *Visibility*—people should be able to see what they have stored.
- *Accessibility*—people should be able to get to what they have stored.
- *Versatility*—people should be able to fit the product to their particular requirements.

To obtain the types of products and quality level required by its core strategy, The Container Store proactively seeks out companies to manufacture to its specifications. Not satisfied with the quality of garment bags on the market, for example, The Container Store worked with a manufacturer to create a garment bag that combined the best elements of all the bags then available. Clear, thicker vinyl, a better appearance, more substantial stitching, and a steel rod to prevent the bag from sagging were among the improvements. The Container Store employees tested prototypes of the bag in their homes. They also brought their heavy clothing to work to hang in the bag and test its strength; they attempted to rip the bag's seams. Passing these and other tests, the bag was put into the stores and has become a strong seller. The story of the garment bag has been repeated many times over the years with other products. The Container Store is not a manufacturer but guides much of its product manufacturing—the only way it can bring unique merchandise that solves customers' storage problems to the market. Customized, quality-controlled product sourcing is an integral substrategy.

The solutions particular products offer are not always obvious. And one customer's lifestyle, requirements, and preferences differ from another's. The Container Store, therefore, emphasizes "solution selling," which manifests itself in merchandising displays, signage, in-store placement of products, and well-trained salespeople who can demonstrate products and propose solutions. The merchandise is carefully arranged within sections flagged with banners, such as *Kitchen*, *Closet*, *Trash*, *Shelving*, *Bath*, *Laundry*, and *Office*. Many products are displayed in several different sections of the store because they can be used to solve multiple problems. A sweater box, for example, also can store office supplies. Plastic trash cans can be used for trash but also to store dog food or to hold recyclables. Individual products not only are sold separately but also often combined and sold as a system. Parents in the store to equip their kids for summer camp living may find a trunk filled with a variety of organizational products for camp. Everything in the trunk is for sale—and so is the trunk.

Store personnel are taught to determine what customers require and to help them find just the right solution. They are expected to demonstrate a product's functions, to show its benefits, to create an air of excitement. Sales trainers are assigned to specific stores for the ongoing development of the staff's solution-selling skills and knowledge.

Many items are displayed without packaging or labels to free the imaginations of the sales staff and customers to devise creative uses for the products. This is fun for employees and customers. Chief Executive Officer Garrett Boone explains:

> Retailing has a theatrical component. We want an air of excitement in the store. This is created by the people in the store, through their interaction with each other and with customers. We want our people to talk to customers, to help them feel the excitement. Speak loudly. Assemble stuff for them. Don't do anything in the back room that can be done on the floor. The store must look good, but even more important it must *feel* good.[7]

Solution selling works only if the products that form the solution are in stock. Integral to The Container Store's strategy is a state-of-the-art distribution and inventory control system. Frequent replenishment of store inventories minimizes out-of-stock conditions.

The Container Store searches for high-traffic store locations that are easily seen from the street. The company believes in visually merchandising the exterior of a store, not just the inside. Its best location is across the street from the Galleria Mall in Houston. The store benefits from the traffic draw of the mall without the parking congestion. More than 100,000 cars a day use the surface street in front of the store, which has 300 linear feet of glass visible from the street. The location possesses what co-owner and vice president of real estate John Mullen calls "street geometry." "Big-box retail stores without glass ignore the emotional and spiritual side of retailing," Mullen says.

Selling boxes and related storage products seems like a simple business. It's not when the mission is to better customers' lives by giving them more time and space. The Container Store has developed and continues to improve an interlocking system of substrategies that is difficult for competitors to duplicate. Benefiting from a strong value system, exceptional leadership, a clear, needs-based core strategy, an integrated system of substrategies, and a commitment to continuous improvement in everything it does, The Container Store competes with a compelling "total product." The company exemplifies the power of strategic focus.

STRATEGIC INNOVATION

Simultaneously managing change and continuity is a complex but necessary challenge that all leaders must meet. Just as strategic focus is a success sustainer, blind devotion to the past is a success killer. The pace of change continues to accelerate in every industry, every market. New technologies and products are coming faster than at any time in history. It was 55 years from invention before one-quarter of the population had automobiles. The telephone required 35 years, television 26 years. It was only 16 years from introduction before one-fourth of the population owned personal computers and only 13 years before they owned cellular telephones. One technology leads to others at a furious pace. The microchip, invented in 1971, already has led to the invention of many "smart" consumer products, including telephone answering machines, pocket calculators, camcorders, compact disc players, personal computers, digital cameras, microwave ovens, pagers, and VCRs. As the costs of these products decline over time and their designs improve, they diffuse rapidly through the population. What once did not exist comes on the market as a luxury and in a matter of a few years becomes a necessity.[8]

Successful companies effect a good fit between what and how targeted markets want to buy, and what and how they sell. As markets change, so must the companies. Indeed, the best companies lead market change; they identify new opportunities just as they are beginning to emerge, develop the internal capabilities and strategies to meet them, and employ creative marketing to encourage customer prospects to act. The great companies usually are ahead of the curve; they lead rather than follow.

Strategic focus is not the enemy of innovation but its ally. Focus gives a company a shot at excellence. A compelling mission offers direction, channels resources, inspires effort, replenishes energy—all requirements of excellence. Excellence also requires innovation, for excellence is a moving target. What is excellent today may be average tomorrow.

The sample companies are simultaneously focused *and* entrepreneurial. They share the core competency of knowing what to preserve and what to change. Focused on their core strategy and true to their core values, they are dynamic implementers of the strategy. These companies are innovative on both the strategic and execution levels, that is, adding new activities and improving the execution of existing activities. The desire to be the best in their chosen business runs deep and compels internal change.

Several of the sample companies have changed their core strategies at some point in their histories. Both USAA and Charles Schwab broadened their core strategies from automobile insurance and securities brokerage services, respectively, to financial services. Miller SQA changed its core strategy to simple, quick, and affordable office furniture rather than retain its predecessor company's strategy of reconditioning used furniture. Enterprise Rent-A-Car started as a car leasing company in 1957 and did not start rentals until 1963. Yet change at the core strategy level occurs infrequently.

Far more common is strategic change at the substrategy level to extend coverage of the market or accommodate shifts in customer wants. Ukrop's was one of the nation's first supermarket chains to sense opportunity in consumers' escalating poverty of time. Working women had less time to shop for food and prepare meals. Food stores lost significant market share to restaurants in the 1980s and 1990s. Meals in a hurry, meals on the run, even meals in the car became part of many consumers' lifestyles.

In response Ukrop's shifted its merchandising emphasis to "solution shopping" with "Meal Idea" centers in the store, ready-to-eat "Dinner for 2" dinner selections, and in-store restaurants serving a wide variety of made-to-order items. Ukrop's sells more fried chicken in the Richmond market than Kentucky Fried Chicken. To attain the levels of food quality and variety required to differentiate its ready-to-eat meals strategy from competitors', Ukrop's built a food manufacturing center, one of its boldest decisions. Producing dozens of ready-to-eat entrees, side dishes, and desserts in Ukrop's Central Kitchen is integral to the company's efforts to combine quality and time-saving in its market offer. The company extends the convenience of its market offer with numerous on-premise services, including one-hour photo processing, dry-cleaning, party-planning, banking, and carry-out catering. It features special store sections, including an international food aisle signed with country flags, a Pet Center displaying all pet supplies in one place, and a Tasting Center for cooking demonstrations. In addition, it extends targeted discounts to customers based on their purchasing history.

Listening for Innovation

What passes for innovation in many companies is actually one-upmanship imitation. Determined to out-duel competitors, companies frequently invest in product refinements rather than truly innovative offerings. True innovation requires a singular focus on customers—rather than on the competition—which is hard to do when numerous competitors are cutting prices, claiming superiority in advertising, and otherwise creating havoc in a market. Yet only customers can lead to radically new ways of creating value for their own benefit. Customers probably cannot describe the nonexistent product that would satisfy their unmet wants; they may not even be able to articulate their wants very well. However, they can comment on what frustrates them about

current offerings. Often embedded in these comments are hints of underserved wants and unmet dreams. Unearthing these hints for creative transformation into new product concepts requires disciplined
listening to prospective and existing customers and to the employees
who serve customers. Occasional surveys are insufficient. Companies
need to build market listening systems.

Listening systems uncover fresh marketplace intelligence, help
guide decision making, and nurture creative thinking. Effective listening systems involve both formal and informal methods, dialogue with
customers, the use of trend data to reveal changing patterns, the dis-
semination of relevant information to all employees, and active discussion and application of findings in work groups.[9]

Listening leads to learning, which sets the stage for innovation.
Genuine innovation is more likely when employees are well informed
about customers, unafraid to try something radically different—even
when it competes with the company's existing offerings—and committed to the organization's long-term success. Charles Schwab Corporation actively nurtures innovation by encouraging managers to listen
intently to customers and by defining acceptable failure:

- It can't put the company at risk.
- Reasonable precautions against failure should be taken.
- Failure must produce learning.[10]

Schwab innovation failures that meet these tests—and they admit to
many—are considered a necessary part of building a strong business.

Schwab makes extensive use of conventional marketing research
methods, such as consumer surveys, but places even more emphasis on
getting face-to-face with customers to listen for a phrase like "I know it's
not possible, but I wish. . . ." Schwab's top management travels exten-
sively to interact with customers in informal settings. Branches host
monthly customer receptions, and each week Schwab polls employees
in different cities to hear their ideas, suggestions, and concerns.

A Maverick Company

Charles Schwab is a maverick company that is not only willing to try
the untried but also eager to do it. It is a company with singular focus

and strong ambition that listens intently to customers. Strategic innovation at a high level evolves from these company characteristics.

The company had a hunch that some investors might wish to bet on the outcome of the 1980 election and kept its trading lines open all night for the first time on the eve of the election. The dramatic response—more than 15,000 trades—handed the company another way to increase the value of its market offer. Co-CEO David Pottruck recalls:

> We took a risk and found out, by a simple trial, that customers really like coming home at night, having dinner and then settling down with their portfolios to make transactions in the privacy and comfort of their homes. We've been open 24 hours a day ever since.[11]

Schwab's mutual fund business took off in 1992 after the company launched OneSource, a service that enables customers to buy more than 800 no-load mutual funds through Schwab with no transaction fee while consolidating their holdings in one monthly statement. Prior to OneSource, mutual fund customers had the option of buying no-load funds from separate sources at no fee or buying a variety of funds from Schwab and paying a commission. Motivated by customers' wishing it were possible to access a single source of mutual funds but pay no transaction fee, Schwab persuaded the mutual fund companies to pay the transaction charges and created OneSource, a $57 billion business at year-end 1997.

Schwab also was a pioneer in online trading, introducing Internet trading in 1996. In effect, Schwab enables customers to access services however they choose—by interacting with account representatives in branch offices or over the telephone and by gathering information and effecting trades through a touch-tone telephone or the Internet. Through Schwab's web site, investors can trade in stocks, bonds, mutual funds, and options; they can work with asset allocation models, obtain stock quotes, and access updated personal account information. Investors also can access considerable information on specific companies, industries, and investment vehicles. Through its web site, Schwab offers MarketBuzz, an electronic gateway to more than 80 third-party information providers and Mutual Fund OneSource Online, which provides current performance data on hundreds of mutual funds.

In 1998, Schwab serviced more than twice the number of on-line brokerage accounts than its closest competitor at the time, PC Financial Network. Spearheading its leadership in cybertrading is the company's willingness to invest significant sums in information technology (between 11 and 14 percent of revenues in recent years) and to compete with its existing higher margin services to better serve certain customer segments. Schwab's senior management believes that virtually all active investors will use computers to manage their investments and that the computer will be to investing what television is to advertising. "We're always looking for new ways to marry technology with the human touch," states Chuck Schwab. "That means that we completely reinvent our technology operations every three to four years."[12]

The most far-reaching strategy shift at Schwab has been its transition from a discount securities brokerage that did not dispense investment advice to a financial service provider that does—cautiously and free from conflicts of interest that stem from commission-based salesperson compensation. Schwab's consumer research in the 1970s and most of the 1980s revealed a large segment of self-reliant investors who had little interest in paying for advice they didn't need. Towards the end of the 1980s, however, the research showed a growing interest in investment help. Wanting to plan proactively for their retirement years, worried about the long-term stability of Social Security, possibly sandwiched between financial responsibilities for both their children and their parents, baby boomers—many of whom were novice stock market investors—wanted advice they could trust. Schwab was well positioned to capitalize on this emerging market opportunity, but the strategic move required shelving its time-honored tradition of not guiding investor decisions. It has made this transition by emphasizing investor education rather than the recommending of specific securities. Among Schwab's advice-giving activities are these:

- The Schwab Mutual Fund Select List, a monthly list of top mutual funds based on long-term performance criteria, and Mutual Fund Report Cards, a rating of funds, prepared by independent research organizations.
- Computer-based asset allocation models based on investors' goals,

risk tolerance, and life-cycle stage. Branch office personnel work with investors using the models.

- Schwab AdvisorSource, which matches investors with fee-compensated investment advisors in their geographic area.

The company feeds its stream of innovations with perpetual paranoia. "We never feel comfortable," states David Pottruck. "Incumbent companies in our industry have never been more at risk as new technology dismisses traditional advantages. Incumbents have to think like startups. If I'm going to lose to a startup, I want to lose to my own. If our Internet business cannibalizes our other business, at least it is ours." Thus far, the company and its shareowners have profited handsomely from perpetual paranoia. Between 1988 and 1997, Schwab's stock increased more than thirtyfold in value. Average annual growth in customer assets was 40 percent between 1993 and 1997. At year-end 1997, Schwab held $354 billion in customer assets. In 1997 alone, Schwab opened 1.2 million new accounts. More than 40 percent of Schwab's total trades are placed online by customers. Chuck Schwab, who started the company in 1971 with a $100,000 loan, is today worth hundreds of millions of dollars.

Strategic focus is a success sustainer. The companies studied for this book benefit not only from a clear set of values but also from a clear, compelling strategy. They have clearly defined their business and tailored a system of activities to implement it and none other—the essence of strategic focus. These companies are dynamic and innovative, always searching for ways to improve the value of their market offers and to extend their distance from competitors. But their dynamism and innovation are channeled; they are focused on delivering a core strategy in service of an enduring customer need. These companies know what to preserve and what to change.

5

EXECUTIONAL
EXCELLENCE

Travelers arrive at the *Sea Lion* docked in La Paz, Mexico, weary from their journeys but anticipating the expedition that lies ahead. Special Expeditions' *Sea Lion* accommodates 70 passengers in 36 cabins. The vessel is large enough to operate in remote environments, yet small enough to reach places inaccessible to larger ships.

Assembling in the ship's lounge for a pre-dinner reception, travelers receive name badges to wear throughout the expedition to facilitate bonding with fellow passengers and with the staff. Expedition Leader Bud Lehnhausen takes the microphone to introduce himself, his staff of naturalists, and the *Sea Lion's* captain, Jill Russell, who, in turn, introduces her officer crew—the mates. Although the ship's staff have led the Sea of Cortez expedition many times, they seem genuinely eager to share the treasures of the area with these passengers. It is a good sign, indeed. So is the delicious dinner that follows.

The next morning the group visits an island off the coast of La Paz. A fleet of motorized landing craft called Zodiacs transports everyone to the island. One of the naturalists leading the group is William Lopez-Forment, a Ph.D. biologist and a spirited, enthusiastic teacher. A citizen of Mexico, Lopez-Forment clearly relishes exposing the natural beauty of his country to his customers on this day. Guiding the group into the rocks, stopping every few minutes for a mini-lecture on particular rocks, vegetation, and wildlife, Lopez-Forment dispenses not only knowledge but also sheer delight in the opportunity to revel in nature's gifts. Finding a desert opal, he shows off the rock as if it were the Superbowl trophy, shouting at the top of his lungs: "It's so perfect, it's not fair." The desert islands in the Sea of Cortez are pristine, rarely visited places. On this day, the only background sounds are the wind, the wildlife, and the waves. It's hard not to be glad you are here.

The group returns to the anchored *Sea Lion* for lunch and then considers three afternoon options: a strenuous hike up the rock formations on the beach, a mild beach walk, or snorkeling. Lee Moll leads the strenuous hike that afternoon. Moll started with Special Expeditions as a naturalist in 1989. Like the other naturalists, she is an independent contractor. She works from three to five months each year for Special Expeditions and also contracts with one other company. Moll has a degree in environmental conservation and has worked in the environmental field for both state and federal government. A group of eight follows Moll up the rocks. Moll stops from time to time to call attention to the vegetation, but the exercise is rigorous. At least some in the group will have sore muscles tomorrow. The climbing requires total concentration; one careless step can cause a slip. Up the hill, with fading sunlight, the sea below is breathtaking. No one seems eager to be somewhere else—including Moll, who brings the group down the hill to the Zodiac craft just as darkness prevails.

In the lounge before dinner comes the nightly ritual of "Recap" when each naturalist briefly presents something the group experienced during the day. Recap is showtime—an opportunity for learning, fun, and bonding between the naturalists and passengers. Many of the presenters use props. Lopez-Forment, for example, displays various commercial products made from prickly pear pads seen during the morning nature walk.

The next few days test the staff's creativity because rough seas prevent the captain from taking the ship to all of the islands planned. Early morning meetings between the expedition leader and captain and the expedition leader and naturalists result in numerous enticing options, including different types of hikes, snorkeling, sunbathing on the beach, and one-hour shore rides on the Zodiacs. Something significant occurred on the Zodiac shore ride. Twice, Bud Lehnhausen stopped the craft to pick up trash from the water that other visitors had left behind. Special Expeditions' staff emphasize in their passenger briefings the importance of leaving the places visited unscathed; vegetation and rock samples should be undisturbed; trash should not be left behind. That Special Expeditions picks up trash from other visitors is a point not lost on its own passengers.

The *Sea Lion* and other Special Expeditions ships are comfortable but not fancy. They feature no swimming pools, no midnight buffets, no dance troupes or comedy acts. Special Expeditions' market offer is wondrous nature in its most authentic and—weather permitting—most glorious state. The staff on board revere nature's gifts and model their reverence with words and deeds. Sharing beautiful, mostly unspoiled places with teachers who explain their nuances and extoll their virtues results in a total product experience for travelers not captured by the term *entertainment*. Travelers interact with nature so closely that their experiences often change their lives.

Whereas many service encounters last only a brief time, Special Expeditions' service lasts for a week or more. The affective—or emotional—content of the service is high. The experiential nature of the service precludes standardized delivery. Service providers and travelers are in close proximity; they are not separated by desks or counters; they explore nature together, ride in the Zodiacs together, eat together. This type of service—called an extended, affective, intimate service encounter by Price, Arnould, and Tierney[1]—is extremely difficult to deliver. The staff are "on-stage" day and night. They cannot feign enthusiasm, cannot just go through the motions, without their customers noticing. The service exchange requires providers to be actively involved with their customers in a way that is more characteristic of friendship than of a commercial service offering.[2]

Special Expeditions' ability to superbly *execute* an extended, affective, intimate service week after week with less than 12 hours separating voyages is central to the company's ongoing success. Company surveys confirm the strength of the total product. Senior Vice President Pamela Fingleton comments on what passengers say:

> You read the surveys from passengers and they have this wonderment about the experience. The lecture staff on board is a key. Passengers seem

in awe of the crew's enthusiasm and how much fun they have. They also notice the care with which the itinerary was developed. I've never heard or seen a comment from a passenger that the trip was not worth the money. We often hear comments such as 'It was a very expensive trip and beforehand I wondered if it would be worth it, but now I see it was worth every penny.'

Special Expeditions and the other sample companies emphasize executional excellence. They not only have focused strategies, they focus on execution. Good execution is not good enough. The firms stress continuous improvement in performing the activities that compose the service; they seek to be demonstrably better than competitors.

This chapter identifies and explores approaches and methods specifically geared to achieving executional excellence. Each subsequent chapter features other success sustainers that also contribute to executional excellence. The success sustainers depicted in Exhibit 1–1 are mutually supportive. Consistent excellence in service performance has many sources. Much of the remainder of the book is germane to executional excellence.

COMPETING FOR THE RIGHT TALENT

A focused strategy—no matter how brilliant—still must be executed. Nothing the sample companies do to support execution is more important than finding the right people to perform the service. In labor-intensive service businesses, the quality of the performers is integral to the quality of customers' experiences. The companies studied for this book simply cannot implement their strategies without exceptional people. These companies don't just recruit employees, they compete for talent.

Finding just the right person means identifying someone who not only has the capability to be successful in the company, to rise in the organization, and to make it a career, but also someone who has the requisite values. The sample companies seek prospective hires with diverse backgrounds and common values. They seek new employees whose personal values fit the organization's values. A poor values fit is a deal breaker no matter how talented a candidate might otherwise be.

The following comments illustrate the importance attached to values compatibility:

- "We look for people who in their soul really care about people." —Tamara McClelland, director of marketing service and customer satisfaction, Midwest Express
- "Operators come from many walks of life. We don't necessarily look for food people. We want a strong work ethic and family-oriented people. We look for people who will fit in our conservative family business. We want people you'd want your children to work for." —Huie Woods, vice president, human resources, Chick-fil-A
- "We have found people who have an affinity for our organization."—Jan Elsesser, executive vice president, sales and marketing, Custom Research Inc.
- "We take the time to find the people who fit our culture."—Natalie Levy, comptroller, The Container Store

Patient Hiring

The sample firms practice "patient hiring." Hiring decisions are considered crucial to the perpetuation of the business and employment candidates typically must pass muster through several screening steps and with multiple interviewers, including line personnel. The standards are high. Midwest Express uses open-ended questions in interviews to reveal candidates' values. Among the questions that may be asked are:

- "Tell me about a time you went out of your way to help another?"
- "Tell me about a time you are proud of?"
- "Tell me about a time you wish you had done something differently?"

These requests are followed by, "Then, what happened?" Candidates who clear this interview undergo further interviews more focused on job skills. Line employees provide input on actual hiring decisions. In 1998, the company was hiring between 50 and 60 people per month from about 800 applicants.

Custom Research looks for people who have the potential to move at least two levels above the position for which they are being inter-viewed. Candidates who clear initial testing and interviewing con-ducted by the human resources department then undergo individual interviews by line personnel. Each member of the interviewing team focuses on different dimensions and questions germane to the position and scores the candidate's responses. The team meets later for a formal debriefing. Typical questions in a Custom Research interview include:

- "Tell me about a time you made a really good decision—the situa-tion and the factors you weighed?"
- "Tell me about a time you had to deal with a difficult situation on the job and how you handled it?"
- "Tell me about an important achievement—what was the situation and what did you do?"

The individuals selected to operate Chick-fil-A restaurants are not employees but independent contractors. They put up $5,000 (actually a deposit that is returned if they leave) and split their restaurant after-expenses profits evenly with Chick-fil-A. Chick-fil-A makes the in-vestment to open the restaurant and guarantees the operator a minimum income of $30,000. The operator agreement, discussed in more depth in Chapter 8, is unusually attractive, and the selection process unusually rigorous. From the 9,000 annual applications for about 80 openings, Chick-fil-A seeks candidates who truly want to op-erate their own business in the restaurant industry, who have ties to the store's locale, who have demonstrated a strong work ethic in prior positions, and whose values fit the company's. The 10-page application questionnaire covers subjects such as personal and work-related goals, past accomplishments, geographic preferences, and demographic in-formation. A telephone screening interview is conducted with the most promising candidates, some of whom are then invited for a head-quarters interview. Multiple interviews and testing occur during this visit. Candidates still under consideration then work for several days in a Chick-fil-A restaurant for a dose of realism. Chick-fil-A will secure five or six in-depth references and conduct other background checks during this period. If the candidate and Chick-fil-A remain interested, the company arranges a second headquarters interview and this time invites the spouse. On the second visit, the candidate sees a different group of people and undergoes more in-depth interviews. The company assesses the spouse's commitment to the business and geographic location.

Few businesses use as rigorous a screening process as Chick-fil-A's store operator selection process. The system works well for Chick-fil-A, which depends on a low operator turnover rate to generate the desired return on its investment in individual stores. Chick-fil-A's annual operator turnover rate of 5 to 6 percent is dramatically low for the restaurant industry, especially quick-service restaurants. Additionally, the company's strategy of product and service superiority requires first-rate store operators. Tim Tassopoulos, vice president of field operations, explains:

> One reason we are successful is excellent products. We continue to bring out innovative products that just taste better. People are our other competitive advantage. Our success is fundamentally based on our operator system. We attract great operators and they attract great team members. An individual restaurant is only as good as its food and the people who serve it. And a chain is only as good as its individual locations.

Adds Craig Hall, who has been the Chick-fil-A operator in the Bryan-College Station, Texas, market since 1987 following a 22-year career in soft goods retailing: "The Chick-fil-A system allows an operator to run a business and share in its results with a $5,000 commitment. You are opening the doors to a lot of potential players compared to one of the big fast-food chains that might require a quarter-million-dollar franchise fee."

First Rule of Execution

The first rule of execution in the sample firms is to hire excellent people to implement the company strategy. Companies such as Midwest Express, Custom Research, and Chick-fil-A are employers of choice. Their reputation attracts more than their fair share of employment candidates to begin with, and the companies further leverage this advantage by aggressively seeking superior candidates. They are ardent career marketers using a host of methods including career opportunity fairs, job hotlines, four- and five-day workweeks, college scholarships, internships, and employee referrals. They aim high and search until they find just the right person. They subscribe to consultant Ron Zemke's view that hiring service performers is like casting a Broadway show. It needs to be done slowly.[3]

The appeal of the sample companies as employers sometimes results in remarkable persistence from applicants. Comments from Midwest Express reservation agents illustrate. States Sonya Wilborn: "I submitted my resume for three years. I wanted to work for Midwest Express—the people with the cookies and great seats." Adds Carrie Ehley: "I applied once and heard, 'We are not hiring at this time.' So I went to travel school to get experience. I then applied again and got a job." And Debbie Kujawa says: "I had two sisters-in-law who worked here. I wanted to work only for Midwest Express. I sent in multiple applications and finally got an interview. I was thrilled. It was totally a blessing."

PRE-GAME HUDDLES

Services are performed directly for customers or for the customers' property. Examples of the former are health care and education; examples of the latter are product repair and dry cleaning. Services performed directly for customers require the customers' participation during the performance. Providers interact with customers, cutting their hair, serving them a meal, singing them a song.

Serving customers directly can be demanding, stressful work. The service provider is "onstage," performing in view of customers expecting them to know the answers to a thousand different questions and managers expecting them to give respectful and professional service even when their customers are disagreeable or rude. Service providers are expected to maintain a high level of energy during delivery even if it is the 38th time or the 138th time they have performed the service that day. What may be a new experience for the customer usually is a routine experience for the provider.

In addition to the emotional strain of being onstage for hours at a time is the physical strain. Many service providers are on their feet much of the day—flight attendants, retail store salespeople, hotel housekeepers. For home games, the front-office staff of the St. Paul

Saints come to work at 8:30 A.M. and finish after the game around 11:00 P.M. In effect, they work two jobs in one day. Between 8:30 A.M. and 2:00 P.M. they work at their desks in street clothes. Then they take a break, reconvening in their Saints shirts—the uniform—at 5:00 P.M. to work the game. "It really helps us mentally to get away for a bit in the afternoon and to change clothes," says Jody Beaulieu, community relations director for the Saints. "We get tired. We are a small staff. But as soon as we start getting ready for the game and see the fans and the players warming up, the adrenaline starts to flow."

Directly counteracting the ever-present mental and physical fatigue is crucial to delivering consistently excellent service. Gathering the service group for a pre-shift huddle can be an effective approach. Just as in sports, huddles are an opportunity for teammates to plan their attack, to recommit to the larger goal, and to recommit to each other. Bringing the group together provides guidance and generates energy for going onstage.

Patriots Checking In

Laughter and smiles are abundant during the daily morning huddle of Paper Valley Hotel housekeepers. Executive housekeeper Paula Walters presides over the informal meeting, reviewing the anticipated number of check-outs and check-ins and discussing specific issues or hotel events. On this day, the New England Patriots of the National Football League will be checking into the hotel for a game the next day with the Green Bay Packers. After sharing banter and answering questions, Ms. Walters passes out room duty lists and keys to each housekeeper. Each will clean 14 to 16 rooms during the shift.

Fifteen minutes before The Container Store opens its doors at 9:00 A.M., the entire staff gathers for its daily huddle that is part informational, part skill building, part team building, and part goal focusing. On this day in late May, Super Sales Trainer Elaine Fuqua helps prepare the staff for a "College Bound" promotion. The staff is given three minutes to fill a toolbox with products students would need for a dormitory room. The staff scatters and then returns with finishing nails, tape, hanging wire, an over-the-door hook, and numerous other products.

Ms. Fuqua asks the staff to discuss why the products they found are good for dorm rooms. She then mentions some of the products the staff missed. Finally, she encourages everyone to talk up what they learned with staff arriving later in the day. The exercise is positive and everyone seems to enjoy it. Store manager Diane Higgins then announces yesterday's sales and discusses sales goals for the day and month: "We strongly believe in sharing our figures," explains Ms. Higgins. "You can't play the game if you don't know what's happening. These are the people who made yesterday's numbers." The Container Store repeats the huddle after the store closes each evening for staff not present in the morning.

Gearing Up for Homestands

Most St. Paul Saints homestands last three to six days. The day before or morning of the first game, the front office staff gathers to review a detailed pre-game timing sheet (see Table 5-1). Entertainment, promotions, community charitable events, game sponsors, special guests, concessions, and stadium operations are discussed in these huddles. Staging any service that draws 6,329 fans to the same place at the same time six evenings in a row is a daunting task. A St. Paul Saints game actually is many different services, including food and beverages, playing a baseball game, providing on-field entertainment between innings, delivering information and entertainment over the public address system, and announcing the game over the radio. The Saints staff needs to get mentally ready to play ball—just as the baseball team does.

MANAGING THE EVIDENCE

One way Midwest Express executes its core strategy of "the best care in the air" is through a carefully orchestrated stream of evidence. Customers experience an air transportation service differently than they experience a tangible product such as a tube of toothpaste, a wrist watch, a book, or an automobile. They taste toothpaste, wear a wrist watch, read a book, and drive a car. They see and touch these products. The physical nature of tangible products helps tell their story. A ser-

TABLE 5–1

St. Paul Saints Pre-game Timing Sheet

3:00	Parking list to Bob Hang banners
4:00	Lot opens Equipment and sound check (manuals and music to booth)
4:30	Saints player pass list to Liz in the ticket office Fan services, souvenirs and concessions set up
5:30	Pre-game entertainment—Filthy Rich Usher assignments Microphone set up
6:00	Main gate opens—PA music on Ushers pass out roster sheet and greet fans
6:30	Ballkids arrive
6:35	Field microphone in place Jill gathers balls for pre-game
6:40	Pre-game announcements Jill greets anthem and first-pitch guests Jill escorts them to the owners' box
6:50	Introduction of the pig
6:52	Introduce ballkids: Josh Zeller & Mark Sweeny Introduce honorary batboy: Joseph Marta
6:53	First pitch (1) MN Brewing representative (2) City Pages representative
6:56	Umps and coaches meet
7:01	Wait for coaches' signal to send the team to the field Send anthem singer to the microphone
7:02	National Anthem—Tonic Sol Fa
7:05	Play Ball!

vice's story needs to be told, too, and a key opportunity for doing so is through the tangibles associated with the service. Although air transportation is intangible—one cannot see or touch it—its associated tangibles can be manipulated to convey a specific story.

No airline does this better than Midwest Express. From the moment a passenger checks in for a flight and is offered a choice of newspapers, Midwest Express uses a succession of physical clues to manage the passenger's experience and instantiate the best care in the air. Boarding passengers see the two-by-two configuration of leather seats and it seems like first class even though it's coach. The plane isn't even aloft and already the service feels different from other airlines that use three-by-three seating in coach class. More physical differentiation comes in the meal service: china plates, paper doilies, individual salt and pepper shakers, and cloth napkins. The food is superior and the wine or champagne free. Flight attendants use a tray to pick up even one napkin. They are taught to hold the wine bottles and present the coffee cups as though they were serving in a fine restaurant. Following the lunch, attendants serve the freshly baked chocolate chip cookies, and passengers enjoy the home-baked cookie aroma wafting through the cabin.

The leather seats, meal service, and cookies are "signature" clues that Midwest Express cares about their passengers. Any single piece of evidence alone would not deliver the perceptual impact that results from combining them. The combination of memorable physical clues forms a credible pattern that is reinforced by the friendliness, competence, and responsiveness of the service providers. The pieces of evidence add up and tell a consistent—and compelling—story. Carbone and Haeckel propose two types of clues. "Mechanics" are the sights, sounds, tastes, textures, and smells generated by *things*. "Humanics" are clues that come from *people*.[4] Midwest Express's choreography of mechanics and humanics embellishes and differentiates the execution of its service.

Nor do the clues end with the flight. One of Midwest Express's partners in its frequent flyer program is MasterCard. Participants receive frequent flyer miles for purchasing with their Midwest Express Master-Card. Each year Midwest Express sends them a note of thanks with a tin of chocolate chip cookies. Hundreds of customers write letters of thanks like this one:

Dear Midwest Express,

Now, it is no longer necessary to fly to enjoy your delicious cookies. All we

*have to do is go to our mailbox. But we will still always fly Midwest. There is
no better airline and we appreciate the comfort and convenience you offer.
Thank you very much for the cookies.*

Significantly, carefully managed evidence communicates not only
to customers but also to service providers. Services are intangible for
the employees who perform them just as they are for customers. Con-
veying the proper mental picture of the service through evidence
guides and encourages employees to perform it well. It is unlikely that
Midwest Express could sustain its remarkably high level of personal
service during flights without the tangibles. The company's values-driven leadership is so strong that its on-board service still would be superior. But it wouldn't be the same. When passengers sit in what looks
and feels like the first class cabin, the service atmosphere influences
not only them but also the providers. A flight attendant does not learn
to use a tray when picking up a napkin in just the right way if the airline doesn't use trays.

Enterprise Rent-A-Car also illustrates the dual effects of intentional
evidence management on customers and service providers. Customer-
contact employees of car rental agencies often dress informally. Enterprise Rent-A-Car employees do the opposite. Men wear suits, long
sleeve shirts, neckties, and polished dress shoes. Women wear dresses
or skirts and hose. They avoid excessive jewelry. Customers often are
pleasantly surprised by the professional appearance of Enterprise employees who pick them up at an auto repair garage or serve them in an
Enterprise office. The employees' appearance presents a good first impression; it is a welcome clue for a customer who may have had a car
wreck earlier that day.

The effect of Enterprise's dress code on employees is no less important. The policy clearly helps Enterprise attract college-educated people to a business—car rentals—that they did not necessarily covet
upon entering college. The dress code also shapes their behavior on
the job. Joanne Peratis-Weber, vice president of the Dallas-Fort Worth
area for Enterprise Rent-A-Car, states: "Our dress code conveys a professional company image. We seek career people rather than people
just looking for a job. We also serve high-powered customers, and
when you are in a suit and tie, you have a different attitude." Adds vice

president and general manager Dick Janicki: "People feel better about themselves when they look good."

FLEXIBLE SYSTEMS

A family arrives at the Valley Inn to check in. A four-year-old girl is holding her pet rabbit in a cage and the hotel has a policy of no pets. The girl's father asks about the hotel's no-pet policy and is told, "For the comfort of our guests, our hotel's policy is not to allow pets. However, this policy is only for adults and does not apply to children."

In most hotels, the family—and rabbit—would have been turned away. Some readers may argue that they should have been, for rabbits can make a mess in a hotel room. Yet the front-desk representative assessed the situation and exercised the greater flexibility afforded by a service compared to a manufactured good. Whereas most goods are manufactured prior to purchase, most services are performed after purchase. As performances, services offer varying degrees of flexibility unlike premade goods. The Valley Inn amended its market offer to accommodate a family with a pet rabbit and, according to the hotel's management, created a guest for life.

The best-run service companies find ways to leverage the flexibility intrinsic to the services they market. They accomplish this with strong values and thin policy manuals; with well-selected, prepared, and empowered service providers; and with systems that facilitate flexible execution. Flexible systems support excellent execution through service customization and adjustable capacity.

Service Customization

Flexible systems enable companies to tailor services to the customers' requirements. Elements of the service that must be standardized for security, safety, financial, legal, or other reasons are defined, and around these definitions a wide solution space is formed to enable "thinking" servers to tailor their performances. Information systems that pool knowledge accessible to all service providers aids the tailoring of service.

USAA's Image system, among the largest in the world, contains current electronic "files" of more than three million members' paper-work, including policies and correspondence. USAA scans into the Imaging system more than three million pieces of mail a year. On a Monday, the busiest day, 30,000 pieces of mail might arrive. Mail that arrives in the scanning room in the morning usually has been inserted in the members' electronic file by mid-afternoon. These files can be instantly accessed by service representatives at any of more than 11,700 Image computer terminals when a member calls to ask a question, insure a car, add a driver to coverage, change an address, or effect any other change.

Although USAA's military clients live throughout the world and move frequently, policy changes are a simple matter. No handoffs to other departments are necessary. It is a one-stop service encounter. "In one five-minute phone call, you and our service representative have done all the work that used to take fifty-five steps, umpteen people, two weeks, and a lot of money," explains retired USAA CEO Robert McDermott.[5] By investing in automated processes and a dynamic information system and by preparing talented employees to skillfully use the processes and system, USAA customizes complex services efficiently and effectively. USAA and its members benefit enormously from flexible systems.

Just as USAA is leveraging smart technology to tailor the service, so is Miller SQA through its 1:1 system. Miller SQA's 1:1 combines a product catalog, competitive product and price information, office system design capability, and order processing—in a laptop computer used by dealer sales representatives. With 1:1, Miller SQA puts knowledge into the system and trains its dealer representatives to use the system rather than trying to teach them the knowledge that is both vast and constantly changing.

The 1:1 system's most innovative capability is its three-dimensional visualization software. The sales representative and customer sit side by side and design the customer's office furnishings—in 3-D, rotating pictures. In effect, the customer can "try on the furniture" through an iterative process, looking at one panel height, then another, or moving furniture around in the available space. The customer becomes part of the design team.

Once the customer and the salesperson agree on the order, the software translates the 3-D picture into a parts list for electronic transmission to the manufacturing site. Customers can select from two-day, two-week, or two-week-plus shipping options. The two-day shipping option—selected by about 10 percent of the customers—is available for a smaller set of the most popular finishes and fabrics.

Using 1:1, the company communicates in the language of the customer with its 3-D pictures, the language of the manufacturer with product numbers for each item to be produced, and the language of the installer who receives installation documents with the furniture. "Our 1:1 is a new art form," says Miller SQA president Gary Van Spronsen.

Sophisticated technology is a tool that facilitates efficient customization of the market offer. Flexibility itself is an attitude. Ukrop's customers who forget their checkbook can still take their groceries home. Managing Director of Retail Operations Roger Williams explains: "We treat customers as honest people. When customers forget their checkbook, we let them take their purchases with them and pay us when they come back. This reinforces a bond between our customers and us."

The Paper Valley Hotel has won the business of most of the National Football League teams that play the Green Bay Packers at Lambeau Field, despite the 30-mile distance between the hotel and the stadium. A key selling point was allowing the visiting teams to stay—and pay—for one night instead of the two-night minimum other area hotels required. A flexible attitude, stellar service reputation, and proactive marketing garnered the business. Dick Bergstrom tells the story:

> Having the NFL teams in the hotel is fun for the employees. They enjoy serving the players. We won the business by sending the teams personalized letters from our management that said, 'We are a full-service hotel with an AAA Four Diamond designation for both lodging and dining. We will be honored to serve your team. We will do it any way you want.'

In 1997 Dial-A-Mattress received a call from Switzerland. The customer needed six sets of bedding delivered to London in a hurry. Although Dial-A-Mattress had no established distribution system in London, it quickly accepted the offer, shipped the bedding by air freight, and made money on the transaction. Most furniture retailers would have said no.

Dial-A-Mattress delivers a mattress to customers' homes when they want it delivered. About 40 percent of customers choose to have their mattress delivered the same day they buy it. Some choose to receive their mattresses within two hours of ordering—which involves an extra charge. Customers who work during the day might have their mattress delivered in the evening or on the weekend; customers can choose any four-hour time frame for delivery. Napoleon Barragan relishes telling the story of a new Chicago resident who moved into an unfurnished apartment and made two telephone calls: to order spareribs from a Chinese restaurant and to order a mattress. The mattress arrived before the spareribs.

Dial-A-Mattress's traffic department coordinates communication among the company, the trucks, and the customers during the delivery process. Staff can reach the drivers by radio and pagers; drivers contact the department after each stop. Thus, the department can notify customers if a driver is running late or notify a driver if a customer is running late. Open from 6:00 A.M. to 1:00 A.M. every day, the traffic department can change delivery instructions or resolve other in-transit issues up to the last minute.

Customers concerned about choosing the right mattress over the telephone can have two mattresses delivered and keep the one they like most. Alternatively, they can try out the mattresses at one of the company's showrooms and then select one. Flexible systems are the key to effective execution at Dial-A-Mattress.

Adjustable Capacity

A common problem for service firms is fluctuating demand patterns. The tax preparation service with more business than it can handle in March and April and not enough business the rest of the year is well aware of this problem. The problem of demand fluctuation confronts goods manufacturing firms, too, but they have the advantage of being able to draw on inventory. Companies that deliver performances usually don't have this option. When a Pioneer Inn housekeeper is cleaning one room, she is unavailable to clean another. When customers are lined up to order at every available cash register in a Chick-fil-A restaurant, newly arriving customers will have to wait.

While the nature of services limits the manageability of demand fluctuations, flexible systems can make a big difference. Ukrop's has developed a Creative Scheduling Program that enables it to share employees based on the daily needs of individual stores. If one store is short personnel, it can borrow from another store. Support Center associates also may help out if needed in a store.

Custom Research delivers services through teams assigned to a specific group of clients. The teams always have multiple research studies underway, each with a deadline. Clients occasionally request unanticipated studies that must be completed in a hurry. Thus, it is not unusual for a team to have too many projects to finish by the agreed-upon deadlines. When this occurs, the team calls a "Rally." Every other team sends a representative to the rally meeting who can commit his or her team to helping. The entire process is transparent to the clients who receive their research on time. Custom Research also uses more informal methods. Often capacity adjustments are effected through simple e-mail requests, for example, "I could really use some help for two hours today" or "I have three hours available tomorrow; does anyone need help?"

Special Expeditions' naturalists are independent contractors who form a labor pool for staffing specific voyages. The naturalists bid for planned voyages that fit their interests and availability. This system enables Special Expeditions to use outstanding naturalists whose availability is limited, such as college professors who can sign on only during Christmas and summer breaks. The flexibility inherent in a pool of independent contractors also facilitates last minute staffing changes generated by demand shifts or the unexpected absence of scheduled staff.

Flexibility as an attitude was clearly illustrated in the Paper Valley Hotel in 1996. During a brief period when the full hotel was short of room attendants because of illness, managers' spouses volunteered to help clean the rooms. Although not every company could imagine help from managers' spouses, every sample company embraces the attitude toward flexibility that motivated such a response.

Excellent service companies understand the need for flexible systems. They understand human nature and business as a dynamic interaction rather than as a rigid system. They intuitively pull on "hidden" resources and evince little anxiety over chaos. Unforeseen circumstances, in fact, bring out the best in a company that embraces flexibility. Specification is not the key to their executional excellence—it's the intrinsic attitude toward flexibility, the intangible operating instructions, the essence rather than the prescription. Flexibility is a philosophy, not a script.

ACTIVE LISTENING

Continuously improving the execution of activities that compose the service depends on knowing what to improve. Active listening to the customers who use the service and the employees who perform it informs executional improvement.

Active listening encompasses ongoing, systematic data gathering from both service providers and users to detect patterns of change in their expectations and perceptions. It incorporates the use of multiple listening methods to tap the strengths of each and compensate for weaknesses. It involves decision makers personally, engaging them in both the listening process and the solution process. It promotes action; it is a means to an end, a tool for improvement.

Service Listening Systems

Active listening can motivate and guide both strategic and executional improvement. The former was considered in Chapter 4; we focus on executional improvement here. Table 5–2, drawn from my earlier work with A. Parasuraman, overviews eleven research approaches a company can use to build a service listening system. No company would use every approach, for too much information creates data overload and obscures the most meaningful insights. Conversely, each method has limitations. The use of multiple methods, therefore, provides a more complete and accurate picture of customers' experiences with the service, employees' experiences in delivering it, and the company's improvement priorities.

Four research approaches included in Table 5–2 apply to virtually all organizations and can be considered essential components of a service listening system: transactional surveys; customer complaint, comment, and inquiry capture; total market surveys; and employee surveys. Combined, these four approaches allow companies to accomplish the following: cover existing customers, competitors' customers, and employees; isolate failure-prone parts of the service system; and generate both transaction-specific and overall service feedback. Additional methods a company might use, if any, would relate to the nature of its service, its strategy, and the specific needs of information users.[6]

From USAA's ECHO to Ukrop's Helpline

All the sample companies use active listening to motivate and guide improved execution. They listen formally and informally to the sounds of their businesses in their own special ways. Here we highlight several approaches.

A primary way USAA listens to its members is through ECHO (Every Contact Has Opportunity). Comments from members—including complaints, compliments, and suggestions—are immediately logged into a computerized database and sent electronically to action agents. The action agents investigate problems and take action directly or pass the feedback on to someone else for handling. Weekly summaries of significant data trends and changes are distributed to management.

ECHO quickly identifies points of vulnerability in the service system. The size of USAA's operation and the immediate filing of member comments in a single, electronic database creates an early-response capability. As ECHO manager Donna Kirby states: "ECHO shows us things right away that we might not have known for a couple of weeks. The system shows tangible evidence of problems and this tangibility creates quicker action."

Additionally, USAA surveys 300,000 members annually to measure their overall assessment of the company. Members who file a claim with USAA also receive a survey on that specific transaction.

Custom Research surveys a new client *before* starting the work to identify the client's principal expectations and plan the relationship accordingly. They ask this key question: "What will we have done to

TABLE 5–2
Research Approaches for Building a Service Listening System

Type	Description	Purpose	Frequency[b]	Limitations
Transactional Surveys[a]	Service satisfaction survey of customers following a service encounter.	Obtain customer feedback while service experience is still fresh; act on feedback quickly if negative patterns develop.	Continuous	Focuses on customers' most recent experience rather than their overall assessment. Noncustomers are excluded.
Mystery Shopping	Researchers become "customers" to experience and evaluate the quality of service delivered.	Measure individual employee service behavior for use in coaching, training, performance evaluation, recognition, and rewards; identify systematic strengths and weaknesses in customer-contact service.	Quarterly	Subjective evaluations; researchers may be more "judgmental" than customers would be; expense limits repetitions; potential to hurt employee morale if improperly used.
New, declining, and lost-customer surveys	Surveys to determine why customers select the firm, reduce their buying, or leave the firm.	Assess the role service quality and other issues play in customer patronage and loyalty.	Continuous	Firm must be able to identify and monitor service usage on a per-customer basis.
Focus group interviews	Directed questioning of a small group, usually eight to twelve people. Questions focus on a specific topic. Can be used with customer, noncustomer, or employee groups.	Provide a forum for participants to suggest service improvement ideas; offer fast, informal feedback on service issues.	As needed	Dynamics of group interview may prevent certain issues from surfacing. Focus groups are, in effect, brainstorming sessions; the information generated is, in effect, brain-storming sessions; the information generated is not projectable to the population of interest. Focus group research is most valuable when coupled with projectable research.

Type	Description		Frequency	
Customer advisory panels	A group of customers recruited to periodically provide the firm with feedback and advice on service performance and other issues. Data are obtained in meetings, over the telephone, through mail questionnaires, or via other means. Employee panels also can be formed.	Obtain in-depth, timely feedback and suggestions about service quality from experienced customers who cooperate because of "membership" nature of the panel.	Quarterly	May not be projectable to entire customer base. Excludes noncustomers. Panelists may assume role of "expert" and become less representative of customer base.
Service reviews	Periodic visits with customers (or a class of customer) to discuss and assess the service relationship. Should be a formal process with a common set of questions, capture of responses in a database, and follow-up communication with customers.	Identify customer expectations and perceptions of the company's service performance and improvement priorities in a face-to-face conversation. A view of the future, not just a study of the past. Opportunity to include multiple decision makers and decision influencers in the discussions.	Annually or semiannually	Time consuming and expensive. Most appropriate for firms marketing complex services on an ongoing, relationship basis.
Customer complaint, comment, and inquiry capture[a]	System to retain, categorize, track, and distribute customer complaints and other communications with the company.	Identify most common types of service failure for corrective action. Identify through customer communications opportunities to improve service or otherwise strengthen customer relationships.	Continuous	Dissatisfied customers frequently do not complain directly to the company. Analysis of customer complaints and comments offers only a partial picture of the state of service.
Total market surveys	Surveys that measure customers' overall assessment of a company's service. Research includes both external customers and competitors' customers, i.e., the total market.	Assess company's service performance compared to competitors; identify service-improvement priorities; track service improvement over time.	Semiannually or quarterly	Measures customers' overall service assessments but does not capture assessments of specific service encounters.

TABLE 5–2 *continued*

Type	Description	Purpose	Frequency[b]	Limitations
Employee field reporting	Formal process for gathering, categorizing, and distributing field employee intelligence about service issues.	Capture and share at the management level intelligence about customers' service expectations and perceptions gathered in the field.	Continuous to monthly	Some employees will be more conscientious and efficient reporters than others. Employees may be unwilling to provide negative information to management.
Employee surveys	Surveys concerning the service employees provide and receive, and the quality of their work lives.	Measure internal service quality; identify employee-perceived obstacles to improved service; track employee morale and attitudes. Employee surveys help answer "why" service performance is what it is.	Quarterly	The strength of employee surveys is also a weakness; employees view service delivery from their own vantage point, subject to their own biases. Employees can offer valuable insights into the root causes of service problems but are not always objective or correct in their interpretations.
Service operating data capture	A system to retain, categorize, track, and distribute key service-performance operating data, such as service response times, service failure rates, and service delivery costs.	Monitor service performance indicators and take corrective action to improve performance as necessary. Relate operating performance data to customer and employee feedback.	Continuous	Operating performance data may not be relevant to customers' perceptions of service. Focus is on what is occurring but not why.

[a]Highlighted approaches normally would be part of any service quality information system.
[b]Frequencies of use vary among companies.

Source: Leonard L. Berry and A. Parasuraman, "Listening to the Customer—The Concept of Building a Service-Quality Information System," *Sloan Management Review,* Spring 1997, pp. 67–68.

make you happy if it's six months from now?" Custom Research sum-marizes the findings from the new client survey in a letter to the client and asks if the information is accurate and complete. Some clients want to know everything that happens in a project and others don't want to be bothered with details. Some want to know about problems, others want to hear only the solutions. Some just want the data, others want recommendations. Custom Research gathers intelligence up-front that enables it to customize each client relationship.

When Custom Research finishes a client project, the account team self-assesses its performance on accuracy, timeliness, and budget in the Project Quality Recap. It also surveys the client's satisfaction with the project. Custom Research's steering committee aggregates the infor-mation from clients and projects to evaluate and improve execution. Additionally, senior management conducts annual client interviews to assess the overall health of the relationship, identify improvement pri-orities, and determine clients' future needs.

Dana Commercial Credit uses customer scorecards in each of its product groups. The scorecards distill customers' service expectations and feedback on Dana's performance, provide an internal performance analysis, record competitive comparisons, and assess strengths, weak-nesses, opportunities, and threats. The information used in the score-cards comes from the field sales force, customer and market research, and internal teams that have mapped and measured service processes, among other sources. The scorecards drive improvement at Dana Commercial Credit.

Also crucial to Dana Commercial Credit's listening efforts is its bi-ennial "People Survey," a study of employees' job satisfaction and well-being. Management chooses the broad areas of survey coverage, and a cross-functional, cross-product employee team selects specific questions within each area from a question pool provided by a con-sulting firm, Stanard and Associates. All employees are invited to complete the survey. The consultant then scores the surveys and ana-lyzes the results. The results are shared with the employees and com-pared to Stanard's five-year, rolling database of more than 200,000 employee respondents from multiple companies. Findings from these surveys have led to significant improvements in internal communica-tions, cooperation across departments and product groups, and employee advancement opportunities. Says Steve Stanard, CEO of Stanard and Associates: "Dana Commercial Credit's intense efforts to improve its internal and external customer service and its quality performance have resulted in the most dramatic improvement in employer satisfaction I have seen in my 20 years as an organizational psychologist."[7]

Ukrop's receives several hundred customer communications in a typical week through its telephone Helpline, comment cards, and e-mail. The comments include complaints, questions, suggestions, and compliments. The Customer Care Center staff who answer the Helpline try to resolve problems that cause customers to call, usually by getting the appropriate manager involved. Linda Lafoon, Ukrop's Customer Care Center manager, comments:

> My goal is to make sure that customer concerns are handled. We want to exceed customers' expectations. For example, if a customer orders a cake and is charged $4 more than she was quoted, we will give her back a $10 gift certificate. Sometimes when customers call, they just need someone to listen to them. Recently, a man whose wife had died called in to find out how to cook. We will do whatever it takes to help the customer.

A summary of all customer communications to the Helpline is prepared weekly for senior management. A detailed description of each complaint and the company's response is included. These summaries often reveal patterns in the comments and lead to corrective actions.

STRUCTURING IMPROVEMENT

Active listening reveals opportunities for improving service execution, but these potential improvements may lie dormant without a means in place for effecting actual solutions. Companies aspiring to executional excellence do not leave improvements to chance. Instead, they create institutional structures to both stimulate *and* process executional innovation. These are integral structural arrangements—committees, teams, work roles, formal programs—that encourage and facilitate continuous operational improvement.

Just Do It

Dana Commercial Credit's "Just Do It" initiative is part of its broader "Ideas for Improvement" effort. Each Dana employee is expected to implement or suggest two improvement ideas per month. In particular, they are expected to continually improve the processes in which they are directly involved—the 25 square feet around their desk. "Just do it" ideas mean those improvements employees implement on their own and later share with the cross-functional administrative team for the Ideas for Improvement program. Ideas with an impact across functional lines are submitted to the administrative team in advance for approval. Employees' involvement in submitting ideas is tracked and reinforced through the company's performance assessment and reward system. Employees are asked during the evaluation period to list the ideas they had during the year that improved the company. A complete record of ideas by category is available on Lotus Notes for use throughout the company.

In 1997, 590 eligible DCC employees submitted 5,970 ideas for an average of 10 ideas per employee. Ninety-eight percent of employees participated and 78 percent of the ideas were implemented. Says Donna Marie Lilly, manager, quality initiatives for the Dealer Products Group, "Everyone is the manager of their 25 square feet. Who knows the job better than the person doing it? This is the bottom line of the Dana style." Adds Barney Schoenfeld, manager of special assets, "I came here from the banking environment, saw the empowerment, and initially thought things were out of control. When you want an idea here, you don't go to management, you go to the person doing the job."

Involving Everyone

In 1991, the Paper Valley Hotel established problem-solving teams in each department, 16 teams in all. The teams met twice a month for two years and successfully completed 80 improvement projects. The process was not ideal, however. Not all the ideas were focused on helping guests, and teams would become discouraged if their ideas were turned down by a management group. Some employees felt left out of the process entirely.

In 1993, a restaurant server asked Steve Tyink if she could join one of the teams. Tyink, the architect of many of Bergstrom Hotels award-winning quality improvement initiatives, checked into the request, told the employee there were no openings and that he would let her know when one became available. "She became irate with me, saying that she had been here a long time and had a lot of good ideas. At that point, I knew what we were doing wasn't correct," says Tyink. "We had involved only 20 percent of the hotel population, instead of 100 percent."[8] The original approach was changed to involve all employees on problem-solving teams.

In addition, the Opportunity for Improvement (OFI) process was added at all three hotels—the Paper Valley, Valley Inn, and Pioneer Inn. The OFI system also involves all employees. Each hotel has an OFI team that meets every two weeks. Team members come from every department and typically consider 15 to 30 of the submitted ideas per meeting. All employees receive OFI "checkbooks" with individual "checks" and stubs (see Exhibit 5–1). Employees who have an improvement idea, fill out a "check" and submit it, keeping the stub to record the outcome of the request. Within one week the OFI team acknowledges the idea and within one month implements it, plans it, or turns it down. Existing employee problem-solving teams and the OFI teams work together closely in generating ideas and seeking solutions.

Issues involving pay, benefits, or personalities are considered inappropriate for the OFI program although employees are encouraged to voice these concerns through other channels. Individual members of the OFI team assume responsibility for shepherding promising ideas and report back to the team at subsequent meetings. Photographs of employees who submitted implemented ideas appear on bulletin boards in the hotels. Drawings for prizes are held at each OFI meeting to recognize individuals submitting ideas. Financial incentives are not part of the program. The spirit of the OFI system is to capture everyone's ideas and to encourage numerous small gains rather than a few breakthroughs.

Hundreds of OFI ideas have been implemented in recent years. For 1997, 564 ideas were submitted, 293 were implemented, 94 were in process at year-end, and 182 were declined. Here is a small sampling of employee ideas implemented since the inception of the program:

EXHIBIT 5–1

Opportunity for Improvement Check and Stub

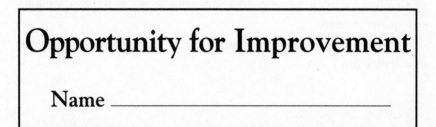

Opportunity for Improvement

Name _____

Steps for Improvement:
1. Complete the "check" & "stub" portion of your checkbook.
2. Forward the "check" portion to the OFI inbox located in the employee lounge.
3. "Check" portion will be returned to you by an action team member. Mark the stub portion "completed," "plan," or "declined."
4. Completed "check" will be recorded in the OFI database (can be viewed on OFI Board and in team meeting).

Inappropriate Categories:
(Thoughts about these are welcome and better handled via other means)
* Personalities
* Pay
* Benefits
Response Time:
* 1 Week acknowledgement & "thank you"
* Completion—time table will be set within team

DATE: _____
SUB. TO: _____
DESCRIPTION: _____
_____
_____

FINAL DISPOSITION:
COMPLETED/PLAN/DECLINED

NAME: _____ DATE: _____
OFI DESCRIPTION: _____
_____
_____
_____

RESPONSE: _____

- Placing lights on the floral sign at the Orchard Restaurant in the Paper Valley Hotel to brighten it with a more festive look
- Black sand instead of white in ashtrays because it looks cleaner
- Smaller packets of parmesan cheese for room service trays because most customers were not using all the cheese in a bigger packet
- Needle containers for diabetic guests to use instead of the wastebasket for used-needle disposal
- Two-sided *Do Not Disturb* hangtags to replace dual-message hangtags (*Do not Disturb, Please Clean My Room*) that pranksters would flip

- A spring tray in linen carts so housekeepers do not have to bend all the way down into the carts to get linen
- Contact lens cleaning solution available at the hotel front desk for guests in need
- Improved signs directing guests to restrooms in the lobby area of the Valley Inn

Spreading Good Ideas

Chick-fil-A's field staff are called business consultants. Consultants are assigned to work with Chick-fil-A operators in particular geographic areas. The consultants conduct scheduled operational visits to the restaurants, but they devote much of their time to conducting workshops for groups of operators and spreading good ideas among operators. "One of our key jobs is to transfer knowledge. I see a good idea in Birmingham and I will spread it to the other stores," explains Chick-fil-A's Wayne Hoover.

The consultants span the boundary between Chick-fil-A and the restaurant operators. The more they can help the operators, the more Chick-fil-A becomes successful. The consultants represent the operators' interests and perspectives at company headquarters, and they help company staff refine new programs for the stores prior to implementation. "We help the operators reach their goals," says one consultant. "We visit 40 to 50 stores a year; the operator is in one store and they will call for some perspective," states another. "It's kind of funny how passionate we can be about a chicken sandwich," says another.

Brilliant strategy is insufficient to drive sustained success. The total product that customers experience from a company is its strategy *executed*. A poorly executed strategy openly invites competitors to imitate the strategy, execute better, and take away the business.

Excellent service companies not only have focused strategies, but they also focus on execution. They continually raise their standards of service delivery and constantly strive for perceived superiority over competitors. The sample companies seek executional excellence in multiple ways. The approaches and methods discussed in this chapter are integral to the pursuit of executional excellence—competing for the right talent, holding pre-game huddles, managing the evidence, embracing flexible systems, listening actively, and structuring improvement. The success drivers featured in subsequent chapters also contribute to executional excellence.

6

CONTROL OF DESTINY

On a Thursday morning, facilities manager Mary Sargent learned that she needed to furnish a satellite office for the California technology company where she worked. Two hundred front-office employees would be moving to the new office within one month. Sargent soon realized she had a problem. She needed the furniture within one month, and each supplier she contacted indicated that a shipment of 200 office systems required a minimum lead time of six to nine weeks.

Only the dealer representing Miller SQA responded differently to Sargent's plight. The next day the Miller SQA representative arrived with a laptop computer and helped Sargent design, specify, and order the furniture systems she needed at a cost fitting her budget. The order could be delivered in two weeks. Together sales representative and customer tried out various furniture combinations in three-dimensional images on the laptop computer. They moved furniture from one area to another, looked at circulation patterns from a bird's-eye view, and added options such as drawer trays while they monitored a running cost tabulation. They continued the process until they found just the right product-price combination. After selecting colors and fabrics, the sales representative transmitted the order electronically to the Miller SQA factory, thus initiating production.[1]

Mary Sargent is like many office furniture buyers. She didn't need choices from a wide array of state-of-the-art furniture. She needed well-made, durable, comfortable, and attractive furniture. She needed

110

reliability. She needed a price that fit her budget. And she needed the furniture—200 systems—soon. She is the perfect customer for Miller SQA and Miller SQA the perfect supplier for her.

Miller SQA is quietly leading a mini-revolution in office furniture by rewriting the value equation for customers like Mary Sargent. Its furniture quality is competitive but offers fewer frills and styles; however, the company's processes are superior and a hard-to-buy product becomes simple, quick, and affordable—SQA.

How did Miller SQA, a wholly owned subsidiary of Herman Miller, Inc., transform itself from a slow-growing division reconditioning and selling used trade-in furniture with sales of $25 million in 1992 to a fast-growing industry maverick with sales of $200 million and an average annual return on assets of 35 percent five years later? How did an industry heretic named Bix Norman, a long-time Herman Miller salesman and manager appointed in 1989 to run Phoenix Designs (renamed Miller SQA in 1995), marshall the political freedom within the Herman Miller organization to lead his mini-revolution?

"We assumed we had the responsibility to be the author of our strategy. Had we asked, the answer probably would have been 'no,'" explains Norman. "Our business model required that we change everything—the way we sold, the technology, the supply of materials into the factory. We had to have the time to build, refine, and prove what is a totally integrated business model. We were extremely conscious of making our numbers to maintain our political freedom."

Miller SQA's ability to control its destiny is one key to its remarkable success. Control of destiny is a success sustainer. Companies in control of their destiny minimize unwanted interference that distracts them from their mission. They not only chart a well-defined strategic direction, they pursue the direction *unfettered*. The senior leaders of a business determine its course—not competitors, not lenders, not institutional shareholders, not unions, not suppliers, not community activists, not the media, not politicians. The senior leaders keep the organization focused on creating superior value for customers, and this focus helps secure the organization's future.

Control of destiny is *independent* action. Companies that sustain success become and stay famous with customers for their unique and valuable market offer. Influences that can undermine the market offer's uniqueness and value are effectively blocked by the independent spirit that enables innovative action. This is the essence of control of destiny.

Controlling a company's destiny evolves from an independent attitude. Bix Norman assumed he had control of Phoenix Design's future, carefully assembled a team of executives to help transform vision into reality, didn't ask permission, made his numbers, and reinvented a division that in recent years has been growing twice as fast as the parent company. Yes, Miller SQA's success helped shield it from interference, but it clearly wouldn't have achieved noteworthy success at first without an independent approach.

All of the other drivers of sustainable success featured in this book contribute to control of destiny. Of particular importance are strong values, strong leadership, and strong focus. Conviction, courage, and clear strategy *facilitate* proactivity and discipline. Control of destiny requires staying centered on the customer. Read slowly the following comment by Tim Hoeksema, chairman, president, and CEO of Midwest Express. Read it several times. These are the words of a values-driven leader who understands the control-of-destiny imperative:

> We've avoided focusing too much on our competitors. We must be aware of what they are doing, but we resist copying what they are doing. Instead, we focus on what the customer wants.
>
> Earlier in the nineties most airlines were losing money, and no-frills airline service was becoming more prevalent. People both inside and outside our company were saying that we had to change to respond to the no-frills trend. We were spending too much on food, we needed to add more seats in the planes, and so forth. We resisted this pressure to look just like our competitors. Instead we stayed focused on what our customers wanted. It's easier to copy competitors, but it's not the best thing in the long run. I could save the company $5 million with one phone call asking for lower quality food, but it's not what the customer wants.
>
> We have a strategy, a vision, a plan. We know who we are. We must stay true to that in all of our decisions.

Midwest Express, Miller SQA, and the other sample companies epitomize independent thought and action. They resist influences or conditions that could weaken their control over the future. They seek success on their own terms. Within the sample, the control-of-destiny attitude manifests itself in different ways, but it is apparent in every company.

STRESSING EXCELLENCE OVER GROWTH

Many companies lose control of their future by growing too fast. Rapid growth weakens the market offer, and this impairs the customers' experience—that is, the total product. Unregulated growth is a particular problem for labor-intensive service companies that create customer value through human performance. These service companies have nothing to fall back on when the rapid addition of new employees, service delivery units, and management layers *undermines* the care with which new employees are selected and trained, the intensity with which company values are taught and reinforced, and the passion with which the company's core strategy is pursued. Companies that sell performances for a living must not allow growth to sap the ability or commitment of the performers.

The sample companies enjoy growth but are unwilling to put growth ahead of operational excellence. For some firms, growth is king. For the sample companies, excellence is king. And because it is, they increase control of their destinies. Even companies like Charles Schwab Corporation and Enterprise Rent-A-Car—two of the fastest growing service companies in the world—stress operational excellence. Both companies have effectively instituted systems and practices that reinforce their core values amidst the rapid growth.

Charles Schwab surpassed $2 billion in revenues in 1997, just three years after reaching $1 billion in 1994. This incredible growth pace would wreak havoc on most firms' executional efforts. And Schwab has no guarantee that it won't wreak havoc within the company in the future. However, the company's strong efforts to hire new employees whose values fit its own, its refusal to pay sales commissions that could put the interests of sales representatives and customers in conflict, and its internal communication investments, such as "town hall" meetings held throughout the system, help maintain a sense of balance in the organization.

Enterprise Rent-A-Car passed Hertz in fleet size and number of locations in 1994 and has been widening the gap since then. When CEO Andy Taylor felt the company needed to focus on customer service in the early 1990s, he made it a priority issue (see Chapter 3). Growth was strong and profits excellent, but Taylor sensed the company was losing its balance between growth and execution. A new customer satisfaction measurement system was instituted and became a crucial part of the company's reward system. "We are a confederation of entrepreneurs," states Taylor. "We started competing for customer satisfaction numbers. You couldn't get promoted without strong customer satisfaction numbers."

Control of destiny requires senior management to identify and commit to an expansion pace that *allows superior execution of the strategy*. For The Container Store, that pace is only a few stores a year. Management will wait years if necessary for an outstanding location to become available in a market they wish to enter. Attracting excellent employees with the right values and equipping them with the skills and knowledge to execute The Container Store strategy also regulate the pace of expansion. Co-owner John Mullen explains: "We could open, say, 10 new stores a year, but we choose not to do that; the limiting factor is finding and training the people at The Container Store level of quality. So we have been opening just a few stores a year." Adds Human Resources Director Nancy Donley: "The hiring of our employees is the most important thing we do. We take a lot of time finding the right people."

Midwest Express also controls its destiny by controlling its growth. Tim Hoeksema explains:

Capital is not constraining our growth. We sit here today with no debt on our balance sheet, and we have managed to grow 20 percent a year. Rather, our desire to preserve our culture and focus on our customer keep us from growing too fast. We can't add 50 percent new people in a year. We can only add about 15 percent.

When we open a new station, we transfer 30 to 50 percent "Midwest Expressers"—our "homegrowns"—who develop the team. With growth, we must be sure that our human resources, infrastructure, and systems can keep pace. ValuJet was growing 150 percent a year and could not keep up. Fast growth does not allow you to control quality, customer focus, or culture.

Placing excellence ahead of growth is not just the CEO's idea at Midwest Express. Staying in balance, preserving the company's special qualities, is deeply embedded in the Midwest Express organization as the following comments illustrate:

- "Other airlines focus on the 'almighty dollar' and build no relationships. We take pride in giving service and that overshadows everything else."—Flight attendant
- "Success is like getting on a basketball. It's not hard to get on, but it is hard to stay on. It's easy to copy our physical strategy, but it's hard to copy the spirit of our employee group."—Pilot
- "We don't want to be forced to be less selective in who we hire just because we need a lot of people."—Customer service representative
- "We don't want growing pains. We need to keep up the team feeling. We don't want an 'old group' of employees and a 'new group.'"—Customer service supervisor
- "We must keep a high level of service. Customers have many choices. We must keep offering the little things that other airlines do not."—Pilot

Ed Shultz, CEO of Dana Commercial Credit, is adamant about *not* growing for the sake of growing. For Shultz, no growth is a far better option than bad growth. "It is acceptable not to do business; it is unacceptable to do bad business," he states. "We don't do deals just for the volume, the growth. Our portfolio doesn't have to grow every year. When you have a mentality that you must grow, you do things that you shouldn't do. When good business is available, we'll grow. At other times, we make good money selling portfolios to companies that insist on growing every year."

ACTING LIKE A PRIVATE COMPANY

A striking finding of the research for this book is how much the private sample companies take advantage of being private and how much the

public sample companies behave as if they are private. Regardless of
their ownership structure, the sample firms act like private companies.
They follow the beat of their own drums. They take a long-term investment view of building their businesses. They prize the creation of
social profit in addition to economic profit. And, as just discussed, they
emphasize execution over growth.

All of the public company CEOs in the sample would agree with
Roberto Goizueta, the late CEO of Coca-Cola, who believed share
value should be increased in a manner that benefited all stakeholders—customers, employees, business partners, and the community.
Goizueta felt his obligation was to benefit *shareholders*—owners holding stock for the long term—rather than *shareowners*.[2]

The only way to build a great company is to do today what strengthens tomorrow. It is a simple, powerful—and elusive—idea. It requires a
delicate, ongoing tightrope walk balancing acceptable short-term financial performance, necessary long-term investment in the company's future, and values-congruent behavior that makes an arduous
journey *emotionally* rich.

Some of the private company owners featured in this book are for-
going millions of public dollars to walk their tightrope at a pace and in
a manner of their choosing. What the Truett Cathy family would be
worth if it took Chick-fil-A public is mind-boggling. Profitable every
year for more than 50 years, Chick-fil-A is one of the most successful
quick-service restaurant chains in the world. Thus far it remains a
happily private company. "People ask me if we are going public and
my answer is 'I hope not,'" says Steve Robinson, senior vice president
of marketing at Chick-fil-A. "If we were a public company, we
wouldn't be doing first-class conferences for our operators, we
wouldn't be closed on Sundays, and we wouldn't be giving away millions of dollars in college scholarships." Huie Woods, vice president of
human resources, echoes the sentiment: "If we were a publicly held
company, we wouldn't be doing half of what we do. Truett is an extremely generous man."

The Container Store also could command millions of public dollars
but has chosen to remain private and unfettered. "So many folks have
told us that we have a great concept and if we don't grow it, we will
lose out to imitators who do. We resisted the pressure and capital has

never been a limiting factor," says co-owner Garrett Boone. "One of the key turning points for our company was *not* giving in to all the people who approached us with offers."

Custom Research and Enterprise Rent-A-Car are two more highly successful private companies that enjoy sole mastery of their destiny too much to pursue public ownership. Jeff Pope, co-founder of Custom Research, explains his and partner Judy Corson's reasoning:

> We do not have to answer to people on the outside. We can do things in the short term that we feel will be good in the long term. We have no pressure of reporting quarterly profits. We can stay on the course we selected without pressure from external sources.

Enterprise Rent-A-Car CEO Andy Taylor offers a similar rationale: "When it comes to tough decisions, we ask what's good for customers, what's good for employees, and then we make the decision. It usually turns out to be a good decision. As a private company we have not veered from our philosophy; being private we are not subject to the grind and I can spend my time interacting with employees rather than investors."

Although private ownership shields outside interference, independence also requires financial resources. Control of destiny requires cash, which leads many firms that can attract public investment to do so. Publicly traded stock also can figure prominently in attracting, motivating, and retaining talented employees—which contributes to financial performance that contributes to control of destiny.

Can well-led companies experience the best of *both* the private and public ownership worlds? Study of public companies, such as Midwest Express and Charles Schwab, and divisions of public companies, such as Miller SQA and Dana Commercial Credit, suggest an affirmative answer. It is possible with exceptional leadership.

Midwest Express, firmly in control of its destiny after going public in 1995, illustrates that control of destiny is an attitude, a guiding philosophy. Essentially, the company has refused to change following its public offering. It did not ramp up growth. It did not become more focused on quarter-by-quarter managing. It did not delay needed investment spending to inflate short-term results.

When Midwest Express executives did road shows for the company's public offering, they advised prospective investors that the company would be managed with a long-term perspective and would seek controlled, steady growth. If the investors wanted fast growth, they should buy another company's stock. "Before going public we were making good and proper decisions. We are using the same thought processes today," explains Tim Hoeksema. The company's strong financial performance to date has made it difficult for anyone to argue.

CONTROLLING CUSTOMER VALUE CREATION

A primary way the sample companies control their destinies is to control processes that directly affect customers' perceptions of quality and value. Although Miller SQA sells through independent dealers, it has put its capabilities into the 1:1 knowledge system that its dealers use in working with customers. More than 1,000 sales representatives from independent dealers are using laptop computers with the 1:1 software. Miller SQA controls its destiny in part by storing value-creating knowledge in one technology system rather than in the heads of more than 1,000 independent sales representatives.

Ukrop's commands market leadership against formidable competitors because of exemplary food quality and excellent customer service. Management clearly understands how the company creates differentiated value for customers and leaves little to chance. Although a relatively small company (25 stores in early 1998), Ukrop's works with resources that produce its own brand products to exacting specifications. Ukrop's beef comes from cattle that have been eating quality feed for the last 110 days of their lives. Ukrop's grows its own shrimp in Honduras. Its coffee is made from beans grown by a family company in California.

Customers notice the superior quality of Ukrop's brand products. Roger Williams, managing director of retail operations, explains why Ukrop's decided to grow its own beef: "We were never truly satisfied with commodity beef. It wasn't consistent in quality. So now we are using family farmers to grow our own beef to our standards. We control everything from genetics to feed. This helps us bring something to market that is different from our competitors."

Ukrop's is a company continually seeking unique options for customers. Major investments in a central kitchen and central bakery to produce consistently high quality, ready-to-eat foods reveal Ukrop's desire to control its own destiny just as much as its strategic alliances with producers. A lemon pie sold in one Ukrop's store is just as good as a lemon pie sold in another Ukrop's store because the pies are made in the same central bakery.

Unlike many retailers, The Container Store does not have vendors ship merchandise directly to its stores. When vendors ship directly to stores, the merchandise arrives at all hours and diverts the attention of store personnel from serving customers. Nor do shelf-stocking activities during store hours make an impressive visual statement to customers.

The Container Store controls all store distribution through its own distribution center. Trucks arrive at a store at 5:00 A.M. where a crew unloads and shelves products before the store opens. Any prep work on the merchandise, such as repackaging, is done in the distribution center rather than the stores. "We don't allow our stores to be in the distribution business," states CEO Garrett Boone. "We want our store employees to focus all of their energies on serving customers."

The sample companies are not keen to outsource anything that affects customer value creation. They are reluctant to put control of their destiny in the hands of another company. Other airlines the size of Midwest Express outsource aircraft maintenance, reservations, and airport services. Midwest Express handles all of these functions itself to maintain quality and, in some cases, also to lower costs. Midwest Express outsources only when absolutely necessary.

In commenting on Special Expeditions' disdain for outsourcing, Maggie Hart, director of operations, captures the essence of controlling customer value creation: "It's hard for us to outsource. We don't like giving up control of anything. It's difficult for us to describe to a partner what makes us different. We really try to understand the places we go, and we agonize over the smallest details. We fall in love with these places and we want to share this feeling with our passengers. Our heart is really in it."

COMPETING AGAINST YOURSELF

The sample companies all face intense competition, yet in a very real sense they compete hardest against themselves. They always are seeking to push beyond existing performance levels, to perform significantly better, to move from what exists to what is possible.

In effect, these companies seek to outdistance themselves, and this helps them control their destiny. Charles Schwab's David Pottruck confesses that he never feels comfortable. Pottruck's comment in a June 1997 interview is illustrative: "We are bringing in $700 million a week in net new assets. In the first six months of this year, we've grown from $252 billion to $303 billion in assets, yet we had a meeting this morning on why we aren't doing better. It is part of our culture."

The St. Paul Saints sell out every home game and have a long waiting list of fans who want to buy season tickets. The Saints present professional baseball as family entertainment in highly creative and appealing ways. The company's spontaneity seems unlikely to slow anytime soon. "We have to keep earning the fan's loyalty," explains Mike Veeck. "We have to keep attempting to innovate at almost reckless speed."

Many companies become more aggressive and innovative when they are in trouble. Survival provokes action. The companies studied for this book are *perpetually* innovative and aggressive. Customers always are changing and so must they. Core values such as excellence and innovation demand action. Great companies always are in motion to become better.

The Container Store's ongoing quest to improve the elfa® storage system and the processes they use to sell and deliver it illustrate the perpetual motion characteristic of all the sample companies. The elfa® storage system consists of strong ventilated wire shelving and drawers, closet rods, and tracks and hanging standards for attaching the system to a wall. The system is custom-designed to fit each customer's preferences and space requirements.

In the mid-1990s, The Container Store approached its supplier about the two companies working together to improve the product. Although the original elfa® system sold well, it was not easy for consumers to install, design flexibility was limited, and it did not differ much from products available in other stores. In particular, the shelves were difficult to put up and level. Each row of shelves required its own screw holes. The Container Store also wanted more flexibility with the shelves, including the ability to create a closet with or without rods.

The result of the collaboration is the "Easy Hang" system available through The Container Store. Easy Hang is simple to install and change. The customer needs to drill holes only to hang a track at the top of the closet wall—eight or nine holes instead of perhaps 50 required for the original system. Hanging standards are hooked on the track, brackets are snapped into place on the hanging standards, shelves are placed on the brackets, and closet rods are fitted into their holders. Drawers are placed wherever desired. What was a formidable, even intimidating, installation task was transformed into a simple job.

But The Container Store's elfa® improvement efforts did not stop with the product. Each year The Container Store has an annual elfa® sale in the six weeks following Christmas. It is the company's biggest sales event of the year, generating as much business as the Christmas season itself. It is a clever strategy; essentially The Container Store has two Christmases instead of one.

The volume of elfa® business during the annual sale poses logistical problems in the stores, however. Selling these storage systems is quite unlike selling manufactured goods off a shelf. Each customer's closet is custom-designed in the store. Tracks, shelving, and rods are cut to the customer's length specifications. From 50 to 100 separate pieces have to be assembled, prepared, and individually scanned.

To improve the overall process for the 1996–97 sale, The Container Store designed a cutting station for the back of the store. A band saw and pneumatic cutter replaced hacksaws and bolt cutters. For the 1997–98 sale, a scanning station also was installed in the back of the store. Orders could be scanned and priced without holding up other customers waiting in line. This improvement especially benefited customers *not* buying a closet system who in prior years could be trapped in a checkout line for 20 minutes. The Container Store also created specialized positions to help facilitate the process. One person might perform several of the functions during slower periods with all positions filled during peak times.

For each of the last several years, The Container Store's elfa® sales have been increasing by 30 percent or more. The 1997–98 elfa® sale was the most successful in The Container Store's history; yet in March 1998, the company began meetings to discuss how to improve future elfa® sales.

Control of destiny is largely attitudinal. If sufficiently determined, companies need not relinquish control of their future to other parties. If they do not allow the lure of growth to impede operational effectiveness, if they stay totally focused on creating superior value for customers, if they continually strive to get better than they are—companies can control their future. Nobody makes the point more compellingly than Jeff Pope, co-founder of Custom Research:

> We do control our destiny. It's more of a mindset than anything else. Judy [Corson] and I have always had a sense that we can tackle any problem and overcome any barrier as long as we work on it hard enough. We are a small company, but this has never limited us. We are clever enough to do anything. To us, control of destiny is living by your wits. You can run out of money, but you can't run out of wit.

7

TRUST-BASED RELATIONSHIPS

"The fans are the magic," states St. Paul Saints General Manager Bill Fanning. "Our job is to provide a fun, fan-friendly, personalized atmosphere that encourages their collective personality to come out. Win or lose, we want the fans to leave with a smile on their faces." Fans highly value the St. Paul Saints because the team provides high value to them—reasonable prices for parking, tickets, concessions, and merchandise, and nonstop, family-oriented entertainment. The game itself is but part of the market offer. The package includes the artwork in the foyer of the ballpark, the band playing at the front gate, the bubble machine spraying fans as they enter the stadium, the on-field autograph sessions before games, the public address announcer who orchestrates the proceedings, the on-field sumo wrestling matches, the nuns who give fans neck massages, the pig delivering baseballs and water to the umpire, and the special game promotions. One of the Saints' best-ever promotions was Halloween in July. They awarded prizes to fans wearing the best costumes. They gave donated candy to kids. The St. Paul JCs, who operate a local haunted house for Halloween, decorated the stadium. They played Halloween music.

The St. Paul Saints illustrate the power of trust-based relationships. By empowering the fans, by giving them a voice in key decisions affecting them (such as whether a new stadium should be built), by offering them abundant value in exchange for their money and time, by naming the team the St. Paul Saints—and not the Twin Cities Saints—a family entertainment company that happens to play professional baseball powers its success with trust-based relationships.

Trust-based relationships characterize the sustained success of the sample companies. A relationship exists when one assesses specific experiences not in isolation but as a progression of past experiences likely to continue into the future.[1] In contrast, the costs and benefits of discrete transactions are evaluated individually, without any reference to previous experiences or those yet to come.

Relationships are important to companies because they are the link to the future—tomorrow's customers, tomorrow's employees, tomorrow's partners. Relationships with employees and business partners, such as suppliers and independent representatives, help a company forge relationships with its customers. The stronger the relationships, the less likely they are to end. Valued relationships last, helping a company control its destiny and perpetuate itself.

Trust is important because a company cannot build true relationships without it. Because service companies market promises—invisible products that customers usually agree to pay for before experiencing— trust is paramount. Customers who buy services must trust a company to keep its promises and conduct itself honorably.

Trust is equally important in creating employee and partner relationships. Just as customers abandon companies they do not trust, so do employees. Even worse are employees who do not leave their jobs but simply quit emotionally. Just as a company makes promises to customers, so does it make promises to employees. When Dana Commercial Credit promises its people that bonuses will be based strictly on their contribution to the company, it is making a promise that is no less real than when Dial-A-Mattress promises a customer standing in an empty apartment that a bedding set will be delivered that day.

Keeping promises also is at the heart of business partnerships. The more than 5,000 independent financial advisors aligned with Charles Schwab Corporation depend on the company to provide reliable back-office support and credible products. Schwab in turn depends on these advisors to serve clients competently and ethically and to send business Schwab's way. Without mutual confidence, the partnership cannot work.

This chapter is organized around the model presented in Exhibit 7–1. Perceptions of a company's competence and fairness contribute directly to a sense of trust, the foundation of employee, partner, and customer relationships. A company's relationships with employees and partners contribute to its efforts to build customer relationships. The greater the trust in these relationships, the greater the commitment to them.

PERCEIVED COMPETENCE

In a series of studies my colleagues, A. Parasuraman and Valarie Zeithaml, and I conducted, customers always rated reliability of service as the single most important feature in judging service quality. The studies covered a wide range of services, including automobile insurance, banking, retailing, computer support, product repair, and securities brokerage.[2] From this research our team learned unequivocally that a service company's *competence* is instrumental in establishing customer *trust*. The risk inherent in buying intangible products becomes a competitive advantage for companies that can earn customers' confidence for dependable, accurate service.

Other researchers also have shown organizational competence to be salient in trust formation. A study of selling partner relationships by Smith and Barclay supports a three-dimensional conceptualization of trustworthiness: character, role competence, and judgment.[3] In a study investigating the use of marketing research services, Moorman, Deshpande, and Zaltman find researcher expertise to be a significant factor in clients' trust.[4] Crosby, Evans, and Cowles show the perceived competence of insurance salespeople to be a significant predictor of customer trust[5] and Doney and Cannon find a similar relationship in a study of industrial buyers' trust of supplier firms and their salespeople.[6]

Customers, however, do not find service competence easily. In an award-winning study of why customers switch service suppliers, Keaveney found that core service failures are the most common cause, cited

EXHIBIT 7-1
Model of Trust-Based Relationships

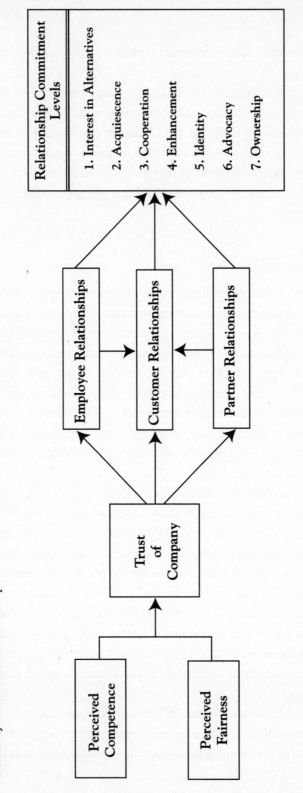

Elements of this model were influenced by two works: Robert M. Morgan and Shelby D. Hunt, "The Commitment-Trust Theory of Relationship Marketing," *Journal of Marketing*, July 1994, pp. 20–38 and Neeli Bendapudi and Leonard L. Berry, "Customer Motivations for Maintaining Relationships with Service Providers," *Journal of Retailing*, Spring 1997, pp. 15–37.

by 44 percent of her sample. Core service failures included mistakes or other technical problems with the service itself.[7]

Service reliability poses some special challenges. Whereas most goods are first manufactured, then shipped, sold, and used, most services are first sold and then frequently produced and consumed simultaneously. Whereas goods-purchasing customers rarely visit the factory where the goods are made, many services require the physical presence of customers for the service to be produced. In effect, jetliners, cruise ships, retail stores, hotels, medical offices, and restaurants are the service factories. Customers' presence in these facilities and their participation in the service process expose them to errors and give them a sense of immediacy.

Moreover, companies that market services requiring the presence of customers ordinarily must locate near the customers, meaning that they must have multiple factories if they wish to grow. Ukrop's is a wonderful supermarket chain but not so wonderful that customers will travel across state lines to reach one of its stores. All the sample companies except the St. Paul Saints must control quality and demonstrate competence in multiple service factories.

Most problematic in consistently demonstrating service competence is the labor-intensity of many services. Human beings deliver a more variable service than machines. This is a reality of the human condition. Not only do people delivering services differ from one another in their service attitudes, personalities, and skills, but the same service provider may provide varying levels of service quality from one customer to the next, depending on a particular customer's attitude, the complexity of the service requested, provider fatigue, or personal problems. In short, labor-intensive services are more vulnerable to failure.[8]

The conditions just described are common. Many companies deliver labor-intensive services in multiple service factories that customers visit. Knowing that service competence is not easily found, customers latch on to it when they find it. Service competence builds the customers' trust in the company's capability to keep its promises.

Service competence also affects employees' and partners' trust in the company. Frontline service employees span the boundary between the company and its customers. They bear the customers' disappointment or wrath when the service fails. They have to solve the problem even when someone else in the company caused it, as is often the case. The service provider's reality is that working for a competent company is easier and more satisfying than working for an incompetent one.

Business partners also depend on a company's competence. Incompetence can spell doom for a partnership on which both parties depend. Dial-A-Mattress significantly strengthened its business when it began offering customers guaranteed same-day delivery in two-hour windows. Company officials thought owner Napoleon Barragan was crazy for proposing this plan because the existing distribution system could not accommodate it. Barragan's approach, however, was to partner with independent trucking companies and custom design a delivery system that would work. This required a leap of faith on the part of the trucking companies and Dial-A-Mattress. Each of Dial-A-Mattress's four trucking-company partners started with a single truck; all have more than 10 trucks now. The trucking firms depend on Dial-A-Mattress to make the sales and Dial-A-Mattress depends on the trucking companies to deliver the bedding units when promised and in a customer-friendly way. This arrangement cannot work without competence and trust among the partners. After all, the only Dial-A-Mattress representatives customers actually see are the truck drivers who are not even Dial-A-Mattress employees.

PERCEIVED FAIRNESS

Two questions individuals often ask themselves before making important choices are "Can promises be kept?" and "Will promises be kept?" Whether it is a packaged goods company selecting a marketing research supplier, a prospective employee considering a job offer from a marketing research company, or a prospective business partner assessing the desirability of a strategic alliance with the research firm, these two questions are pivotal. The first concerns competence, the second fairness. Competence and fairness contribute directly to trust, which leads to loyalty. Trust is the basis for all significant relationships for it counterbalances risk and vulnerability.

Company fairness is an individual's perception of the degree of justice in a firm's behavior. Much of the time, fairness lies dormant as a consumer, employee, or business partner issue. Two conditions generally are necessary to elicit positive or negative fairness perceptions: the individual feels vulnerable and the company's behavior triggers a fairness or unfairness perception. As discussed, the inherent role of promises in services, employment, and partnerships induces vulnerability. Intangibility intensifies "purchase" risk.

Individuals feel most vulnerable when they lack information, expertise, freedom, or recourse. Fairness becomes an issue when a firm's behavior exceeds or violates the person's fairness expectations or norms. These norms can best be understood through a language of justice developed by social psychologists:

- Distributive justice refers to the outcome of a decision.
- Procedural justice concerns the process used to determine the outcome and the interpersonal treatment of individuals during the process.[9]

These justice categories, summarized in Table 7–1, relate to the fairness perceptions of customers, employees, and partners. The potential for a distributive or procedural breakdown is pervasive. Events need not be dramatic to trigger a perception of service unfairness although any one of three conditions can intensify reactions: *severe consequences* (the penalty is high); *recurrence* (the event has happened before); and *controllability* (the behavior was intentional).[10]

When fairness becomes an issue, individuals often react in an immediate, intense, and enduring way. One perceived act of unfairness can destroy a relationship forever. Conversely, one perceived act of fairness can be so distinctive and memorable that it anchors a trust-based relationship for years. Recall the earlier story of the Valley Inn allowing the little girl to keep her pet rabbit in her room. The family and pet rabbit were moving into town. Allowing the rabbit into the hotel was a just decision under the circumstances—and a smart one. The little girl's father is a senior executive of a local company and has since used the hotel for numerous corporate functions and guests.

Fairness is not legality. This point is driven home by a 1997 Conference Board survey of 62 American companies revealing mistrust of management and low morale to be the most significant factors affecting employee-management relationships.[11] In interviewing more than

TABLE 7–1

Categories and Principles of Justice

Justice Categories	Principles	
Distributive Justice		
The outcome of decisions or allocations	• Equity	Participants' rewards equal their contributions to the exchange
	• Equality	Participants are entitled to the same outcome
	• Need	Participants' rewards are proportional to their needs
Procedural Justice		
The procedures or systems used in determining outcomes	• Consistency	Behavior the same across all processes and over time
	• Bias Suppression	Prevention of self-interest
	• Accuracy	Minimization of information errors
	• Correctability	Allowing decision appeals and reversals
	• Representativeness	Values reflect all subgroups
	• Ethicality	Consistent with ethical and moral values

Source: Adapted from Kathleen Seiders and Leonard L. Berry, "Service Fairness: What It Is and Why It Matters," *Academy of Management Executive*, May 1998, pp. 8–20.

250 people from the 14 sample companies, I found no evidence of mistrust of management. These companies operate at a higher standard of conduct than legality and this accounts for the absence of mistrust. In matters small and large, decisions are guided by the principles of fairness and trust. When Midwest Express went public in 1995, it did not have a legal obligation to reserve one million dollars in stock to grant to employees based on their seniority. But it did it anyway at the insistence of chief executive Tim Hoeksema. The same criteria used to allocate stock to employees were applied to Hoeksema and other senior

managers. Dan Sweeney, director of business performance at Midwest Express, considers the employee stock grant a turning point for the company: "It was management's recognition that employees' hard work got us to this point."

TRUST OF COMPANY

The true strength of a company is measured by the strength of its relationships—with customers, employees, business partners, and other stakeholders. Relationship strength or commitment concerns the duration *and* quality of stakeholders' involvement with the company. The ultimate goal for any company should be to organize and use resources supplied by stakeholders to create added value for these stakeholders, including the company itself. Without the commitment of stakeholders—the customers who provide revenue, the employees who provide labor, the institutions that provide financing, the firms that provide goods, materials, equipment, and services—a company cannot realize its value-creating goal and cannot survive.

Trust is the glue that enables a company to organize and use resources effectively in creating added value for stakeholders. An unseeable force, trust is all-powerful for companies that depend on their credibility to survive. Yes, companies can substitute contracts for trust, but contracts do not produce the level of stakeholder loyalty and involvement that trust engenders. Contracts specify obligations and constraints; trust elicits dedication. Contracts are a matter of legality; trust is a matter of the heart.

Trust exists ". . . when one party has confidence in an exchange partner's reliability and integrity," write Morgan and Hunt.[12] Moorman, Deshpande, and Zaltman offer a similar view of trust ". . . as a willingness to rely on an exchange partner in whom one has confidence."[13] Both definitions fit Rotter's view of trust as "a generalized expectancy held by an individual that the word of another . . . can be relied on."[14]

Trust is confidence. To trust the other party is to have confidence in its capability and willingness to keep its explicit and implicit promises. The companies studied for this book sustain their success with trust. Trust may be their single most formidable weapon. These are "high-trust" companies that have built strong, enduring relationships with their principal stakeholder groups. Relationship strength comes from mutual benefits; from giving and getting; from open, honest, frequent communications; from compatible values. Good intentions cannot be in doubt.

The inherently intangible nature of services, employment, and partnerships paves the way for trust-based relationships. Trustworthy companies reduce uncertainty and vulnerability. Confidence feels good.

An important benefit of trust is tolerance. My colleagues and I have found that customers' service quality expectations exist at two levels: *desired* and *adequate*. The desired level reflects a blend of what the customer thinks the service "can be" and "should be." The adequate level reflects the minimum service the customer finds acceptable. Separating these two service expectation levels is the customer's *zone of tolerance*, as shown in Exhibit 7–2. Service above the zone is superior, within the zone satisfactory, below the zone unacceptable.

EXHIBIT 7–2
The Zone of Tolerance

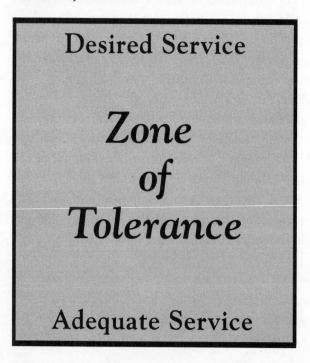

Desired Service

Zone of Tolerance

Adequate Service

The zone of tolerance varies from customer to customer and, potentially, from transaction to transaction for the same customer for reasons documented in earlier publications.[15] Trust plays a central role in the size of tolerance zones for customers, employees, and partners. *The bond of trust increases tolerance for a misstep.* A mistake or failure on the part of a trusted other is more likely to be viewed as an aberration. Trust creates a reservoir of goodwill that in bad times allows an opportunity to rebuild, restore, redo.

EMPLOYEE RELATIONSHIPS

Companies that market performances must be prepared to invest in trusting—and being trusted by—the performers. Labor-intensive service companies that do not build trust-based relationships with their employees cannot build them with customers either. When the product is a performance, company-employee relationships facilitate company-customer relationships.

High employee turnover drives a stake in the heart of a company's relationship marketing efforts. Excessive turnover negates customers' efforts to develop any kind of personal relationship with a firm because they must continually deal with different service providers. Moreover, high turnover discourages companies from investing much in employees' skill and knowledge development because they lose the investment when employees leave. It is a classic paradox. Insufficient investment in employees leaves them unskilled and emotionally unprepared to deliver excellent service, and they quit or are fired. The large percentage of employees leaving the company discourages more investment. Because service quality—and customer retention—suffer from so many new, inexperienced, and poorly prepared employees, profitability is hurt, further reducing resources available to invest in employees' success. High employee turnover is the central culprit in what Schlesinger and Heskett call "the cycle of failure."[16]

Even more destructive than employee turnover to customer relationship building are employees who stay on the job physically but quit emotionally. Service work is emotional labor.[17] Excellence in serving requires listening, helping, caring. It requires performing at a high level of discretionary effort day in and day out despite inevitable bouts of discouragement, fatigue, and inappropriate customer behavior. It requires commitment to the task, to the customer, to co-workers, and to the company. It requires personal leadership and risk taking to find ways to help customers when all paths seem blocked.

Ed Shultz, Dana Commercial Credit's CEO, understands the imperative of trust-based employee relationships in service businesses:

> I run Dana Commercial Credit like a family. I don't see any difference. I have 750 people on the payroll; most of them are heads of households. They deserve to be treated fairly, to have someone care about them. To me, it's personal. If you ever act unfairly and damage people's careers for some short-term gain, you will lose their trust. And if you don't have a trusting relationship with your people, you can't get them to take risks.

Professor Sandra Robinson studied the impact of employee perceptions of unfulfilled employer promises on employees' contributions to their companies. Robinson surveyed a sample of graduate business school alumni three times during a 30-month period. She found that companies violating employees' trust receive a lesser contribution from those employees and that violated trust in the workplace is not easily rectified. Robinson also found that employees with a high level of trust in the company at the start of their jobs were less likely to perceive a trust violation during their first year than less trusting employees. The study also reported on how employees with high and low initial trust reacted to perceived trust violations. When employees with low initial trust perceived an apparent violation, they experienced a greater decline in trust than employees with high initial trust.[18] Robinson's findings are consistent with the zone of tolerance effect proposed in the previous section.

The sample companies have established trust-based employee relationships through rigorous attention to being trustworthy. As Dana Commercial Credit's Ed Shultz puts it: "You have to convince your people that you are an honest person, and the best way to do that is by being an honest person." Regardless of size, the sample companies function like *extended families*. Family behaviors underlie the internal company trust found in this study.

Family Gatherings

Members of strong families gather periodically to communicate, share, celebrate, resolve problems, console, help, or enjoy one another—and so do members of strong organizations. Enterprise Rent-A-Car brings together its managers for an annual meeting that is as much a rally and celebration as it is a conference. The purpose is to reinforce the company's culture, values, and sense of family. Owners Jack and Andy Taylor will walk through the entire banquet hall to shake hands. And they encounter a lot of hands to shake—3,300 people attended in 1997. Chick-fil-A sponsors an all-expenses-paid, four-day business meeting each year for restaurant operators and all full-time headquarters employees and their spouses. Celebration, recognition of top performers, annual business direction, and values reinforcement are principal goals of the gathering.

Charles Schwab Corporation includes every single employee in its annual "Town Hall" meeting. Senior management discuss the company's direction, reinforce its values, and answer questions. The meeting occurs in three to six cities during several months. Employees participate personally or via satellite video or telephone hookups. "We believe relationships are driven by shared values at Schwab," explains Mark Thompson, senior vice president. "Face-to-face interaction is a powerful way to perpetuate our values."

Ukrop's holds an annual picnic for associates at the farm of the company founders, Joe and Jacquelin Ukrop. The event truly is a family affair. Employees bring spouses, children, grandparents, aunts, and uncles—5,400 people attended in 1997. Picnic goers play softball, volleyball, tennis, and golf; bands play music; kids play games. A Parade of Champions honors associates who have been recognized by customers or vendors for demonstrating Ukrop's values. The picnic is a festive, memorable family gathering, as human resources manager Cheryl George explains: "Our founders, Mr. and Mrs. Ukrop, sit in the pavilion and greet all of the associates. James and Bobby Ukrop also shake everyone's hand. Just picture all of the associates and their families saying a prayer together and eating together."

Ukrop's also has "roundtable" meetings four to six times a year for managers to discuss leadership, business, and personal issues. More than 140 managers participate in these meetings. The managers meet in small groups with a facilitator. People who do not normally interact with one another in the course of business are grouped together. Jim Blackwell, managing director of retail operations who has been with Ukrop's more than 30 years, recalls a particularly valuable roundtable session:

> We were all told to write about our favorite childhood hero and why this person was our hero. It was interesting to listen to everyone talk about it and what that hero had contributed. It really helped each of us relate to times when things seemed so simple. Then we talked about our favorite childhood memories. This gets you close to everyone in the room. So when disagreements happen, we understand each other better. It connects the links to the chain. It increases team bonding.

Team meetings at Midwest Express often include a segment called "Check-In." Participants share personal issues that may be causing stress in their lives and preoccupying them at work. The sessions increase understanding, camaraderie, teamwork, and trust.

In November 1997, Special Expeditions held a special three-day workshop for its management and field leadership. With its ships operating year-round throughout the world, getting together for face-to-face communications is not easy. But in late 1997 the company held a necessary family meeting in Washington state. The company was moving into new markets such as a Galapogos Islands voyage with an Ecuadorian partner and testing new concepts such as a golfing tour. It had recently acquired a 110-passenger ship, the *Caledonian Star*, which was bigger than its other ships. Concern was mounting in the field that the company was losing sight of its mission.

Tom O'Brien, director of environmental affairs for Special Expeditions, proposed the meeting to owner Sven-Olof Lindblad, who was supportive. About 90 members of the Special Expeditions "family" attended—management, expedition leaders, naturalists, ship captains. On the first evening, participants introduced themselves and described their work for the company. The creativity and camaraderie of the field staff was abundantly evident. "It was a magical hour and a half," states O'Brien. The next morning Sven-Olof Lindblad presented a detailed history of Special Expeditions and the expedition travel industry and discussed the future of both. This, too, was a key moment. "Everybody knew that Sven came from where they had come from. They all realized the values were there and that the company was in good hands," adds O'Brien. On the last evening, some of the staff wrote a farewell song. According to O'Brien, this was a "tremendous bonding moment that will forever be part of Special Expeditions' culture."

Family Familiarity

In strong families, the parents are accessible and approachable. They are real people, not portraits on a wall or in an annual shareholders' report. It is easy and comforting to be in their presence. Relationships are personal, genuine, and loving. The same is true in strong organizations. The leaders are accessible, approachable, and caring. Relationships are personalized. Mutual respect is abundant. And organizational trust is nurtured.

The sample companies are "first name" organizations. At The Container Store, Garrett Boone is just "Garrett," Kip Tindell just "Kip," and Sharon Tindell just "Sharon"—to everyone. Napoleon Barragan is universally referred to as "Nap" at Dial-A-Mattress. In the corridors of Chick-fil-A's Atlanta headquarters or in its restaurants across the country, employees and operators speak warmly about "Truett." Dana Commercial Credit's Ed Shultz hosts "Lunch with Ed" sessions to give small groups of Dana people the opportunity to question him about the company's strategy—or about how to prepare mushroom soup (Shultz is a gourmet cook). A management trainee can walk into any executive's office at Enterprise Rent-A-Car's St. Louis headquarters, which is what branch manager Scott McDonald did when he was a trainee: "I went to St. Louis and walked right up to Andy's office."

A group of Midwest Express flight attendants were asked about the high level of trust in the organization. The answer was: "It comes from knowing people in management like Tim personally. The personal relationship is a lot better than a signature on a piece of paper. We know that Tim is genuinely a good person and would never do anything for the sake of business that violated his beliefs." Adds Frank Brenner, who started at Midwest Express as a ramp agent: "When the president of the company shakes your hand on your first day and says, 'Hey, you're working for the best now'—WOW! I've never experienced anything like that before."

Family Honor

The sample companies encourage organizational trust by believing in members of the organization. They create trust by trusting. Just as families do not expect members to cheat, neither do high-trust companies expect employees to do so. Some employees may indeed cheat but this is considered an aberration that does not require management looking over all employees' shoulders.

Miller SQA factory employees do not use time clocks. They are automatically paid for 40 hours a week. When they miss work, they record the missed time in the computer. Each year employees are granted 24 hours for personal time such as medical appointments. Additional hours are deducted from the employee's bank. The calculations are done on the honor system.

Jennifer Grassano, a sales coach and bedding consultant for Dial-A-Mattress, works out of her home part of the week. Her husband, Kenneth, also works at home as a Dial-A-Mattress bedding consultant. The Grassanos have a work cubicle in their home just like in the company's call center. Several other married couples have similar arrangements. A typical plan is one spouse working from 8:00 A.M. to 4:00 P.M., the other from 4:00 P.M. to midnight. Clearly, the arrangement requires the trust of the company. The main purpose is to enable parents to work while raising children. Says Jennifer: "I like not having to travel to work and being able to get the children ready for school. It's a wonderful thing because I can be there for my kids and still work. Plus, it is a learning experience for the children. The only thing is, I don't want my kids to think they can go to work in their pajamas." She adds: "A parent is always there for the children, an agent always there for Dial-A-Mattress."

A single act of trust can have lasting effects. Christine Sharratt, a senior vice president of Custom Research, remembers such an act: "I made a mistake once that cost the company $30,000. I was sick about it. Jeff [Pope] and Judy [Corson] never once came to me and said, 'What in the hell did you do?'" Although Pope and Corson may have forgotten the incident over the years, Sharratt remembers it well. The owners' faith in her made a deep impression.

Family Fairness

Fairness, consistency, and evenhandedness are hallmarks of strong families—and high-trust companies. Companies build organizational trust through equal treatment of managerial and nonmanagerial personnel. And if the treatment is unequal, it is the managers rather than the nonmanagers who must meet a higher standard. As Enterprise Rent-A-Car President and CEO Andy Taylor comments: "We have no double standard for managers versus nonmanagers or headquarters personnel versus field personnel. We are all treated the same."

The sample companies promote from within. Incumbents whose efforts have brought the company to its present state of success taste its fruits rather than outsiders. The companies recruit people who share their values, then promote from within.

The companies also pay for performance. Employees' salaries at The Container Store are pegged to their value to the company rather than their specific job function. Thus, employees can be in the role that suits them best without sacrificing income opportunities. Fernando Ramos is a case in point. Ramos was a store manager for more than three years, but the administrative tasks were not right for him. His passion is selling on the retail floor. So a new position for selling and training was created for him. "I go to all the store openings to show the new people how to generate excitement on the sales floor," explains Ramos. "I hate to be behind a desk. My deal is working on the floor. My salary hasn't changed; why worry?"

Dana Commercial Credit's bonus program is based strictly on merit. Employees are evaluated at the end of the year and receive bonuses based on their contribution to the business. Management takes the performance evaluation and bonus allocation process seriously and devotes considerable time to it. Bonus recommendations for each employee come from immediate supervisors through product managers and the company's operating committee to senior management. "Our people understand the best way to get a bonus is to reflect Dana's value system—customer satisfaction, innovation, finding a better way to deliver the service," states chief executive Ed Shultz. "Our senior management spends three days and reviews every person on the payroll. Our principal objective is to make sure bonuses truly reflect performance."

Custom Research Inc. faced a dilemma after it won the Malcolm Baldrige National Quality Award in 1996. Jeff Pope and Judy Corson had promised to take all employees to the Washington, D.C. awards ceremony should Custom Research win the award. They were unaware that each winning company was limited to 50 guests. Corson and Pope used some principles of family fairness. They held a drawing for the seats in each area and job level to insure that people throughout the company attended the ceremony. On the day of the ceremony, employees not attending enjoyed a special celebration. The ceremony was broadcast live to the office by satellite. The staff shared a catered lunch and received massages and manicures. Then they closed the office and everyone went home early. The people who went to Washington carried a large photo of a staff member who stayed behind. Audrey Omlid did make the trip—she is considered by all at Custom Research to be a world-class receptionist.

Family Fun

Members of strong families enjoy being with one another and they enjoy celebrating achievement. Families invest time and money in having fun together and so do high-trust organizations. Fun is a great trust builder because it conveys caring. Only companies that care would invest in employees' having fun on the job. Only companies that care would thank employees for their hard work by investing in their laughter and smiles.

The companies studied for this book all have hard-work, high-achievement cultures. But fun always is in the air. Custom Research has good-news meetings, pet day, indoor golf tournaments each Minnesota winter, and treat tables (cookies, M&Ms, potato chips) in work areas. "We believe in carbohydrates," says researcher Carolyn MacLeod.

Ukrop's holds an annual company Olympics. Six-member teams from throughout the organization compete in fun events for gold, silver, and bronze medals. The photos of winning teams are posted in store information centers. The company sponsors bowling and golf tournaments and held its first awards and variety show in 1998. Service award dinners and luncheons are held. Several times a year, employees recognized at the annual picnic wear their "Parade of Champions" shirts to work. "We are always thinking of ways we can celebrate," explains Debbye Mahan, who manages human resources for Ukrop's support center. "We think of how we can thank employees. You don't have to invest a lot of money. It's all about showing that you value them."

The Container Store actually has a Fun Committee, which was established after the size of the corporate office tripled. Management sensed that employees were losing touch with each other in the bigger building. The Committee decorated the home office with photos of products and merchandise displays, named each conference room after the company's foundation principles, and planned fun lunches. The Fun Committee also sponsors the Annual Chili Cookoff which occurs in the home office during Halloween. Departments combine efforts to build elaborately decorated booths, cook a pot of chili, and dress in thematic costumes. In 1997, the accounting department chose a pumpkin theme, making pumpkin chili, cornbread, and dessert, dressing as pumpkins, and decorating their booth like a pumpkin patch. Employees secretively guard their thematic ideas until the morning of the contest. The judges, wearing the appropriate judicial attire of long black robes, award prizes for the best food, costumes, and booths. Nancy Donley, human resources director, explains the rationale for the Fun Committee: "Fun activities help us to get to know one another on a different level, play a vital role in helping new employees learn about our culture, and help us preserve our culture as we grow."

The offices of the Frequent Flyer Department at Midwest Express are next to windows on the first floor of the company's headquarters building. Outside the building is a sidewalk. Staff member Randy Beres had the idea that each department member should write something on the sidewalk, which is visible from the window. One day everyone wrote messages or drew pictures with chalk on a square of sidewalk to express their thoughts. Steve Mathwig, the department manager, traced his body and wrote, "Hello, welcome to work." Beres comments:

"Fun is important in this department because in our line of work we can spend a lot of time listening to problems."

Relationships with Employees

A powerful lesson for labor-intensive service companies is that building employee relationships must precede building customer relationships. Employees with "just-a-job" attitudes do not have the personal commitment to their work and company to perform at a level that generates customer commitment. The sample companies have far more "relationship employees" than "just-a-job" employees, and this offers them a significant competitive advantage.

Trust is the foundation for any strong relationship, including company-employee relationships. High-trust organizations truly do act like strong, extended families. Trust is everything; it is paramount; it is precious.

PARTNER RELATIONSHIPS

Company partners, such as suppliers and independent representatives, figure in company-customer relationship-building efforts just as employees do. Company-customer relationships are secured by the benefits customers receive from staying in the relationships. Business partners help provide these benefits.

The market offer from Dial-A-Mattress of purchased-by-phone, promptly delivered bedding has worldwide appeal, not just in the company's present markets. Thus, Dial-A-Mattress is well underway in expanding its distribution nationally and internationally through company-owned operations, franchising, and retailer alliances. Here is how the retailer alliance approach works. An independent retailer in a local market agrees to display and deliver the bedding for Dial-A-Mattress. The retail partner must be willing to advertise Dial-A-Mattress's 1-800 number. Local customers call Dial-A-Mattress, which makes the sale. The local retailer then delivers the mattress from its inventory. The local retailer pockets 80 percent of the selling price, Dial-A-Mattress 20 percent. The process works the other way, too. A customer moves to an area in which Dial-A-Mattress has its own distribution and is referred by the local retailer. Dial-A-Mattress sells and delivers the bedding and takes 80 percent of the revenue; the local retailer receives 20 percent.

In past years Dial-A-Mattress has received thousands of calls from prospective customers who saw or heard its advertising—or heard word-of-mouth advertising—but who did not live where the company had distribution. Dial-A-Mattress also is facing intense competition in its home market as a result of its visible success. By 1998, 38 competitors were selling the same bedding brands as Dial-A-Mattress through 1-800 numbers in New York area markets. Both the opportunity and need to expand are clear.

The key for Dial-A-Mattress is selecting retail partners that operate as competently and ethically as it does. Retailer alliances are conceptually simple and executionally complex. Selling mattresses over the telephone is all about keeping promises and earning trust. Just as Dial-A-Mattress recruits employees who share its values, so must it find retail partners with these values. If it does, the company has a good chance of realizing its market share goal of 10 percent of the U.S. bedding market.

Several studies reveal the key benefits of trust-based partner relationships. Kumar, Hibbard, and Stern studied the relationships between a large manufacturer of replacement automobile parts and 429 of its retailers. They found that the retailers indicating a high level of trust in the manufacturer were more committed to the relationship, less likely to have developed alternative supply sources, and generated significantly higher sales of the manufacturer's products. They also found that trust increased tolerance, consistent with the zone of tolerance effect proposed earlier in the chapter.[19] Nirmalya Kumar writes:

> What really distinguishes trusting from distrusting relationships is the ability of the parties to make a *leap of faith:* they believe that each is interested in the other's welfare and that neither will act without first considering the action's impact on the other. . . . Trust . . . creates a reservoir of goodwill that helps preserve the relationship when, as will inevitably happen, one party engages in an act that its partner considers destructive.[20]

Dyer and Chu have explored the economics of trust in a study of the eight largest automobile manufacturers in Japan, South Korea, and the United States and 435 of their suppliers. The researchers studied how much the suppliers trusted the manufacturers and measured the cost of mistrust. Their findings indicated that in all three countries, higher levels of trust resulted in substantially lower costs for both manufacturers and suppliers. In the United States—where supplier relationships exhibited the least trust overall—the manufacturer with the lowest trust levels devoted nearly one-half of its face-to-face time with suppliers to non–value-adding activities such as negotiating prices or contracts or assigning blame for problems. The manufacturer with the highest trust rating devoted only a quarter of this time to such matters. Purchasing personnel at the latter company handled more than twice as many goods in dollar value as the least-trusted manufacturer. The researchers also found that trust paved the way for the manufacturers and suppliers to share information and ideas. They concluded that trust not only saves money in relationships but also adds value because it encourages the sharing of resources.[21]

Partners can help a company operate more efficiently and effectively. They can help a company serve its customers better and bring new customers to the company. But the relationship must be beneficial for both partners. A strong relationship must be mutually perceived and mutually beneficial.[22] A company's competence and fairness engenders trust which engenders the necessary cooperation for effective partnerships. Relationship marketers cooperate with partners to compete for customers.[23]

The Donut Strategy

Enterprise Rent-A-Car offices typically call on primary referral sources every week. Because Enterprise focuses on the replacement market for car rentals, branch offices diligently build relationships with local businesses that can refer customers who need rental cars, particularly automobile dealerships, body shops, insurance companies, and hotels.

How do you call on major accounts weekly without being a nuisance? Enterprise brings food for their employees, usually donuts but possibly bagels or fruit trays, too. On a hot day, Enterprise might show up at the service department of a car dealership with cokes or ice cream sandwiches in an ice chest. The company has been known to rent ice cream trucks and drive them to major accounts for an afternoon treat.

The usual fare, however, is donuts—often brought in Enterprise Rent-A-Car's own donut box with the company's logo. Joanne Peratis-Weber, vice president of the Dallas–Fort Worth area, estimates that she spent $50,000 on donuts in 1997 for 27 Enterprise branch offices. And she considers the investment a bargain: "It encourages regular contact with our customers. It is an easy way to introduce new employees to an account. When we arrive with donuts, we are not an interruption; they are glad to see us. It is an inexpensive way to say 'thank you.'"

New Enterprise employees quickly learn the heart of the company's marketing strategy: never take referral sources for granted and thank them for their business every time. Other rental agencies have tried to imitate Enterprise's approach but have not generated the same impact. The donuts are but a symbol of mutually valuable relationships. Enterprise helps the dealerships, body shops, insurance agencies, and hotels please their own customers. They call the body shop for the insurance agency to see when a car will be ready. They go to the body shop to pick up a customer needing a rental car. If an account phones a Texas branch office for a rental car needed in Oklahoma, the Texas office handles all the arrangements.

The marketing strategy calls for Enterprise to be an extension of referral accounts, to represent them while serving their joint customers well. The donuts symbolize the sense of partnership, the sense of trust built from a record of performance. Dick Janicki, an Enterprise vice president and general manager, comments: "It doesn't matter what you sell. We happen to rent cars but it really doesn't matter. It's the people who make the difference in any business. We become friends with people at our accounts because we can help each other out."

The Advice Strategy

Charles Schwab Corporation was founded to provide an efficient, cost-effective, and conflict-free way for investors to buy and sell securities they knew they wanted to buy and sell. Investors who did not need advice should not have to pay for it. Brokers should be noncommissioned to remove conflicts of interest. The original strategy brought Schwab a long way and revolutionized the securities brokerage business as discussed in Chapter 4. But in the 1980s the company's market research showed a growing percentage of investors wanting advice in managing their financial affairs. This posed a challenge for a company founded on a nonadvice model. To turn away investors needing advice was to send them into the world of commissioned salespeople—what Chuck Schwab calls "the lion's den."

The company's response was to build a network of independent *fee-based* financial advisors to whom Schwab would refer clients requiring advice. The partnership concept has worked extremely well, and Schwab currently has more than 5,000 independent financial advisors in its network called Schwab Institutional. More than $100 billion invested in Schwab accounts are managed by these advisors.

Most of the financial advisors in the network are small businesses. Schwab provides not only referrals but also back-office transactional and record-keeping systems at no cost to the advisors. All of the back-office systems needed to operate are available from one source; because Schwab distributes all the major mutual funds, it is a one-stop shopping opportunity for the financial advisors to make transactions for their clients through a "turnkey" operating system.

In effect, Schwab is the wholesaler, the financial advisors the retailers. On its wholesale "shelves" are a wide variety of investments from which the advisors can construct client portfolios. Both parties to the relationship benefit. Schwab has extended its reach to advice-seeking investors and brought in about one-third of its total assets in so doing. The financial advisors on the other hand have a support system; they have a partner. The arrangement is not easily executed, however.

Managing trust in such a large and complex partnership network is challenging. Schwab is a huge company; most network members are small businesses. Schwab works on the trust issue by regularly interacting with network members at advisory board, regional, and national meetings. The annual Schwab Institutional Conference is the largest conference for fee-based investment advisors in the United States.

Schwab follows a policy of "open architecture" to systematically share financial services market information with its financial advisor network. For example, Schwab tracked the growing number of smaller investors with portfolios under $100,000 seeking investment advice and developed an academic, research-based computer software model to help these clients in its branch offices. The software model standardizes the advice given across branches. Schwab's entry into this business created some tension within its advisor network because it appeared that the firm was competing with the advisors. Schwab's sharing of market data showing many small investors turning to other sources of financial help—for example, Intuit or Microsoft software—helped to moderate the issue. Other issues will arise in the future. They are inevitable in such complex organizational arrangements. Managing the trust of its independent financial advisor partners is one key to Charles Schwab Corporation's future success.

CUSTOMER RELATIONSHIPS

Companies create trust-based customer relationships through the actions of their employees and partners and through company strategies and policies. Repeat business nourishes a company's vitality. Feargal Quinn, a successful food retailer in Ireland, refers to this maxim as the "boomerang principle: the main task in business is to bring the customer back."[24]

Attracting new customers to a business is only the beginning. The best companies view new customer attraction as the launching point for developing and enhancing a long-term relationship. Companies can expand market share three ways: attracting new customers, increasing business with existing customers, and retaining current customers. Building relationships with existing customers directly addresses two of the three possibilities and indirectly addresses the other.

Relationships benefit customers as well as the firms. This is especially true for customers of services. Services that are consequential, involving, complex, delivered on a recurring basis, and variable in quality from one provider to another have particular relationship appeal to customers. Services with some or all of these characteristics—importance, involvement, complexity, continuity, and variability—are common. Financial, professional, transportation, and health-care services are just a few of many categories of services with these characteristics. Customers are motivated to remain as customers when they buy these types of services and have an excellent experience. Not only does the auto repair firm seek loyal customers, customers seek an auto repair firm that evokes their loyalty.[25]

Customers reduce risk, save time, and reap social and other benefits by forming relationships with companies offering services possessing the characteristics enumerated above. In a two-phase study, Gwinner, Gremler, and Bitner find that customer confidence—reduced anxiety, faith in the trustworthiness of the service provider—is the most important benefit to customers of maintaining a relationship with a service firm. Social benefit, including personal recognition by employees and customer familiarity with employees, is the second most important benefit.[26] Other researchers echo the importance of social benefits in commercial relationships. Barlow writes that "it fundamentally appeals to people to be dealt with on a one-on-one basis."[27] Jackson stresses that relationship marketing addresses the basic human need to feel important.[28] Czepiel suggests that because service encounters also are social encounters, ongoing contacts between providers and customers naturally assume personal as well as professional dimensions.[29]

Relationship customers also can expect the company to become more knowledgeable and skilled in serving them over time as a result of experience effects. A series of customer-company encounters should facilitate more customizing of the service to customers' specifications.

Service companies able to establish strong customer relationships benefit enormously. Industry price competition is rampant for every service category studied for this book. Genuine customer relationships are by far the best way to counterattack price competition. As Dial-A-Mattress founder Napoleon Barragan puts it: "I used to advertise that I would beat any price in town. I was fortunate to find a way to compete with service so I could charge a reasonable price."

Strong relationships normally provide some price cushion because of the nonprice benefits customers receive from the relationship. By definition, relationship customers are not buying a commodity service. The price cushion may be thin, but it generally exists in strong relationships. Midwest Express, which has built strong relationships with thousands of frequent flyers traveling from and to its hub cities, knows it must be price competitive. But its management also knows it does not need to match every competitor price cut either. Service customers who strictly are price-buyers—a minority of customers in most markets[30]—are not candidates for relationship marketing in the first place. They are deal-prone customers who are continually seeking the low price offer.

Reichheld and Sasser have shown across a variety of service industries that profits climb steeply when a company reduces its customer-defection rate. Based on an analysis of more than 100 companies in two dozen industries, the researchers found that firms could improve profits from 25 percent to 85 percent by reducing customer defections by just 5 percent. Loyal customers generate more revenue for more years, and costs decline because the expense of acquiring new customers to replace defecting customers is less.[31]

Service firms that serve customers competently and fairly and establish trust use all three approaches to build market share. They not only do more business with existing customers and retain them longer, but also they attract new customers from positive word-of-mouth communications. The strongest trust-based customer relationships generally possess three qualities: structural solutions, friendship rules, and continuous learning.

Structural Solutions

Companies create a solid foundation for maintaining and enhancing customer relationships when they offer customers valuable benefits that are not readily available from other suppliers. Strong relationships are built on real solutions to important customer problems. Structural solutions are designed into the company's service delivery system rather than depending upon the relationship-building skills of individual service providers. The structural solution binds the customer to the company instead of—or in addition to—particular service employees who may leave the firm.

Much of Midwest Express's total product—the point-to-point routing, no middle seats, full meals served on china, chocolate chip cookies baked on board—is structural. Passengers flying coach receive a "first-class" experience. It is a valuable, differentiating service—especially for frequent flyers for whom traveling is a chore.

Friendship Rules

Professors Michael Argyle and Monica Henderson have defined several fundamental rules of friendship. These include providing emotional support, respecting privacy and preserving confidences, and tolerance of other friendships.[32] Trust-based customer relationships honor these friendship rules. Excellent service companies may not have a personal relationship with their customers, but they are effective in personalizing service transactions and counteracting the anonymity that customers so often experience with companies. Relationship companies look for ways to please their customers, to do something extra or special for them, just as friends would do for one another. As in friendships, relationship companies do not take advantage of customers. They respect, honor, and trust them. They value the relationship and invest time, effort, and money in strengthening it.

From the sample companies come numerous stories that reflect friendship rules. Space permits the telling of only a few. During a Richmond snowstorm, ice slid off the roof of a Ukrop's store and damaged a customer's car. Ukrop's was not legally responsible for the damage because it resulted from inclement weather. The company paid for the car to be fixed anyway. Ukrop's does not deliver groceries, but a customer called a store to ask if two food trays could be delivered for a neighbor who had a death in the family. The assistant manager personally delivered the food trays.

Custom Research prepares "surprise and delight" plans for its clients to exceed their expectations. For example, Custom Research mapped the entire research process with one client to avoid duplicating steps and to save the client time and effort. A client contracting only for tabular data might also receive presentation charts at no extra charge.

When an American Airlines strike seemed imminent in 1997, Special Expeditions contacted every potentially affected customer booked on one of its voyages and sent them backup plane tickets on alternative carriers. Special Expeditions told its customers to use the tickets if necessary and to send them back if not used. The strike didn't occur, but customers were impressed by Special Expeditions' proactivity and concern. Maggie Hart, Special Expeditions director of operations, tells a story about the company's ship, the *Sea Lion*, suffering a problem with the steering controls. The engineers worked through the night, but the ship would be late getting to Vancouver to pick up passengers. The company owner, Sven-Olof Lindblad, called an old friend, the renowned wildlife artist Robert Bateman, who has a home overlooking the water at Fulford Harbor. Passengers were ferried from Vancouver to Fulford Harbor, fed dinner, and entertained at the Bateman home. The *Sea Lion* arrived and everyone boarded a little after midnight in the greatest of spirits.

Continuous Learning

Customers can teach companies how they want to be served. Relationship companies that capture and use this knowledge make it more difficult for customers to leave the relationship. As Peppers and Rogers write: "Whoever knows a particular customer best has the advantage with that customer."[33]

Continuous learning about customers hones service to them with each transaction. Custom Research maintains "client books" that contain information helpful in tailoring the service to individual client requirements. The client book becomes a living document that captures new intelligence as it becomes available, including client feedback on individual projects and the overall relationship. All information that can help Custom Research staff know more about how to serve a client goes into the client book.

The client book serves multiple purposes for Custom Research. It accelerates the learning curve for new staff on an account. It becomes a briefing book for staff preparing for client visits or to write a proposal. It is a single depository of feedback and other information on how the client wants to be served. It is a documented record of the health, strength, and evolution of a relationship. Explains Executive Vice President Jan Elsesser, "What is exceeding client expectations today will be only meeting them tomorrow. We continually gather feedback from clients."

Information technology facilitates efficient learning about customers and the performance of key relationship marketing tasks by:

- Tracking the buying patterns and overall relationship of existing customers
- Customizing services, promotions, and pricing to customers' specific requirements
- Coordinating or integrating the delivery of multiple services to the same customer
- Providing two-way communication channels—company to customer, customer to company
- Minimizing the probability of service errors and breakdowns
- Augmenting core service offerings with valued extras
- Personalizing service encounters as appropriate[34]

Ukrop's was the first supermarket in the United States to introduce a frequent shopper program—Ukrop's Valued Customer (UVC) program, introduced in 1987. The foundation for the company's relationship marketing efforts, the UVC program illustrates not only continuous learning through information technology but also structural solutions and friendship rules.

By using their bar-coded UVC membership cards when checking out, customers accrue automatic savings and Ukrop's tracks household purchases. Membership cards come in three versions: as a wallet card similar to a credit card, as a smaller keychain card, and as a bank debit card issued by First Market Bank with branches in Ukrop's stores and jointly owned by Ukrop's and National Commerce Bancorporation. Customer benefits revolve around their use of the card. Through monthly newsletters and other mailings, members are informed of member-only product discounts that are electronically granted when checking out. A specific store aisle is dedicated to the monthly UVC specials. Members can select a charity to receive a percentage of their spending with the UVC card. By using their card, members automatically are entered in periodic store sweepstakes promotions ("Win a trip to the NCAA Final Four basketball tournament") and can qualify for a free Thanksgiving turkey (based on spending in the weeks preceding the holiday). Members also receive discounts from other local businesses.

The ability to apply continuous learning about individual household purchasing patterns is one of the program's strongest features. Monthly newsletter specials are targeted to the needs of specific households. Thus, a loyal yogurt customer may receive a coupon for a free Yoplait yogurt. Ukrop's has incorporated a Baby Club into the program that gives members a $10 certificate for every $100 they spend on baby products using the UVC card.

The UVC program takes much of the anonymity out of food shopping. Loyal customers develop personalized relationships with store employees, and they develop electronic relationships with the company as a whole. The program is a way for Ukrop's to talk to the nearly 300,000 households that used the UVC card during any 12-week period in 1998. Ukrop's publishes a glossy magazine for its members twice a year that includes recipes, sweepstakes promotions, electronic coupon specials, vendor-sponsored promotions, and seasonal editorial content, such as "Alternatives for the Allergic."

The UVC program benefits are compelling, which is why within two weeks of a new Ukrop's store opening in Fredericksburg, Virginia, in 1997, 89 percent of the sales were through the UVC card. In 1998 about 30 percent of Ukrop's customers accounted for 71 percent of its sales. "We need to take good care of this 30 percent. We need to keep our best customers shopping with us," states Scott Ukrop, vice president of sales and marketing.

LEVELS OF RELATIONSHIP COMMITMENT

Customers, employees, and partners may remain in relationships with a company either because they desire the relationship or because they perceive no suitable alternative. The level of commitment to a relationship depends on the extent to which it derives from dedication rather than constraint.[35] Trust-based relationships foster dedication.

Relationship commitment can be conceptualized across a range of commitment levels from interest in alternatives to feelings of ownership (see Exhibit 7–1). Customers, employees, and partners who remain in relationships because constraints bar leaving (for example, other services are perceived to be too expensive or local companies are not currently hiring) are prone to defect should the constraints be removed. The relationship is necessary but not valued—and consequently *interest in alternatives* is high.

Acquiescence is the degree to which one party to a relationship complies with the other party's requests.[36] It implies passive agreement to maintain the relationship. Both constraints and dedication can lead to acquiescence. *Cooperation* involves parties in a relationship working together to achieve mutual goals. It is characterized by active participation in making the relationship work. Cooperation is a natural outcome of trust-based relationships.

Enhancement refers to broadening and deepening relational bonds with the other party, to invest in strengthening the relationship beyond its current status. Buying additional services from the company or assisting the firm with its marketing are examples. Parties to a relationship they would like to leave are unlikely to invest in enhancements that raise exit barriers. Closely related to enhancement is relationship *identity*, the extent to which one party thinks of the relationship as a team[37] and considers the other party in proprietorial terms, for example, "my broker," "my airline." *Advocacy* concerns the party's willingness to be an advocate for the company, to promote it, and, if necessary, to defend it from detractors.[38]

Emotional *ownership* of the company, the highest level of relationship commitment, is an extension and combination of cooperation, enhancement, identity, and advocacy. Trust can help a company build relationships with customers, employees, and partners that are so intense they feel and act like owners of the business and may actually become financial owners. This is what has happened with the companies studied for this book and the next chapter includes a section on employee ownership attitudes. Emotional ownership from a customer perspective is illustrated in the following story told by Jerry Scott, director of customer service training at Midwest Express, who earlier had worked for Eastern Airlines: "Coming to Midwest Express was a culture shock. For example, a customer came running up to the counter in New York. I just braced myself for the worst because at Eastern only the upset customers ran up to the counter. But this customer just wanted to thank Midwest Express for taking such good care of its passengers. This was my baptism at Midwest Express and it set the tone for my career."

Trust is powerful. It is so powerful that companies relying on human performance to create value cannot achieve sustained success without it. Trust provides the foundation of service companies' efforts to establish enduring, commitment-rich relationships with customers and with employees and partners who perform for customers.

The confidence of customers, employees, and partners is a service company's most valuable asset. This is a fact of life for companies that market promises for a living. Unless they keep their promises, there is no living to be made. Great service companies by definition are high-trust companies.

8

INVESTMENT IN
EMPLOYEE SUCCESS

Cora Griffith is a waitress for the Orchard Cafe in Appleton, Wisconsin's Paper Valley Hotel. She is superb in this role, appreciated by her first-time customers, famous with her regular customers, revered by her co-workers. She came to the Orchard Cafe in 1985 after moving back to Wisconsin from Arizona where she had her first waitressing experience. "I still remember my first day as a waitress. I was scared to death. I was so shy. Being a waitress brought me out of my shell." Prior to moving to Arizona, Cora lived in Kaukauna, Wisconsin, and worked for more than nine years as an executive secretary. When she moved back to Wisconsin she knew she wanted to stay with restaurant service and joined the waitress staff at the Orchard Cafe.

Cora loves her work and it shows. She is comfortable in a role she believes is the right one for her. She has not applied for openings at Christie's, the hotel's four-star restaurant, preferring the informality of the Orchard Cafe. "At the Orchard Cafe, I can laugh and talk and just be more relaxed," she says.

Cora implements nine rules of success, the first of which is to *treat customers like family*. First-time customers are not allowed to feel like strangers. Cheerful and proactive, Cora smiles, chats, and includes everyone at the table in the conversation. She is as respectful to children as she is to adults and makes it a point to learn and use everyone's name. "I want people to feel like they're sitting down to dinner right at my house. I want them to feel they're welcome, that they can get comfortable, that they can relax. I don't just serve people, I pamper them."

Another success rule is to *listen first*. Cora has developed her listening skills to the point that she rarely writes down customers' orders. She feels she can pay closer attention to her customers when she is not writing. She listens carefully and provides a customized service: "Are they in a hurry? Or do they have time on their hands, feel a little lonesome, and just want to talk? Do they have a special diet or like their selection cooked a certain way?"

Cora strives to *anticipate* her customers' wants, replenishing beverages and bringing extra bread and butter in a timely manner. Her regular customer who likes honey with her coffee gets it without asking. "I don't want my customers to have to ask for anything, so I always try to anticipate what they might need."

Simple things make the difference is another of Cora's success rules. She manages the details of her service, monitoring the cleanliness of the utensils and their correct placement on the table. The fold of the napkin must be just right. She inspects each plate in the kitchen before taking it to the table. She provides crayons for small children to draw pictures while waiting for the meal. "It's the little things that please the customer."

Cora applies her *work smart* rule by scanning all of her tables at once, looking for opportunities to combine tasks. "Never do just one thing at a time," she says. "And never go from the kitchen to the dining room empty-handed. Take coffee or iced tea or water with you." When she refills one water glass, she refills others. When clearing one plate, she clears others. "You have to be organized, and you have to keep in touch with the big picture."

Keep learning manifests itself in Cora's ongoing effort to improve existing skills and learn new ones. She and other members of the staff learned to commit orders to memory from a waitress who once worked in the Orchard Cafe. "She encouraged all of us to believe that we could learn to do it. I wanted to learn how to do it. At first it was difficult, but little by little I got better."

Success is where you find it is reflected in Cora's contentment in her work. She finds satisfaction in pleasing her customers; she enjoys helping other people enjoy. Her positive attitude is a positive force in the restaurant. It is hard to ignore. "If customers come to the restaurant in a bad mood, I'll try to cheer them up before they leave." Her definition of success: "To be happy in life."

Cora is a team player, an *all for one, one for all* employee. She works the day shift (6:00 A.M. to 2:00 P.M.) and has been with many of the same co-workers for more than eight years. The team supports one another on the crazy days when 300 conventioneers come to the restaurant for breakfast at the same time. Everyone pitches in and helps. The wait staff cover for one another, the managers bus the tables, the chefs garnish the plates. "We are like a little family. We know each other very well and we help each other out. If we have a crazy day, I'll go in the kitchen towards the end of the shift and say, 'Man, I'm just proud of us. We really worked hard today.'"

Cora's ninth rule is to *take pride* in the work. She believes in the importance of the work and in the need to do it well. "I don't think of myself as 'just a waitress.' . . . I've chosen to be a waitress. I'm doing this to my full potential, and I give it my best. I tell . . . anyone who's starting out: take pride in what you do. You're never just an anything, no matter what you do. You give it your all . . . and you do it with pride."[1]

Cora Griffith is a success story. She is loyal to her employer and dedicated to her customers and co-workers. She is a perfectionist who seeks continuous improvement. Her enthusiasm for her work is abundant, her spirit unflagging. Her energy radiates through the restaurant. She operates at a high level of discretionary effort every single day. She is proud of being a waitress, proud of "touching lives."

If the restaurant industry had a "hall of fame," Cora Griffith would be a strong candidate, although she would be the first person to nominate one of her teammates. In my research for this book, I met many service providers of the same caliber as Cora Griffith, many service workers who love to serve and who excel at it. How do great companies get employees like Cora Griffith?

First, they hire well, as discussed in Chapter 5. They compete for talented people whose values match the company's. They compete for people who will be excellent "volunteer" workers because the reality of service work is that much of it is discretionary. The difference between an average or acceptable waitress and Cora Griffith comes from Cora's extra effort.

Hiring well is but the first step, followed by the commitment to building true relationships with employees as discussed in the last chapter. And still more resources go into transforming a new employee's potential success into actual success—the subject of this chapter.

Cora Griffith is a better waitress than she might otherwise have been because of her employer's willingness to teach her, trust her, and listen to her. When asked if she would have been as good a waitress had she worked for another restaurant, she replied:

> I have always wanted to do my best. However, Dick and John Bergstrom really are the ones who taught me how important it is to take care of the customer and who gave me the freedom to do it. The company always has listened to my concerns and followed up. Had I not worked for the Orchard Cafe, I would have been a good waitress, but I would not have been the same waitress.

Great service companies invest in employees' success. Many firms, tormented by high employee turnover, avoid investing in employees because of their propensity to leave. The sample companies take the opposite approach, investing in infrastructure, tools, and incentives necessary for employees' success. These companies invest in personnel who stay rather than save on those who leave. They establish high performance standards for their employees—and equip them to meet the standards successfully. So many firms operate with modest expectations of employees' performance. Not the companies studied for this book. They expect superior achievement and invest in getting it.

This chapter is organized into three categories of employee investment as shown in Exhibit 8–1. Integral to sustainable service success are investments that enable employees to get off to a strong start, continually develop their service skills and knowledge, and feel like part-owners of the business. This is the reality of Cora Griffith and many other service providers interviewed for this book. The companies' investment in their employees' success directly contributes to the companies' success. These dynamics form a cycle of success.

STRONG BEGINNINGS

The sample companies invest in getting new employees off to a strong start that lays a foundation for the future. They capitalize on the fact that new employees are invariably eager students who are nervous about their new job and anxious to learn the basics, gain some confidence, be accepted by co-workers, and start contributing. The initial days and weeks of employment offer a wide-open window for learning about the company's values, traditions, history, strategy, customers, competitors, policies, and procedures. Like actors on a stage, service providers need to know the play; to perform their role well, they need to know where their part fits in the overall performance.[2]

Companies such as Midwest Express and The Container Store invest significant resources in new employee orientation, viewing this as an irretrievable opportunity to teach the underlying philosophy, values, and context of the business—as well as the necessary getting started procedures—while an employee's experience slate is clean. To

EXHIBIT 8–1
Investing in Employee Success

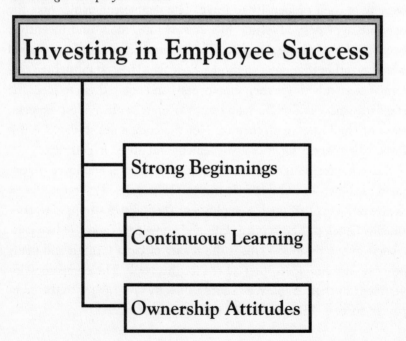

discourage employees from forming bad habits and negative thoughts, it makes sense to begin with good habits and positive concepts. These companies structure new employee orientation, extending it over multiple days and designing it to evoke emotional commitment to the core strategy, promote core values, and forge coworker bonds. Managers help teach, focusing as much on "what" and "why" as "how." The educational scope is the company as a whole—"the play"—rather than merely the specific job. All new employees participate; these are not optional sessions. New employee orientation is an essential first step in an ongoing educational journey at success-sustaining companies.

Taking Off at Midwest Express

Midwest Express conducts a two-day orientation program for 25 to 30 new employees every three weeks. All new employees attend together—a pilot, a baggage handler, an aircraft groomer. The program simulates the experience of taking a flight. Employees receive their invitation to attend in the form of an airline ticket. A boarding announcement is made prior to the first session. Lunch is served on a parked Midwest Express plane. Participants eat the same meal that actual passengers would eat that day. "We do this so everyone can feel the pulse of our business," explains Art Director James David Marks, who is on the team that developed and runs the program.

The agenda revolves around company values such as mutual respect, honesty and integrity, responsiveness, and customer service. Each course module focuses on a specific value. The mutual respect module emphasizes the benefits of a diverse work force and includes segments on stereotyping and how it feels to be excluded from a group. The customer service module features veteran employees who relate personal service stories that were especially rewarding. Most of the segments involve interactive exercises and group discussions.

Graduation ceremonies include remarks by Tim Hoeksema or other members of the senior leadership team, the company's television commercials, and graduation music. Attendees sign their graduation certificates, which enumerate personal commitments such as "I will focus on providing our customers with superior customer service," "I will treat customers, supervisors, and co-workers with respect," and "I will be honest in my dealings with my customers and co-workers." Following the ceremony, the new employees "are hyped and ready to go," states Director of Human Resources Mary Blundell. She adds: "It is so neat to see the bond that develops in two days among 25 people who will work in various parts of the company. Many have asked us if they can have a reunion."

The orientation program was designed by a team of eight employees (both managers and nonmanagers) who met weekly for more than a year during the development phase. The team continues to evaluate and refine the program. "They all were passionate about the values of Midwest Express and wanted the orientation to emphasize them. The goal is to help new employees be successful at Midwest Express," says Mary Blundell.

Foundation Week at The Container Store

The Container Store refers to their new employee orientation as Foundation Week. All new full- and part-time employees participate. Different Foundation Week programs are organized for store, distribution center, and home office personnel. Foundation Week for store employees consists of three basic parts: pre-orientation assignments, Orientation Day, and four additional consecutive days of in-store learning. The pre-orientation assignments include reading the employee handbook, current company literature and benefits information, the scheduled activities for the week, and completing paperwork. Completion of these assignments is required prior to participating in Orientation Day.

The store manager and typically several other staff conduct Orientation Day, which begins with the new employee's participation in the store's daily "huddle." The rest of the day is organized around the contents of the employee handbook: company history, foundation principles (values), company guidelines and employee expectations, and the philosophy of selling as customer service.

Other members of the store staff instruct during the next four days, covering in detail subjects such as telephone service, visual sales, register selling, and inventory coordination, with extensive discussion about how each subject relates to customer service. An overview of each merchandise section of the store also is included. Only after completing these additional four orientation days may new hires be placed on the regular staffing schedule and begin specialized training for their first position.

Foundation Week represents a considerable investment in new employees. Barbara Anderson, manager of employee relations and community services, explains the rationale:

> If we are going to preserve the wonderful culture of our company, we have to immerse new employees in it from the very beginning. Other companies do not do business the way we do. Many of our new employees have worked for other firms that have let them down. When they first hear about our culture, they want to believe it, but they have learned to be cautious. Our Foundation Week doesn't completely resolve this problem—trust takes time. But it does speed things up. The store manager spending the entire day with new hires makes a huge statement.

CONTINUOUS LEARNING

A strong orientation learning experience commences an ongoing education journey in the companies studied for this book. Companies such as Charles Schwab Corporation, Miller SQA, and Ukrop's operate their own corporate "universities." Dana Commercial Credit provided each employee an average of 60 hours of in-house training and tuition-reimbursed education in 1997. USAA spent approximately $5 million dollars in 1997 to provide employees a college education or to prepare them for insurance or job-related certifications. This spending is in addition to on-the-job training employees receive.

The sample companies invest aggressively in continuous employee learning for at least four reasons, all linked to encouraging personal achievement and professional success on the job. First, continuous employee learning reinforces the firm's core values; it keeps the foundation of the house strong. What better way exists to nurture values such as excellence, innovation, and respect than investing in the personal growth of those expected to live these values on the job? And what better way exists for a company to demonstrate its commitment to these values than investing in employees' personal development? By sponsoring the college education of more than one-third of its entire work force, USAA is *living* its values of excellence, respect, and social profit.

Second, education motivates. Employees' willingness to perform at a high level of discretionary effort is inextricably linked to their self-perceived skills and knowledge. Learning builds self-confidence, which is a powerful motivator. Service providers naturally gravitate to those activities for which they feel most competent—and dodge those for which they feel unprepared. So often, service providers who appear *unwilling* to serve customers actually are *unable* to do so. They lack the requisite skills or knowledge.

Third, investment in continuous employee learning recognizes the infinite nature of personal development. No one ever is fully trained or fully knowledgeable. Learning is a journey, not a destination. Service providers have only two capability options: to progress or to decline. In a dynamic world of new technologies and methodologies, static capabilities are declining capabilities.

Fourth, continuous employee learning professionalizes the service delivery role.[3] Professionals are expected to continue to learn, to deepen and broaden their skills, to expand their base of knowledge. Professionalism is not the automatic by-product of a specific job function or title. Professionalism is an attitude that derives from self-esteem and manifests itself in how one acts in the presence of others, such as customers or co-workers. Both the content of learning and the sense of forward motion that accompanies learning contribute to self-esteem and professionalism.

Learning is an alternative to staleness, boredom, burnout, and ineffectiveness. It is stimulating and rejuvenating. It renews the spirit of serving; it replenishes energy. Applying newly acquired skills and knowledge to the job is especially rewarding. Learning coupled with application generates enthusiasm for more learning. Personal growth contributes to personal happiness, which is critical to delivering service at a consistently high level. As Liisa Joronen, who built Finland's SOL Cleaning Service into one of northern Europe's most admired companies, asks, "In a service business, if you're not happy with yourself, how can you make the customer happy?"[4]

Core Curriculum

Ukrop's offers a curriculum of both required core courses and elective courses through its Center for Retail Food Studies. All full- and part-time associates attend four core courses in their first year, spaced about three months apart: Healthy Start (Ukrop's' orientation session), Values, Superior Customer Service (manufacturing employees take a course called Quality instead), and Teamwork.

The Values class features presentations by Chairman Jim Ukrop and President and CEO Bob Ukrop. The content of the two-hour class includes the company's history, philosophy, shared values, competitive environment, strategy, and decision-making approach. Explains Vice President of Operations Bob Kelley, "When I used to work at Philip Morris, I never met the president of the company. Here, we assure that every one of our 5,500 employees will meet the chairman and CEO."

Other classes in Ukrop's curriculum include The Game Plan (a course on strategy), Shrink Busters (how to minimize perishable waste), Perfectly Packed Groceries (bagging techniques), Supermarket Operations (a three-and-a-half-day overview of the retail food business and Ukrop's operations), and Manufacturing Operations (a three-and-a-half-day overview of food manufacturing).

Ukrop's executives teach most of the classes, and the company provides dedicated classrooms in Ukrop's Support Center. Ukrop's does not hire full-time trainers, preferring to use its own managers to develop their presentation skills and to reinforce credibility. They publish a new course catalog quarterly. In 1997, the headcount in all Ukrop's classes combined was about 10,000—a remarkable statistic for what essentially is a local supermarket chain. Kathy Meadows, manager of human resource development for Ukrop's, is herself a study in personal development. Meadows started at Ukrop's in 1986 as a part-time cashier.

Boot Camp

Rigorous preparation of employees to sell and serve customers characterizes the sample firms. In-depth, immersion learning worthy of the label "boot camp" is the price of admission to the ranks of first-line service providers at companies such as Dial-A-Mattress and Miller SQA. Employees who pass the boot camp tests—literally and figuratively— are better equipped for the physical, mental, and emotional tests that await them in the service role itself.

Dial-A-Mattress not only has to prepare new sales hires to sell bedding but to sell it over the telephone. Many customers who call Dial-A-Mattress never have purchased a mattress sight unseen before, and they are not at all sure it is a good idea. The bedding consultant's challenge is to create mental pictures for customers, to lead them through a selection process based on individual needs, to create a level of confidence that results in a sale. Success in the role requires high energy, persistence, creativity, listening skills, product knowledge, verbal skills, keyboard skills, and a customer-centered philosophy.

Dial-A-Mattress prepares new sales hires with an intensive program averaging six consecutive weeks of training and education. (Customer service representatives undergo a similar program that typically is several weeks longer.) Trainees spend the first four weeks of the sales course predominantly in a classroom setting; during the remaining weeks, they train in the Call Center, selling with the assistance of an assigned mentor.

Role-playing is a principal learning method. Training and Recruitment Manager Phildelis Cooper-Snell plays audio tapes of actual exchanges between a bedding consultant and a customer and asks the class how they would have handled the situation. Many of the role-play episodes present difficult situations, for example, a customer who twice has returned a delivered mattress, still is not satisfied, and wants her money back.

Product knowledge sessions taught by Dial-A-Mattress vendors also are crucial given the importance of in-depth understanding of product components and differences when selling mattresses over the telephone. The class takes field trips to the New Jersey plants of both Simmons and Serta to observe mattress construction. Other training methods include lectures, side-by-side observation of experienced bedding consultants, hands-on computer sessions, and watching and discussing videotapes on customer behavior and selling skills.

Dial-A-Mattress recruits more people than they need because only about half of the new hires complete the course. Some leave on their own, others don't pass muster with Cooper-Snell, who states:

> Some people can retain the information but can't apply it. Some just are not the right people for our operation, which relies on its reputation for honesty and integrity. I want to make sure the people can be successful in our company. I take such pride in having new people come though the training and go on to be successful in the company. It is an awesome feeling. They are like a bud and then they blossom.

Those who finish the course participate in graduation day and receive a certificate of completion. Dial-A-Mattress senior managers congratulate the graduates and welcome them to the company at the ceremony.

Miller SQA offers an 11-week educational course for dealer salespeople who sell the company's product line. In 1998, 21 learning modules composed the course. The purpose of the course is to convert office furniture salespeople from traditional industry selling practices to the Miller SQA approach of collaborative selling through a laptop computer. Each trainee equipped with a laptop computer and the 1:1 software works with a trainer over the telephone for the first six weeks. The weekly sessions last from one to three hours as trainees gain product knowledge and learn to use the 1:1 system. The seventh week, held at the Miller SQA plant, includes three days of intensive review with an emphasis on experiential learning, i.e., performing on the laptop computer. The next several weeks involve more over-the-phone classes. During the final week, trainees go on sales calls with an experienced Miller SQA sales representative. They must use the system to place an actual order before they graduate.

Because Miller SQA's fundamental business approach differs from industry practices, its educational challenge is not to hone or refine a sales representative's selling skills but to take that person to a new realm: computer-aided, collaborative selling and service. Given the challenge of changing people's mindsets, Training Manager Mabel Casey and her associates have devoted considerable resources to designing an interactive, experiential format and creating an atmosphere of fun. The college metaphor is used throughout the program. Participants attend "Freshman Orientation," experience "Spring Break," receive a camera when they visit the plant to create a photo album, earn "currency" on-site to buy merchandise at the "campus store," and read a campus newspaper online. Says Casey: "In most industry training programs, you sit in a room and hear people talk about furniture but it's not like that at all here; it's interactive—you have to take part. We hear again and again 'It's fun.'"

Individualized Development

Charles Schwab Corporation and Custom Research are two of the sample companies that assess the competencies of individual employees and offer a customized development program based on the assessment. Schwab uses a 360 assessment process with senior executives and middle managers to identify both their strengths and development opportunities on 22 separate competencies. Peers, subordinates, and superiors contribute to the competency assessment of the specific individual. No one sees the results except the person being assessed. The sole purpose of the assessment is to guide the individual in crafting a development plan. Senior executives work with a coach in creating their plan; middle managers take a course on how to create a development plan.

Schwab's senior executives were the first to go through the assessment process. Middle managers undergo an 18- to 24-month development period following their initial 360 assessment and then undergo the assessment again. Individual development plans include both formal educational experiences (courses offered by Schwab University and various university executive programs) and action learning experiences (specific activities to demonstrate mastery of competencies). Schwab is developing a certification program for middle managers leading to the designation "Master Manager."

Individualized development planning is available to all Schwab employees with targeted curriculum available for each job category. Schwab University offers dozens of courses from which individuals can design a development plan, including numerous courses on communications, organizational effectiveness, leadership, information technology, investing, and finance. Schwab University delivers education in headquarters and regional service center classrooms, through a partner for certain computer courses, over the company's Intranet, and via CD-ROM. In 1998, about 65 percent of Schwab's total employee population took at least one course from Schwab University. Eileen Schloss, vice president, organizational learning at Schwab, explains the underlying philosophy of Schwab University: "The heart of our firm is our core values and culture. This is the water we swim in. Schwab University shares and perpetuates these values in the spirit of continuous development for all employees. We want to reach every employee and make a career development covenant with them."

Custom Research also is an ardent practitioner of individualized development planning. Each CRI employee meets with his or her manager annually to identify short- and long-term advancement goals and to plan a personal development program for reaching these goals. The employee and manager then meet throughout the year to review progress on the plan. These regular "checkups" involving two people help the employee stay on plan even when the company is very busy—which is most of the time.

Custom Research offers a broad curriculum of internal courses on subjects such as report writing, understanding financial statements, delegating, teamwork, performance management, basic and advanced statistics, research design, and creative problem solving. The company also sends employees to outside courses on subjects such as writing, presentations, time management, and supervision skills.

To broaden their experience, CRI employees also are assigned recommended outside reading and targeted work projects, and they are periodically moved within the company. To be promotable at CRI, employees must gain experience in several different areas of the business. The company services its clients through account teams and team members below manager periodically change functions within the team and move to a new team every several years. Each year CRI team and department managers hold a "draft" to reassign or promote selected employees to the teams. Moving to a new team accelerates the personal development of employees who experience new managers, co-workers, clients, and projects. The principal challenge is to accommodate team needs for experience and continuity while making these shifts. Explains Laura Olson, who started as a CRI telephone center employee while in college and by 1998 had served on two account teams, "We want client continuity so we try to balance what is best for the client and best for the employee."

Exhibit 8–2 presents the 1998 development plan for an actual Custom Research employee with the employee's and manager's names re-

EXHIBIT 8–2

Individualized Development Planning at Custom Research

Fiscal Year 1998 Development Plan for (employee) Prepared by (manager)

Long-Term Goal: Research Manager

Short-Term Goal: Senior Research Associate

Training Goals for Fiscal Year 1998

1. Handle implementation of three to four projects on own.
2. Handle at least one focus group project.
3. Continue to develop report writing skills.
4. Develop estimating skills.

Outside Training

1. None at this time.

CRI Training

1. Contract services training: Field Operations (one to two days)
                                              Sample Processing (two days)
2. Advanced statistics training
3. Research design training
4. Write two to three research reports.
5. Complete estimating module and handle 10–15 bids during the year.
6. Come up with four ideas to improve either quality or efficiency on the team.
7. Travel to the field on at least two projects.
8. Business reading:
    a. Read two general business books during the year. These may be selected from the Recommended Reading List or may be another selection applicable to our business. Check with manager to okay selection. Prepare a brief summary of key points in the book and discuss with manager.
    b. Read at least one weekly business periodical.
    c. Attend at least one book discussion group.
    d. Attend Lunch and Learn programs.

moved. The employee had been with CRI for four years at the time this plan was prepared. The exhibit illustrates the precision of individualized development planning at CRI. It also reveals the company's underlying commitment to investing in employee success. Custom Research offers no low-skill jobs. Continuous learning is a prerequisite for employment.

They Call Me "Coach"

Coaching is a common method of employee development among the sample companies. Individual employees are assigned to a coaching role either as their primary responsibility or as an additional one. In The Container Store organization, full-time staff known as Super Sales Trainers (SSTs) work with store personnel on product knowledge and solution-selling skills. Each SST is assigned two stores in the chain. Less formal coaching also occurs daily in every store; it is part of The Container Store's culture. Sharing with others is a core value in the company. Salesman Fernando Ramos, who does considerable coaching, astonishes new employees when he states: "I want to teach you everything I know." "We are all trainers," adds SST Elaine Fuqua.

New Midwest Express flight attendants undergo a six-week training regimen, which includes two weeks with an assigned coach. The experienced flight attendants who serve as coaches are formally trained for this role. New flight attendants benefit from one-on-one tutorials and the coach gains the satisfaction of sharing knowledge. Midwest Express also has a Quality Assurance Service Representative (QASR) program for its reservation agents. Selected by their peers, the QASRs also are reservation agents. When in the QASR rotation they coach other agents who are handling difficult transactions. Explains reservation agent Sonya Wilborn: "Sometimes you need feedback and guidance. The QASR program is very helpful because it means that someone always is available to help."

Jennifer Grassano is a bedding consultant (BC) and coach at Dial-A-Mattress. Three days a week she works as a BC and one day as a coach to other BCs. She usually works independently with three or four BCs on a coaching day. She selects her candidates by reviewing

the productivity of the sales staff during the prior three months, looking for people who appear to be slumping or in a rut. Grassano's first
step is to monitor the BC's telephone work with customers. She will
listen for about an hour and make notes on each call. The BCs understand that at certain times their sales calls may be monitored, but they
do not receive advance notice when they will be monitored for that
would defeat the purpose.

Once Grassano finishes the monitoring, she calls the BC aside for a
coaching session, reviewing strengths as well as areas for improvements. As a BC herself, Grassano understands how difficult it is to
maintain a high energy level and convey enthusiasm when handling
60 calls in a shift. She likes to suggest new tactics and phrasing to the
BCs to "spark up their presentation." One BC under Grassano's tute-
lage was not responding effectively when customers asked why one
mattress was more expensive than another. Grassano stressed the need
to paint pictures in the customer's mind:

> Customers are at our mercy when buying bedding. They don't know the
> difference between one coil system and another. It is just like buying a
> carburetor for my car. I don't even know what a carburetor looks like. We
> have to use very descriptive words to help bedding customers make the
> decision that is right for them. Tell the customer that the more costly
> mattress has richer, finer padding with a blend of silk and wool. Don't just
> say the mattress has more layers of padding.

Following the initial coaching session, Grassano follows up with the
same individual about two months later. She can then compare performance in the three months preceding the coaching session and the
two months following it. "People want proof," she says.

Grassano believes her experience and productivity as a BC give her
credibility as a coach. "If I am not doing well as a BC, then who am I to
be a coach? I have to lead by example. I would be much less effective if
I was a full-time trainer." Like all great teachers, Grassano relishes the
opportunity to share her knowledge, to pass on her craft. In the delicate, tightrope-walking act of helping salespeople improve even when
they don't think they need to, Grassano has earned respect in the Call
Center. "They tease me and call me coach. I'll wear a baseball cap. I
sent everyone a memo comparing us to the Yankees. We are a team,

too. And we not only need home run hitters, we need singles hitters. After all, if someone hits a single before the home run, you get two runs instead of one."

Off to College

No company believes in continuous learning more than USAA. The company is noted for the significant investment it makes in job-related training courses. Its course to prepare employees to be account representatives lasts 10 weeks, for example. Equally impressive, however, is USAA's investment in employees' college education. All full-time employees on the job for more than a year are eligible for full college funding. They must attend a local accredited institution and pursue studies related to their work, usually a business degree. USAA also funds distance learning programs located within the state in which the employee works.

USAA pays tuition bills directly rather than reimbursing employees later. Employees who do not pass or finish a course must pay back the money. USAA will pay for one undergraduate and one graduate degree per employee. It also pays the tuition for employees who wish to take individual college courses but not enroll in a degree program.

Many college classes are taught on USAA premises in more than 60 classrooms. Employees can use USAA Resource Centers to do their homework or prepare presentations on the computer. They can avail themselves of the services of college advisors who are on site. USAA even offers college scholarships for employees' children—a longer term effort to invest in human capital.

How does USAA justify the more than $2.6 million it spends annually on its college studies program? Karen Wolfshohl, manager of college studies, explains:

> It has always been our culture that employees are our most important resource. They are the decisive factor in our competitiveness as a financial services provider. An educated work force is our only option given the force of change, especially technology change, in our business. I tell our employees that they need an education just to stay current in the job they presently hold. Otherwise, they are losing ground.

OWNERSHIP ATTITUDES

Employees who feel like part-owners of a company are more likely to do what is necessary to sustain the company's success. Owners not only have more to gain if a company succeeds, they have more to lose if it fails.

Ownership in its truest form is a state of mind. It is emotional attachment, personal responsibility, and pride. Financial ownership can contribute to the state of mind but cannot guarantee it. A financial stake alone does not create the emotional connection associated with true ownership attitudes.

A story from Midwest Express illustrates the psychological foundation of ownership attitudes. The airline had persevered for a long time to acquire the rights to fly to New York's La Guardia Airport. The gate area eventually assigned to the airline was a mess. The company planned to hire an outside firm to refurbish the 3,000-square-foot space but Midwest Express's own employees wanted to do it. They came in on a Saturday and replaced the tile, repainted the walls, and cleaned. This is what owners would do. This is an ownership attitude.

Ownership attitudes are revealed in the following comments of individuals interviewed for this book:

- "In January 1996, we had a huge snowstorm and I wasn't able to leave my home. I called all of our customers that day to see who got their bed and who didn't. I was struck by how many customers praised our drivers for their determination to make the delivery."—Maureen Renneberg, assistant director of sales, Dial-A-Mattress
- "My goal in life was to own a business. I've been able to do this at Enterprise. I have autonomy to build my business. I don't follow any book that says this is how you have to do something. They have allowed me to meet my dreams here."—Joanne Peratis-Weber, regional vice president, Enterprise Rent-A-Car
- "You feel connected to the product you put out. You care. You don't feel like a little pawn doing the hard work and others are taking credit. You feel appreciated. You are important here. People know you."—Lisa Gudding, account manager, Custom Research

- "The itinerary says La Paz on the 10th and on the 15th. In between is up to me. I have an amazing amount of authority to run the trip. I get highs from sunrise and sunset and from seeing the animals. Perhaps there are CEOs who are 32 who have as much authority as I have, but I bet they are not having as much fun."—Jill Russell, ship captain, Special Expeditions
- "We wear an ETC pin (Extra Thorough Care) to remind us to lay our hand towels and organize customers' things on the bathroom counters."—Mary Ellen Scieszinski, housekeeper, Pioneer Inn
- "A customer called and very officially said that he wanted to make a change. He told me that his wife had just died. And then he started crying. I told him that we could help him and not to feel bad about crying. I made sure that we took care of everything."—Berniece More, service representative, USAA

Inclusion is a central factor in these forceful ownership attitudes. Being part of something bigger—something important. Being in the loop. Being accountable. Being in control of the job that needs to be done. Being expected to think on the job, to be creative, to be resourceful. Being part of the team.

Employees develop ownership attitudes when they are treated like part-owners of the business and expected to act like part-owners of the business. These employees manage themselves to a significant degree while creating value for their internal or external customers. They are more likely to work hard, account for their own performance and the company's, and take prudent risks to build a stronger business. A company realizes the full potential of ownership attitudes when its success is also the employees' success.[5]

Low-Secret Companies

"We want everyone working in our stores to be informed to the same degree as the store manager," emphasizes Beth Barrett, vice president of operations for The Container Store. "Customers say 'I was dealing with George, the store manager.' Well, George isn't the store manager but he acts like he is." The Container Store, like the other sample firms, is a low-secret company. The company shares virtually all information with all employees, including daily, month-to-date, and year-to-date sales comparisons for each store. The company internally publishes its yearly profit goal, which is linked to its profit-sharing goal.

Through its daily huddles in the stores and distribution center, through in-store bulletin boards with space reserved for each day of the week, through frequent visits from headquarters personnel, through daily faxes and e-mail, through ongoing education and training sessions and regular company meetings, The Container Store invests in employees' success by showering them with information. "We want everyone to know everything," says Diane Higgins, a store manager for more than 10 years and currently a visual sales trainer. "The more people know about the organization, the more they will care," says Jon Wavra, operations manager for Chicago-area stores. "If there is anything we can do to enhance communication, we will do it," adds Nancy Donley, human resources director.

Sharing information conveys trust, reinforces personal accountability, builds pride, and evokes commitment. Trust, accountability, pride, and commitment stem from belonging and belonging—in part—stems from knowing. From its first day in business, Custom Research has shared all financial information other than salaries with all employees. Explains co-founder Judy Corson, "If you have total information about the company and its financials, you feel that you are part of the whole." Adds partner Jeff Pope, "Before starting CRI, I was a vice president at a large research company and didn't even know the company's volume."

Miller SQA has developed and refined new approaches to foster internal communications as it has grown to more than 500 employees. One effective approach is the use of Town Criers to fill the grapevine proactively. The Town Criers all are full-time employees who assume an internal communications responsibility in addition to their regular duties. They attend monthly company information meetings and then pass this information on to their assigned work group; they also serve as spokespersons on business results and issues to other employees as the need arises. They obtain answers to employees' questions prior to the monthly information meeting and clarify incorrect information when encountered. The Town Crier approach helps Miller SQA maintain regular face-to-face communications in the company. "People want to know what is going on and they want to be heard," says Finance Vice President Bob Enders. "Employees feel connected here; they have a voice here."

Wide Solution Spaces

Being treated like a part-owner of the business is not a walk on the beach. With ownership comes responsibility to make decisions, assume risk, and lead. Owners operate in wide solution spaces; they have license to maneuver, innovate, take chances, try something new when something old doesn't work. Owners have authority—and the performance expectation that they will use it to strengthen the business.

One way the sample firms invest in employee success is by giving them the decision space to succeed. This is what is meant by wide solution spaces. Employees are trusted to put on their track shoes and run to the solution; they in turn trust their managers to be fair when creativity backfires and mistakes occur. A company can create wide solution spaces only in a climate of trust. States Jan Elsesser, executive vice president of sales and marketing at Custom Research: "Mistakes occur, of course, but ours is not a blaming culture. It is okay to make a mistake at CRI; we focus on continuous improvement, on finding a better way, on fixing the process." Adds Bix Norman, who led the transformation at Miller SQA, "There is a profound awareness on my part about the destructiveness of intimidation and threat. I am most effective in a position of confidence and security, and I presume this is true for others."

Trust is pivotal and thus so are its sources, competence and fairness, as discussed in the last chapter. And so are the sources of competence and fairness, including smart hiring, training and education, effective internal communications, and core values such as respect, teamwork, integrity, and social profit.

In addition to laying a foundation for organizational trust, humane core values play another important role in widening solution spaces: they eliminate the need for thick rulebooks. To the degree that strong values guide employees' behavior, companies can function with fewer rules. Values-driven leadership supplants the need for rulebook management. Employees of The Container Store know that they are supposed to fill the other party's basket to the brim; they really don't need many rules. Employees of the St. Paul Saints know that fun is good; they, too, need few rules to guide their decisions. Try it. If it works, do it again. If it doesn't, then don't do it again.

Defining solution space boundaries reinforces the guiding power of core values. Innovation is part of every Dana Commercial Credit person's job through the company's "Ideas for Improvement" initiative (Chapter 5). Ideas that reach across functional lines require advance approval. "Just do it" improvements are those that fall within the 25 square feet around an employee's desk. In effect, Dana Commercial Credit employees are CEOs of their own 25 square feet of space.

Midwest Express's frequent flyer staff are guided by two categories of rules: those that cannot be broken under any circumstance and those that can be bent or broken depending on the circumstances. Departmental member Jill Schuetz explains: "We have the ability to make our own decisions. For example, a guy was a few miles short for a free trip. I was able to give him the extra miles so that he could fly to his girlfriend and propose. I had the power to do this."

Sharing the Wealth

Every company claims that its employees are its most important asset, but the most admired companies in the world show they really mean it, writes *Fortune* Magazine.[6] One important way excellent companies demonstrate their commitment to employees is by sharing with them the wealth they helped to create. Through employee stock ownership plans, stock grants, profit-sharing, bonuses, and above-average wages, the sample firms offer employees a financial stake in the companies' success. The better the firm performs, the richer the employee's payout. Those who create the success enjoy its rewards.

Ownership attitudes, as discussed earlier, have multiple sources. They are a product of far more than money. Yet money plays two crucial roles in encouraging and sustaining ownership attitudes. First, owning means investing one's emotional resources, energy, time, reputation, and perhaps financial assets. The greater the investment of personal resources, the greater the sense of ownership. People who truly invest themselves in a business expect—and deserve—to participate in its financial success. Second, a company that generously shares its wealth with employees earns their trust in doing so. Few, if any, actions a company takes are more instrumental in building or destroying trust than its money decisions—how it earns money and how it distributes money. Trust is the foundation of employee ownership attitudes, the strongest level of employee commitment possible.

Eighty percent of Dana Commercial Credit's employees are shareholders. Forty percent of Charles Schwab Corporation's stock is owned by its own employees. Every Midwest Express employee received stock when the company went public in 1995. In these and other sample companies, literal ownership contributes to psychological ownership.

The Container Store consistently allocates 18 percent of its revenues for salaries and wages and has for 20 years. Salespeople at The Container Store make about double the industry average. The company could easily justify bringing the percentage wage and salary contribution down given its strong annual growth rate of 25 percent. However, it has held fast at 18 percent to share the wealth with those who create it, to compete for the most talented people, and to strengthen employee relationships. The company's annual store employee turnover rate is between 10 and 15 percent, an unusually low figure in retailing. As President Kip Tindell explains, "We have to attract and keep the best people because we sell the hard stuff. Anyone can be an order taker. But we sell products like absolutely leakproof travel bottles that are more expensive than ordinary bottles. It's a joy to sell this type of product, but it requires excellent people to do it."

Chick-fil-A invests in the ownership attitudes of its restaurant operators with its unique profit-sharing arrangement. Chick-fil-A invests the capital to put a new operator into a "turnkey" operation. The operator commits $5,000—which actually is a deposit, to be returned if the operator leaves the system. The two parties then split monthly net profits from the restaurant fifty-fifty. The operators are guaranteed a minimum income (currently $30,000) as they build their business. They pay Chick-fil-A an operating fee of 15 percent of revenues that covers equipment rental and administrative and support service expenses.

The deal is beneficial to the operators and to Chick-fil-A. Operators can open their own business without capital and without going into debt. They gain access to the brand, products, and systems of one of the most successful restaurant chains in the world. They are independent business people, but they are not alone. As Chick-fil-A's field operations vice president Tim Tassopoulos puts it, "You're in business for yourself but not by yourself." Most importantly, because of the fifty-fifty profit sharing arrangement, Chick-fil-A has a strong vested interest in helping operators become and stay successful. Chick-fil-A makes money when its operators make money.

Chick-fil-A benefits from the deal because it can attract extremely talented people to operate its stores with an ownership commitment. Chapter 3 introduced Craig Hall, the operator of Chick-fil-A stores in Bryan and College Station, Texas, who started at Chick-fil-A in 1987 after more than 20 years of experience as a retail manager. Hall, an effective leader, tireless marketer, and involved community citizen, operates his restaurant like the owner he is. He is in charge and he is committed. "I am committed to the task," he says. "It is my life." He also is very successful, a top operator in the Chick-fil-A system. Craig Hall's competing against a neighboring quick-service restaurant that has had three managers in one year is not a fair fight. By creatively sharing wealth, Chick-fil-A has operators of the caliber of Craig Hall who are running its stores. "We have a lot of Craigs," says Steve Robinson, senior vice president of marketing at Chick-fil-A. "How many fast-food brands have people like Craig Hall? It goes back to our unique operator deal that Truett created that has not fundamentally changed in over 30 years."

All Miller SQA employees participate in a monthly bonus program based on Economic Value Added (EVA) as the fundamental performance measure. Net income after taxes less capital costs is calculated each month. Half of this sum goes to the parent company, Herman Miller, Inc. Another 10 percent goes into Miller SQA's 401K retirement plan. The balance is shared with all employees.

Miller SQA assigned EVA coaches to help factory employees understand how such factors as productivity increases, percentage of return goods, and materials and inventory costs affect EVA. Miller SQA's culture emphasizes on-time shipments and quality workmanship. Throughout the plant are "information trees"—vertical signposts—with performance data and messages hanging from "branches," such as "99.6 on-time shipments last week." If on-time shipment performance falls below 99 percent, a green sign becomes a red one. When Miller SQA employees turn on their computers, the first thing they see is the company's on-time shipment performance the day before and week-to-date. Factory employees also know how many chairs they need to make during their shifts for the company to make a profit—and for them to make their bonus.

Miller SQA workers know what is important in their company, they know their goals, they know how they are performing against these goals, and they know they will benefit if they perform well. They are in the loop, on the team, part of something bigger; Miller SQA's success is their success.

———

The companies studied for this book enjoy a competitive advantage with customers, in part, because they enjoy a competitive advantage with employees. They invest in their employees' on-the-job success—their feelings of inclusion and participation, their skills and knowledge, their self-confidence and sense of achievement, their financial rewards—and through this investment sustain their own success. When the product is a performance, serving customers well first requires serving the performers well. In labor-intensive service businesses, customer success is a function of employee success.

9

ACTING SMALL

A letter from one of my students captures a key service success sustainer: acting like a small organization regardless of actual size.

April 27, 1998

Dear Dr. Berry:

I just wanted to let you know about a superior service encounter that my wife experienced. My wife and I have rented cars many times from almost every major rental company. Last week she had to rent a van for a school field trip and by chance she chose Enterprise. The service she received was the best ever and far beyond any other rental company.

Here is what happened:

1. *She was unsure if she made the reservation with Enterprise (she forgot). She called Advantage just to check, and she was on hold for 10 minutes. When she called Enterprise, they confirmed her reservation in under one minute.*

2. *My wife was under a lot of pressure. She could not get to Enterprise until 5:50 P.M. and they close at 6:00 P.M. She called them at 5:40, and they said they were expecting her and would stay after closing if necessary.*

3. *When we got to Enterprise at 5:50, my wife had forgotten her license. Enterprise again stated that they would stay over and it was absolutely no problem.*

4. *Finally, they gave her a 25 percent discount because the rental was for a school district.*

This is great service . . . the best example of great service I have had this year.

Thanks for your class,

Dennis L. Mann

Enterprise Rent-A-Car has a larger automobile rental fleet and more branch offices than any other car rental company. It is a big company, a multibillion dollar company. Yet it served the Manns without a hint of bureaucracy, without a hint of the rigidity customers so often experience with large chain operations. On this day, with this customer, Enterprise acted like a start-up, entrepreneurial venture hungry for business.

What powers Enterprise Rent-A-Car's remarkable success is that the company as a whole functions as a startup entrepreneurial venture hungry for business. This chain doesn't act like a chain; it is an international company that builds customer, employee, and partner relationships locally, a firm with thousands of employees who operate the business as though they own it. Enterprise Rent-A-Car is a big company but it acts small.

Acting small with customers means to act fast, seamlessly, flexibly, responsively, personally. It means knowing the customer and custom-fitting the service. It means caring. It means commitment.

Acting small with employees means creating a community. It means a shared vision, a collaborative mission. It means teammates and teamwork, individual and collective accountability. It means building trust-based relationships. It means nurturing ownership attitudes and a "can-do" spirit of action.

Acting small is Miller SQA's indoor "Street" in its headquarters building where office and factory workers mingle. It is the first-name culture at Midwest Express and numerous other sample companies. It is The Container Store's daily employee "huddle" in its stores and distribution center. It is Charles Schwab Corporation's "Town Hall" meetings. It is USAA's application of information technology enabling service providers to immediately access a member's integrated and complete file and provide quick, customized, seamless service. It is Dana Commercial Credit employees assuming total responsibility for the 25 square feet around their desks. It is expedition leaders and ship captains for Special Expeditions never having to call the home office for permission to change an itinerary to seize unforeseen opportunities. It is Ukrop's offering individual customers targeted specials on specific products they buy regularly and sending employees birthday cards signed by Bob and Jim Ukrop with a $50 check inside.

Bill Cooney, USAA's deputy CEO for property and casualty insurance, encourages employees to continually ask these fundamental questions and to take charge of the answers:

- Is it easy for customers to do business with us? If it isn't, why? Change it.
- Is it easy for us to do business with ourselves? If it isn't, why? Change it.

As discussed in Chapter 1, most companies become more rule-driven, bureaucratic, and difficult for customers and employees to navigate as they grow. USAA and the other sample companies have been unusually successful in fighting these tendencies and moderating their pernicious effects. One of the ways these firms drive their success is by making it comparatively easy for customers to do business with them and for employees to do business with each other. These sample firms are not immune to creeping rigidity introduced by scale, but they fight it harder and more boldly than most companies.

To be sure, company bigness has its competitive virtues, including more complete service lines, broader geographic coverage, operational support infrastructure, bargaining strength with suppliers, and bigger promotion budgets. The problem with scale is the side effects. The key is to minimize the disadvantages of scale while capitalizing on the advantages. It is a *central* challenge for all growth companies, as Starbucks Coffee Company CEO Howard Schultz explains in his book *Pour Your Heart Into It:*

We're opening so many stores that people are starting to feel we're approaching ubiquity. The danger is that the bigger the company gets, the less personal it feels, to both partners and customers. If our competitive advantage has always been the relationship of trust we have with our partners, how can we maintain that as we grow from a company of 25,000 people to one of 50,000? . . . How do we grow big but maintain intimacy with our people? This is the toughest dilemma I face as the leader of Starbucks.[1]

How can service companies that depend on energized, resourceful, committed people to deliver value to customers reap the benefits of smallness when no longer small? The answer lies in a blend of values-driven leadership, innovative structure, customer- and employee-focused information technology, and ownership attitudes.

A CONFEDERATION OF ENTREPRENEURS

Enterprise Rent-A-Car had more than 3,600 branch offices in mid-1998. Most of these offices employ fewer than a dozen people. The company opens a new branch office almost every business day and is located within 15 minutes of 90 percent of the U.S. population. In bigger cities, an Enterprise office will serve a one- to two-mile area. In smaller towns and rural areas, an office will serve around 25,000 people.

Delivering service through many smaller offices rather than fewer larger offices is not the full story, however. Small offices in large chains often reflect chainlike behaviors, including soulless, by-the-book, homogenized service. Enterprise Rent-A-Car branches are run by entrepreneurs who share in the profits they generate. These ambitious, competitive, entrepreneurially minded managers are expected to build a business, are given wide berth in how they go about it, and are rewarded handsomely if they succeed.

The company scours college campuses for talented young people who want to run their own businesses. The fainthearted need not apply. "It takes a different person to do what we do," explains Dick Janicki, a vice president and general manager in Austin, Texas. "Our managers handle everything—the customer service, marketing, hiring. You have to love the action. You must be prepared to have fun. And you must have a confident, 'no-hill-I-can't-climb' attitude. People with these qualities thrive in our environment."

Enterprise Rent-A-Car is a confederation of entrepreneurs—thousands of them running local businesses, building relationships with local customers and referral sources, making local real estate decisions, participating actively in local communities. Many companies claim to be decentralized and are not; Enterprise Rent-A-Car is *devoted* to decentralization. Says Callaway Ludington, assistant vice president of marketing: "Our people are extremely empowered. We do not tell our local operators what to do. We support them running their own businesses." Adds Rob Hibbard, vice president of rental development: "At corporate headquarters we keep a lean staff. We have only a handful of executives and enough information systems people to run the technology. Almost all of our people work outside of our headquarters." States CEO Andy Taylor: "Our managers in the field call the shots. We provide the resources and consultation in the headquarters, but we are not the generator of ideas."

Enterprise Rent-A-Car benefits from both smallness *and* largeness—a principal factor in its sustained success. It operates local, entrepreneurially run businesses supported by a strong core value system, a solid financial base to fund growth, national advertising, and a highly sophisticated computer network that links all offices by satellite. The computer system, known as "Ralph" (Rapid and Logical Paper Handler), is composed of 24 IBM AS 400 computers—the largest single-location AS 400 installation in the world. The system processes one million separate communications an hour during peak periods.

The computer system supports Enterprise employees in tracking the repair of a customer's car, determining insurance company billing instructions, and knowing each and every car's location at all times. Branch employees can locate cars available at nearby branches and trade or pick up cars for customers as necessary. Once customers have rented from Enterprise, the paperwork requirements for the next rental are minimal; the needed information can be accessed again through a telephone number, enhancing customer recognition and service anywhere in the country. Many insurance companies have a direct link to Enterprise's system, enabling them to authorize rentals without making a phone call.

Enterprise's philosophy of operating many branches gives more people the chance to be a manager. With its small-office approach, it gives employees the opportunity to work in intimate, collaborative environments. With rapid growth, it offers employees significant advancement opportunities beyond the branch office. With locally centered operations, it benefits from better understanding the needs of referral sources and renters and building personal relationships with them. With an entrepreneurial, competitive, pay-for-performance culture, it fosters an insatiable hunger in local markets to find more customers and grow the business. No company studied for this book benefits more from strong employee ownership attitudes than Enterprise Rent-A-Car. In speaking about Enterprise managers throughout the system, Dick Janicki comments: "We all are very competitive and want to do well. We do not want to finish on the bottom of anything. You always know where you stand compared to other managers. You want others to do well, but you always want to do a hair better. There is a lot more business out there."

COMPANIES WITHIN THE COMPANY

Custom Research is a highly successful business by any measure. Its marketing research clients include Coca-Cola, Procter & Gamble, and many other prominent companies. It won the Malcolm Baldrige National Quality Award in 1996. It has made money every year of its existence.

Four pivotal decisions have contributed directly to CRI's sustained success. One was the decision to apply for the Baldrige Award, which provided a road map for many systemic improvements to the company's operations. As co-founder Judy Corson states: "The Baldrige helped us grow up. It gave us the theoretical framework to improve our internal processes."

Deciding to focus all of the firm's energies on serving larger clients needing multiple research projects during a year also was significant. This decision paved the way for relationship marketing. "We are up front with prospective clients and tell them we are seeking a relationship and looking for a volume of business," explains Jan Elsesser, executive vice president of sales and marketing. "Whether they want a relationship or are strictly price buyers helps determine whether a prospective client is a good fit for us."

Another key decision was to be a technology leader. The company became one of the first in the industry to use computer-assisted telephone interviewing in the late 1970s, the first to place a personal computer on every employee's desk in the late 1980s. In 1987, CRI created a separate department to apply technology in marketing research. "We are always pushing the envelope on technology," states Executive Vice President Diane Kokal.

The hardest decision, also implemented in 1987, was restructuring the company to serve clients through cross-functional teams. The short-term cost during the transition was inefficiency. The long-term effect is what one Baldrige examiner described as an "almost obsessive focus on the client."

At this writing, CRI has nine teams of five to nine people. Each team handles the functions necessary to complete a research study and serves specific clients exclusively. The teams have separate P&L statements and their own profit, client satisfaction, productivity, and performance goals. "They are running their own little businesses," says Judy Corson.

The teams are repositories of knowledge about clients' needs and preferences because of the continuity of service. The teams systematically seek client feedback and maintain "client books." When clients visit the office, the entire team meets with them. Teams use client-specific databases that contain multiple survey questions reflecting the client's questionnaire style and preferences.

Increasingly, CRI teams are linking up electronically with their clients, including electronic distribution of completed research reports. Some clients put requests for research proposals in CRI's electronic mailbox, CRI responds electronically, and the proposal is accepted without a spoken conversation between provider and client. The electronic connection, however, does not depersonalize the service. The client's immediate access and the company's direct response enhance the one-on-one dimension of acting small.

Team members also wear pagers and clients always can reach someone on the team in an emergency. In effect, CRI team members are an extension of a client's staff, the essence of acting small.

Team members take great pride in their accountability to clients and to one another. They feel a sense of ownership for their team, clients, and CRI. The following team member comments illustrate:

- "I like being on the team. You feel like you belong. Everyone knows what's going on."—Stephanie Parent
- "You don't feel like you've handed something off to another department and it will come back eventually. There are no black holes."—Christine Sharratt
- "There are no slugs. Everyone pulls their weight."—Lisa Gudding
- "We don't take a cookie-cutter approach even though we may have done hundreds of a certain type of study. We take ownership. Everyone accepts responsibility and jumps in to help."—Rhonda Lind
- "When a client needs something in an hour, we work together to solve the problem."—Jeanne Wichterman
- "The client has everyone's name and number. If Susan is not here, John is."—Patricia Hughes

Custom Research is a substantial company in the marketing research industry with 1997 year-end revenues of $26 million. Yet it feels like a small company to both clients and employees. It is a company built on relationships. The synergy of the Baldrige framework for continuous improvement, technological prowess, large clients with relationship potential, and cross-functional teams to manage the relationships has enabled the company to effectively compete on value rather than price. Between 1987 when CRI adopted the team structure and added its technology department and 1997, the company's productivity as measured by sales per employee doubled.

Custom Research's case study illuminates an important lesson: *most great service companies are high touch and high tech, not one or the other.* "We have nine smaller companies within a small company," states cofounder Jeff Pope. "Our technology investments key our responsiveness to clients and cycle-time reductions. Teams and technology have helped us become one of the most productive and financially successful firms in our industry."

DO YOU KNOW ME?

In 1998, USAA completed its restructuring into cross-functional customer insurance teams—known in the organization as CITs. Pioneered by the Oklahoma CIT, which began operations in August 1995, the essential idea is to organize around customers rather than functions. USAA had built huge departments to handle insurance policy services, underwriting, claims, and other functions. From the company's perspective, the functional structure meant specialization, which meant efficiency. From the customer's perspective, it meant more telephone transfers and wasted time and energy.

With the CIT structure, service providers are cross-trained to handle automobile *and* property insurance policy service *and* claims. Service providers belong to a team serving a specific geographic area. The Oklahoma CIT, for example, serves all USAA customers living in the state. The team knows the state's culture, weather patterns, insurance issues, even how local sports teams are doing. Each day, a CIT member reads the state's largest newspaper, *The Daily Oklahoman*, to keep abreast of developments. Newspaper clips are posted on the bulletin board. Michael Burns, director, claims process reengineering, who leads the Oklahoma CIT, comments:

> Because we know the most frequent types of claims people have in Oklahoma, we are able to give much better information and advice to our customers. For example, you can count on hail storms in Oklahoma, and we educate our customers on how different kinds of roof shingles hold up in these conditions. By being attuned to the Oklahoma environment, we can help customers make more informed decisions. We can give more than just 'plain vanilla' answers.

Individual CITs serve designated customer regions ranging from a specific metropolitan area (e.g., Chicago), to a single state (e.g., Oklahoma), to a combination of states (e.g., Wisconsin and Iowa). Customer insurance teams are the centerpiece of a systemic effort to create, in the words of deputy CEO Bill Cooney, "a small company soul inside a big company." Cross-functional employees with specialized knowledge about a specific region leverage a streamlined service delivery model and information technology to pursue the goal.

USAA is establishing alliances with closely screened firms in local markets to handle automobile and property repairs for its members when they choose to use such a service. Here is how STARS (Streamlined Appraisal and Restoration Service) is designed to work: a USAA member who has a car accident calls the CIT on a toll-free number and is assigned a service representative. The representative arranges for the car to be towed to an affiliated auto repair service and for a rental car to be delivered to the customer. The repair service is authorized to repair the vehicle immediately rather than waiting for estimate approval. The repair service bills USAA directly, as does the rental car company. One phone call from the customer initiates a stream of coordinated services designed to get the customer back into his or her vehicle as quickly and effortlessly as possible. What automobile owner would not be interested in such an arrangement?

USAA's application of information technology also helps the company streamline and customize policy service. As discussed in Chapter 5, USAA's imaging system processes customer correspondence into electronic files on the same day it is received. Thus, when customers call to change or add a policy, or to ask a question, their files are complete and electronically accessible to the representatives who take the calls. With a click of the computer mouse, a representative can fax information and documents to customers. The company aims for a 20-minute turnaround on faxes sent by customers.

USAA also has implemented a customer needs-based sales and service information system that automatically identifies gaps in members' insurance coverage. This customer-specific information is displayed on the computer monitor once the representative pulls up the customer's name.

USAA's high-tech teams help a big company streamline, customize, and personalize service delivery—in other words, act small. Bill Cooney makes a strong point in this comment: "From an operations perspective, we take the business apart and ask, 'Is it easy, simple, and fun for the customers to do business with us?' Time is currency. You give customers more time and it's like giving them more money. Customers want to make only one call. We must be intensely focused on enabling them to do this."

SMALL THROUGH SEGMENTATION

At year-end 1997, Charles Schwab Corporation served 4.8 million active customer accounts holding $354 billion in assets—a large company by any measure. However, in recent years Schwab has begun segmenting the market to enable the company to act smaller.

Two primary segmentation criteria are assets in Schwab accounts and trading activity. Customers investing $500,000 or more in Schwab accounts qualify for "Priority" services; more than $1 million invested merits access to "Priority Gold" services. Investors trading more than 24 times a year qualify for Schwab's "Active Trader" program.

A Priority Service or Active Trader customer benefits from a variety of customized services, including alerts on investment opportunities triggered by individual client preferences and late-breaking news and price changes delivered via fax or e-mail. Access to specialized trading services (e.g., Schwab Priority Bond Service, Global Investing Service), additional information sources (e.g., *Standard & Poor's Stock Guide*, *Argus Update* newsletter), and waived fees (e.g., IRA and asset management account fees) are among other benefits.

For many Priority Service and Active Trader customers, however, the most significant benefit is access to the small team of Schwab personnel assigned to serve them. Although these customers are among millions of accounts, they call a special 1-800 number and work with the same team of brokers over time. The specially trained brokers use a database containing information on each customer's history and holdings. Each Priority Service team of 12 people serves 4,000 to 5,000 households. Each Active Trader team of eight to 10 members serves 800 to 1,000 households.

This structure enables Schwab to serve Priority Service and Active Trader customers, the top 20 percent of its customer base, as a large-small company, much like Enterprise Rent-A-Car and USAA. Frequent traders who want discounted transaction costs, quick access to competent and familiar securities brokers, and targeted information, such as stock alerts and company investment reports, can have it all through Active Trader. The combination of high-touch and high-tech benefits in Schwab's segmented market offers enables the company to compete on a value-added basis rather than strictly on a price basis.

SMALL SHIPS AND SHEPHERDS

"We've worked very hard to treat passengers as individuals," states Sven-Olof Lindblad, president of Special Expeditions. "Acknowledging the individuality of travelers is even more important to our success than where we go." Special Expeditions staff never use the term *cruise* because it connotes large ships, inflexible itineraries, passive entertainment, and anonymous service. Special Expeditions' market offer is the converse: small ships, flexible itineraries, active education, and personalized service.

Each Special Expeditions voyage differs from all others for ship personnel and passengers because the crew and expedition staff have an unusual amount of freedom to respond to opportune moments and create a special experience. For ship personnel, the rulebook is thin and the guidelines clear: give people an adventure, seek out extraordinary possibilities, treat people as individuals, never shortchange safety, and create an experience that you would enjoy if you were a traveler. Says Lindblad: "Our staff has as good a time as the passengers; they are inspired by the guests, the geography, and the opportunity to be creative."

Special Expeditions' largest ship, the MS *Caledonian Star*, accommodates 110 passengers. The small ships fit the company's strategy of enabling travelers not only to see a whale from the ship but also to have a more intimate association with whales from inflatable Zodiac landing craft. The company nurtures the passengers' personal exploration of the natural world. Occasionally this can be as extraordinary as the encounter related here in an excerpt from a ship's log.

Each of us was deeply moved by our interaction with the friendly grey whales. We looked into their eyes and they into ours. We touched and caressed the skin of their faces. We played with 30-ton creatures, whose rolling and flapping flukes suggested as much delight as our jumping about the Zodiac and shouting. We shared in meeting intimately with whale beings that have flourished on the earth for 45 million years, far beyond the dawn of anything resembling human beings. There is healing in being present to the beauty and mystery of the natural world. My friend Lou Gold, who is struggling to preserve the Siskiyou Ecosystem of southwest Oregon, signs his letters "Touch the earth and be healed." Touching the whales must be an intravenous megadose of healing. Theodore Roszak writes in his book *The Voice of the Earth:* "Sometimes the voice of the earth breaks through to us in an instant of realization that flashes across the eons, reminding us of who we are, where we come from, what we are made of. For an instant we touch the cosmic continuity that is easily lost in the frenzied affairs of the day."

This account is the essence of Special Expeditions' reason for being; such an experience is possible only in a travel company that operates small ships and craft to personalize adventures. The passenger who shared this experience, Dr. Martin Albert, practices medicine in Charlottesville, Virginia, and occasionally serves as a Special Expeditions ship doctor. He wrote the passage in the *Sea Lion's* log during its trip along the Pacific Coast of Baja, California, on March 15–23, 1997.

In addition to the crew, four to seven naturalists travel on board a Special Expeditions ship, depending on the particular itinerary. This unusually high staff-to-passenger ratio is a function of the company's core values and strategy. Naturalists eat with the passengers, provide a running commentary while leading small groups on nature walks and hikes, direct scuba diving excursions for small groups, and present a talk each evening at "Recap" (see Chapter 5). "We look at each itinerary and decide what staffing level will bring the trip to life for the passengers," explains Director of Operations Maggie Hart. "We need seven to eight naturalists to deliver the kind of experience we want to create on the Amazon trip, for example. The Amazon is like a big 'highway.' You need to get out on the Zodiacs and into the tributaries. A strong staff is vital to identify and interpret the wild life and indigenous cultures."

Special Expeditions has a "shepherd" for each of the major geographic areas it visits. The shepherd is an expert on the region and plays the lead role in developing and refining the overall itinerary. The shepherd envisions a destination, works with operations and marketing to transform the vision into reality, serves as a liaison between a host country and the company, and plays an active role in improving the program each year. Explains Sven-Olof Lindblad, "Every itinerary is a living organism as we keep learning; each year we agonize over what next year's itinerary should be because someone always is coming back with new information. The shepherd is the one person in the company everyone can go to about a particular itinerary."

Special Expeditions presently has six shepherds. Each holds another full-time position in the company. Being a shepherd is an informal position. Because the shepherds have extensive field experience and knowledge, are widely respected internally, and know how to navigate the organization, their presence simplifies change and speeds implementation in a company that is delivering service throughout the world. The shepherds give change a focal point within Special Expeditions, helping the company to act small.

Organizational scale offers competitive advantages, but so does organizational smallness. Smallness can be particularly helpful in labor-intensive service companies. For customers, patronizing a small company can mean less red tape, a more customized service, and more personal attention. For employees, working in a small firm may mean a greater sense of teamwork and community and more personal accountability. Personal performance is more evident in a firm with six people than a firm with 6,000.

Large service companies that act small for customers and employees enjoy the competitive advantages of both scale and smallness. Small companies that retain nimbleness, responsiveness, teamwork, and personalization as they grow and mature preserve qualities that are crucial to their ability to compete.

All of the companies studied for this book, including multibillion dollar companies such as Enterprise Rent-A-Car, Charles Schwab Corporation, and USAA, behave like small companies. Their values, leadership, structures, nurturance of employee ownership attitudes, and high-tech/high-touch strategies support small company actions. Harnessing the virtues of organizational smallness contributes to the sustained success of service companies.[2] When people are a key part of the total product, acting small is big.

10

BRAND CULTIVATION

Shoe problems often bring customers to The Container Store. No, The Container Store does not sell shoes. Nor does it repair shoes. What it does is help customers store and organize the shoes they are not presently wearing. The average female customer of The Container Store owns at least 40 pairs of shoes. How to organize high heels, flats, sandals, athletic shoes, and boots so they can be easily found when needed, how to prevent the shoe piles that impede walking into a "walk-in" closet, how to keep shoe mates together—these are the kind of problems The Container Store loves to solve. The company's clear plastic shoe boxes that hold individual pairs may be the answer. Or the customer may prefer the shoe cubby product, or an over-the-closet-door shoe bag, or shoe shelves that can be incorporated into the elfa® wire storage system described in Chapter 6.[1]

Most consumers buy more products than they dispose of each year. The Container Store is a store sent from heaven for consumer-accumulators. Its products do not save lives, but they do save time, space, and stress. Customers who are neatniks love The Container Store because it celebrates the rightness of their lifestyles. Customers whose closets, kitchens, offices, and garages are in perpetual disarray love The Container Store, too. Why? Because the store gives them hope.

Since its founding in 1978, The Container Store has positioned itself as the original source for storage and organization products. The company that invented the category has been true to it for more than 20 years. Communication tactics change, but the essential, defining message remains the same: get organized, save time and space, simplify your life. The Container Store drives the message home with billboards, catalogs, radio and newspaper advertising, special promotional events, public relations and community outreach, and proactive, competent in-store service. Consistency, cleverness, creativity, and color (blue and yellow) characterize The Container Store's brand development efforts.

The company is an ardent user of billboards, paying top dollar to locate them just before the expressway exit to reach the store, in the highest traffic areas of a market, and, if possible, so close to the store that they are extensions of the store front. The company advertises on billboards continuously but changes the headline every eight to 12 weeks so the message doesn't become invisible. "Customers look forward to seeing our billboard advertising," says Melissa Reiff, vice president of sales and marketing. And what advertising message might customers see? A sampling of past billboard copy from The Container Store illustrates:

- The First Place To Look When You Can't Find Anything
- We Can Help You Get at Least One Car in Your Two-Car Garage
- Bike Racks to Spice Racks
- Kitchen a Mess Hall? Do an About-face. Get Organized.
- Closet a Shoebox? Add a Few More Feet. Get Organized.
- Store More

The Container Store mails between one and two million catalogs to its in-house customer list four or five times a year primarily to stimulate store traffic, build the brand, and pave the way for new markets. "Our catalog enables our customers to pre-shop before coming to the store," explains Melissa Reiff. "Customers frequently bring the catalog with them to the store, with items checked off."

The company's catalogs support the annual elfa® sale, Christmas, and the end-of-the-summer sales period ("Summer is over, it's time to get organized again"). Much of the radio and newspaper advertising also occurs at these times. The company targets college students' dorm-room needs and advertises in college newspapers. After hours on a summer Sunday evening, The Container Store sponsors an in-store shopping party exclusively for college-bound students and their parents. Every item in the store is discounted.

The Container Store does not enter a new market quietly. Executives refer to a new store opening as a "launch," fully expecting the new store to become a top sales producer immediately. The firm begins the process of establishing a presence in a new market eight months prior to actually opening the store. A key early step is a rigorous process for selecting a nonprofit community group to help create local buzz about the company. The selected organization works with company staff and a local public relations firm on the new store launch. The Container Store may evaluate a half-dozen local nonprofit organizations to find the one that best fits its own culture. Atlanta's High Museum of Art, the Denver Center Theater Company, and the San Diego Zoo are among the nonprofits that have helped The Container Store open new stores, including assisting with the requisite invitation-only, pre-opening gala parties. The company donates 10 percent of launch weekend sales revenue to its community organization partner. "We definitely give away too much time and money—and we are proud of it," says company President Kip Tindell. "We become very enthusiastic about the nonprofit groups we work with."

The Container Store cultivates its brand through steadfast adherence to its core strategy, a consistent message, creative advertising, and community partnerships. Most of all, the company builds its brand by living it through the service-mindedness of its stellar employees. As Melissa Reiff states: "Our core competency is service, and we reinforce this in every action we take, in every communication piece we create, in every decision we make. Articulating The Container Store brand is the responsibility of all employees."

The companies studied for this book cultivate their brands—to communicate their "reason for being" to customers and other stakeholders, to stand apart from competitors, to compete with reputation. Managerial and nonmanagerial employees alike are quite conscious of the need to build the brand, to not only preserve it but strengthen it, every day, with every customer. The conscious cultivation of the brand by customer-contact employees in the field in addition to marketing executives in the home office is a distinguishing characteristic of the sample companies and a key factor in their sustained success.

BRANDING THE COMPANY

Branding plays a special role in service companies because strong brands increase customers' trust of the invisible. Strong brands enable customers to better visualize and understand the service. They reduce customers' perceived monetary, social, or safety risk in buying services that are difficult to evaluate prior to purchase. Strong brands are the surrogate when the company offers no fabric to touch, no trousers to try on, no watermelons or apples to scrutinize, no automobile to test drive.

In packaged goods, the product is the primary brand. However, with services the company is the primary brand. The locus of brand impact differs for service companies because services lack the tangibility that facilitates packaging, labeling, and displaying. It is not possible to package and display a St. Paul Saints baseball game in the same way as Kodak packages and displays film.

Even more significant are the relative roles tangible products and intangible services play in creating value for customers. Impact shifts from product brand to company brand as service plays a greater role in determining customer value.[2] Folgers Coffee customers buy the product brand. Most are probably unaware that Folgers Coffee is a division of Procter & Gamble. It is not relevant to the purchase decision. The locus of brand impact is with the product. Customers patronizing a Starbucks store, however, buy the company brand. Their service experience with Starbucks figures prominently in their assessment of value and perception of the brand. Starbucks founder Howard Schultz clearly understands the source of brand power in a service business:

> Our competitive advantage over the big coffee brands turned out to be our people. Supermarket sales are nonverbal and impersonal, with no personal interaction. But in a Starbucks store, you encounter real people who are informed and excited about the coffee, and enthusiastic about the brand. . . . Starbucks' success proves that a multimillion-dollar advertising program isn't a prerequisite for building a national brand—nor are

the deep pockets of a big corporation. You can do it one customer at a time, one store at a time, one market at a time.[3]

Service branding becomes clearer when we understand its components. Exhibit 10–1 depicts the relationships among the presented brand, brand awareness, brand meaning, customer experience, and brand equity. The bold lines indicate primary impact and the dotted lines secondary impact.

The *presented brand* is the company's controlled communication of its identity and purpose through its advertising, service facilities, and the appearance of service providers. The company name and logo and their visual presentation, coupled with advertising theme lines, are core elements of the presented brand. The presented brand is the brand message a company conceives and disseminates. The effectiveness with which a company presents its brand contributes directly to *brand awareness,* which is the customer's ability to recognize and recall the brand when provided a cue. The percentage of customers in New York City who mention Dial-A-Mattress when asked "what companies come to mind if you need to buy a mattress?" is a measure of the company's brand awareness in the market.

Brand meaning refers to the customer's dominant perceptions of the brand. It is the customer's snapshot impression of the brand and what is associated with it. Brand meaning is what immediately comes to consumers' minds if you mention Target and then Kmart. Most consumers have different perceptions of Target and Kmart, even though both companies are general merchandise discounters. Brand aware-

EXHIBIT 10–1

A Service Branding Model

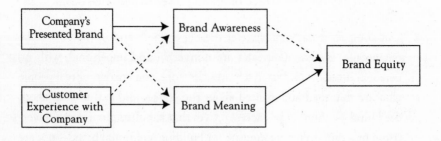

ness is high for both companies; brand meaning is different.[4] The fundamental difference between brand awareness and brand meaning is illustrated by Chick-fil-A versus Kentucky Fried Chicken, by Charles Schwab Corporation versus Merrill Lynch, by Midwest Express Airlines versus Northwest Airlines. These companies are well known by customers in their respective target groups, yet their images are quite different.

The presented brand also contributes to brand meaning but not as strongly as the customer's actual experience with the company. The presented brand has the most influence with new customers who have had little or no direct experience with the company's service to shape their impressions. The presented brand and word-of-mouth communications are a new customer's only evidence of what the company stands for. However, as customers experience the company's "total product," these experiences become disproportionately influential. Customers' experience-based beliefs are powerful. A presented brand can generate greater brand awareness, stimulate new customer trial, and reinforce and strengthen brand meaning with existing customers. A presented brand *cannot,* however, rescue a weak service. If customers' service experiences differ from the advertising message, customers will believe their experiences and not the advertising. In services marketing, customers' disappointment with the service closes the door that traditional brand marketing helps to open. The Container Store's billboards are clever, its catalogs informative, its public relations forceful. Yet all of this effort is wasted without superior performance in the stores. Customers are not going to buy an elfa® closet system in a store without good service no matter how enticing the catalog pictures. Elfa® is not a product consumers buy off a shelf like Folgers Coffee.

Customer experiences also can contribute to brand awareness through word-of-mouth communications. Typically, word-of-mouth will not be as influential as a company's own marketing communications, hence the dotted-line relationship between customer experiences and brand awareness. The most likely carriers of favorable word-of-mouth communications are customers well pleased with a company's service. The more outstanding and unique the service, the greater the likelihood of word-of-mouth messages. The opposite effect also is true: the more horrible the service, the greater the likelihood of unfavorable word-of-mouth. Word-of-mouth occurs under these conditions because of the natural inclination to share valuable information.

Brand awareness and brand meaning both contribute to *brand equity* for experienced customers but not to the same degree. Just as customer experiences disproportionately shape brand meaning, so does brand meaning disproportionately affect brand equity. Brand equity is the differential effect of brand awareness and meaning combined on customer response to the marketing of the brand.[5]

Brand equity can be positive or negative. Positive brand equity is the degree of marketing advantage a brand would hold over an unnamed or fictitiously named competitor. Negative brand equity is the degree of marketing disadvantage linked to a specific brand. Negative brand equity explains why Holiday Inn sponsored television commercials in 1997 portraying hotel housekeepers using chainsaws to destroy a Holiday Inn room and then totally refurbishing it (see Chapter 1).

The service branding model shown in Exhibit 10–1 differs in degree, not kind, from a packaged goods branding model. The customer's actual experience disproportionately shapes brand meaning and equity for goods, not just for services. The principal difference in the two models is the salient role of service performance. In labor-intensive service businesses, human performance, not machine performance, plays the most critical role in building the brand.

The sample companies compete with strongly positive brand equity. They benefit from branding distinctiveness and message consistency, from performing their core services well, from reaching customers emotionally and associating their brands with trust. These companies have high "mind share" with targeted customers, which contributes to market share. Their success invites intense competitive reaction and frequent imitation, yet all 14 sample companies have thrived for years. Why? Because "a product is something that is made in a factory; a brand is something that is bought by a customer. . . . A brand is unique."[6] The sample companies illustrate four principal ways of building brands, as shown in Exhibit 10–2.

EXHIBIT 10–2
Cultivating Brand Equity

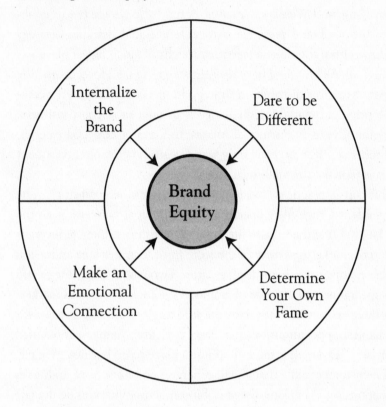

DARE TO BE DIFFERENT

Service companies with the strongest brands reveal a conscious effort to be different, a conscious effort to carve out a distinct brand personality. Top brand builders almost always are mavericks that defy convention and forge new paths to reach and please customers.

Strong brand firms *never* market their offer as a commodity, enacting Tom Peters's assertion that "commoditization isn't inevitable."[7] Invention rather than imitation rules branding efforts. The brand presentation is different. The customer's total product experience also is different. The brand occupies a distinct place in the customer's mind.

Chick-fil-A, which operates in 35 states and South Africa at this writing, exemplifies the "dare to be different" principle. Competing against large national television advertisers such as McDonald's, Burger King, and Wendy's, Chick-fil-A has little choice but to establish a distinct brand presence. Any conventional branding strategy will drown from the sheer advertising weight of much bigger players.

Chick-fil-A's branding heritage is in shopping mall food courts, the company's original distribution strategy. In this environment, the company's principal marketing challenge is to offer food court visitors a compelling, visually distinct *alternative* to a sea of fast-food eateries. Mall rents are dear, and the only way to earn a favorable investment return is to make the mall the medium.

Chick-fil-A practices "inside-out" marketing in its mall stores. The independent Chick-fil-A operator is the principal marketer with the mandate to bring the store to life as an advertising medium, to leverage the latent marketing power of the store front, counter area and menu boards, point-of-purchase displays, store layout and cleanliness, and the appearance and attitude of employees. Chick-fil-A's mall marketing strategy is to transform the store into a television screen that will command shopper attention, encourage trial, and stimulate unplanned purchases. "The mall is more than just a place to do business. We pay for the customer traffic that a mall generates and have to capitalize on this opportunity," explains Steve Robinson, senior vice president, marketing, for Chick-fil-A. "We continually ask our operators: 'What are the messages you are providing from your store that are distinctive, unique, and compelling?'"

To leverage Chick-fil-A's food quality superiority that is consistently documented in blind taste tests with competitive products, mall stores regularly invite food court visitors to sample the product—the venerable small-piece-of-chicken-on-a-toothpick tactic. "We encourage the operators to use every possible method to get the taste of the product in people's mouths," adds Robinson.

Chick-fil-A's branding challenge both intensified and changed when the company expanded distribution beyond the mall with free-standing "street" stores. Now the company truly is competing against the major fast-food brands. Hungry mall shoppers select from available restaurant alternatives in the mall. Hungry people in their homes, workplaces, or cars have a much wider choice set and creating "mind share" becomes an imperative. McDonald's, Burger King, Wendy's, Pizza Hut, and Taco Bell have a compelling reason to spend significant dollars on advertising. Chick-fil-A, with fewer stores, regional distribution, and a network of independent store operators who fund the advertising, cannot spend nearly as much. Creating a distinct, appealing brand personality was the only way to break through the clutter of competitive advertising.

Like The Container Store, Chick-fil-A is a committed billboard marketer. Competitors are aggressive television advertisers and use billboards primarily as directional signs to the restaurants. Chick-fil-A likes billboards because in most markets it cannot afford broadcast media alternatives. It would rather dominate one medium than spread its advertising resources thinly in multiple media. Even with little or no broadcast advertising, Chick-fil-A believes outdoor advertising still can help build a distinctive brand.

Billboards are the medium, however, not the message, and they require unique creative content to be effective. Chick-fil-A's creative breakthrough came in the form of cows who urge consumers to "Eat Mor Chikin." (See Exhibit 10-3 for samples of the billboard execution.) The cows give Chick-fil-A a distinctive brand personality that did not exist before. Created by Chick-fil-A's Dallas-based advertising agency, The Richards Group, the Chick-fil-A "Cows" remind consumers "that they don't have to eat a hamburger today" and present Chick-fil-A as the alternative.

What began as a billboard campaign is now the centerpiece of the company's presented brand. The best brand marketing gives customers a return on their investment of time and attention; it gives customers something back.[8] This is what the Chick-fil-A cows do. They are fun, humorous, different. They are understated, just like Chick-fil-A. They do not intrude. These animals put a smile on consumers' faces while giving a quick-service restaurant chain a more distinct and human identity. Says Steve Robinson, "Because we don't spend a lot of money on advertising, what we do spend must have an impact. Me-too advertising won't break through the clutter. The creative side of what we do has to be excellent and it has to be distinct." Adds marketing professor Ken Bernhardt, a long-time consultant to Chick-fil-A, "It isn't just advertising weight that counts."

EXHIBIT 10–3

Brand Personality at Chick-fil-A, Inc.

Advertisements courtesy of Chick-fil-A, Inc.

DETERMINE YOUR OWN FAME

Strong-brand service companies stand for something that is important to targeted customers; their brand not only differs from competitive brands, it represents a valuable market offer. The sample companies use branding to convey their "reason for being." As discussed in Chapter 4, they have asked and answered the question "What do we want to be famous for with customers?" They capture and communicate the answer through their brands.

Service companies with strong brand equity are providing a service that customers truly value, are performing it demonstrably better than competitors, and are effectively telling their story through communications that create awareness, stimulate trial, and reinforce customers' experiences. Over time, these companies become famous for their defining excellence, aided not only by their own controlled messages but also by customers' word-of-mouth communications.

Thirty percent of Dial-A-Mattress's customers are referrals. The company's core service strategy makes it so simple to acquire a new mattress that many first-time customers are astonished. The conventional method forces the customer to find the time and energy to visit one or more furniture stores, test multiple mattresses by lying or bouncing on them, sort fact from fiction in the selling process, and arrange for delivery in three or four days. Instead, a customer can telephone Dial-A-Mattress, speak with a bedding consultant who has participated in a six-week training regimen (see Chapter 8), receive the mattress within two hours if desired, and send it back with the driver if not fully satisfied. The astonishment factor stimulates customer word-of-mouth, which Dial-A-Mattress encourages by giving purchasers discount coupons for their friends. Explains founder Napoleon Barragan, "A new customer who calls us in the morning to buy a mattress is skeptical. When she receives her mattress that afternoon she is happy she called, and Dial-A-Mattress becomes a topic of conversation."

Dial-A-Mattress advertises on television and radio with a consistent message: buy Sealy, Serta, or Simmons brand name mattresses over the telephone, subject to your approval, save money, and receive your mattress when you want it, within two hours if you wish. The advertising often ends with the tagline: "Dial 1-800-MATTRES, and leave the last 's' off for savings." The advertising purposely is simple and direct. "We deal with facts in our advertising," says Jay Borofsky, vice president of the national division. "We offer a good value to customers and have no reason to stray from the facts."

The combination of frequent television and radio advertising, a consistent message, word-of-mouth communications, and publicity generates awareness of the Dial-A-Mattress brand. Late-night talk show host David Letterman once called Dial-A-Mattress on camera during the show, requesting that a mattress be delivered to his car in Manhattan. Dial-A-Mattress made the delivery on camera.

The company's name also contributes to brand awareness. Dial-A-Mattress is a great name because it simply, yet distinctively, conveys what the company sells and how to buy it. Because of the powerful influence of customers' actual service experiences on brand meaning and brand equity, a service company can overcome a mediocre name. A good one certainly helps, however, as Dial-A-Mattress illustrates.

The Midwest Express brand also captures and communicates a valuable market offer. Midwest Express wants to be famous for "the best care in the air," its signature statement in all advertising. The company's advertising strategy includes clearly stating, as often as possible, factual support for this assertion. Advertising consistently refers to the airline's nonstop, single class of premium service with comfortable leather seats, no middle seats, delicious food, and caring, personal attention. Advertising usually mentions the airline's top ranking by independent organizations, such as the Zagat Airline Survey or Conde Nast Traveler. The company also stresses its competitive fares that are comparable to the regular coach fares of other airlines; this message counteracts impressions that it must be expensive because of the high quality service.

Midwest Express likes to advertise on television in local markets. Explains Advertising Manager Jim Reichart, "Our differences translate well into television. We *like* to show coach—the leather seats, the smiling faces, the great food, and the glass and silverware."

Unlike the Dial-A-Mattress name, Midwest Express is not a great company name. The airline flies to the Southwest, Southeast, and both coasts. Moreover, the word "Express" suggests a commuter airline, which definitely is not Midwest Express. The company is proud of its

Wisconsin roots and seeks to convey Midwestern values of caring, friendliness, community, and commitment in its marketing communications. Its advertising also features one of its jets—with its signature dark-blue-on-white color motif and distinctive logo on the tail—to counteract the commuter airline impression.

Although Midwest Express is not a great name, it is a great brand. No company from the sample better illustrates the disproportionate impact of customers' service experiences on brand meaning and equity. Among passengers who have experienced the airline's service, an ordinary corporate name evokes the image of first-class seats, good food, chocolate chip cookies, and caring personal service. The name holds rich, differentiated meaning and the company is not about to change it.

MAKE AN EMOTIONAL CONNECTION

In January 1998, the Harlem Globetrotters played their 20,000th basketball game in the small town of Remington, Indiana. Renowned for their ball-handling wizardry, comical routines, and old-fashioned silliness, the Globetrotters make an emotional connection to the customer. The Harlem Globetrotters is a magical brand—a brand that evokes images of fun and laughter, respect and decency, hard work and good values. Globetrotter players are graded by the team owner on their charisma, punctuality, and ability to promote the brand. Cursing, pouting, and rudeness are forbidden. Players sign autographs after the games. "We're all aware of how precious the brand is," says Paul "Showtime" Gaffney, who performs the clown prince role once played by Meadowlark Lemon. "Each and every night, the people in the stands don't care if you just stepped off a 10-hour bus ride. They want you to be your best, and we want to be our best."[9]

Great brands always make an emotional connection with the intended audience. They reach beyond the purely rational and purely economic level to spark feelings of closeness, affection, and trust. Consumers live in an emotional world; their emotions influence their decisions. Great brands transcend specific product features and benefits and penetrate people's emotions.[10] As Charlotte Beers, chairman emeritus of Ogilvy & Mather, writes: "The truth is, what makes a brand powerful is the emotional involvement of customers."[11]

Brands that connect with customers' emotions are those that reflect customers' core values. In effect, the brand captures and communicates the values customers hold dear. Corporate values cannot be faked in services branding. As the branding model (Exhibit 10–1) reveals, company-controlled marketing communications is but part of brand development; the company's true values emerge in the customer's actual experience with the service. Marketing communications cannot establish nonexistent values.

Enterprise Rent-A-Car connects emotionally with employees of local body shops, auto repair firms, and insurance companies by taking donuts to them week after week, by building personal relationships, and most of all, by keeping their explicit and implicit service promises. Chick-fil-A's "Cows" invite the customers' affection, but the effort is negated if customers' experiences with the service contradict the feeling. Midwest Express could portray chocolate chip cookies in its advertising, but far more powerful is actually baking them on board for passengers and serving them with a warm smile.

Brands that connect emotionally are authentic summations of a company with a soul. The brand captures and conveys that soul. As Starbucks founder Howard Schultz writes: ". . . the most powerful and enduring brands are built from the heart. They are real and sustainable. Their foundations are stronger because they are built with the strength of the human spirit, not an ad campaign."[12]

It is instructive that low price is not a central element in the ongoing advertising of any of the 14 sample companies. Even Dial-A-Mattress, which competes against dozens of price-screaming mattress retailers, does not give price messages a starring role in its marketing communications. Owner Napoleon Barragan scoured the telephone directory yellow pages for various pricing claims and made a list, e.g., "Lowest prices in town," "We will never be undersold," "We will give you a free . . ." Barragan took the list to his advertising people and asked them never to use any of the claims.

Companies that emphasize price in their advertising forfeit the opportunity for an emotional connection with their customers. Customers do want their money's worth and most customers are interested in a bargain. Yet price-dominated marketing messages ring the emotional bell of few customers. Price advertising may be about value, but it is not about *values*; it does not stir the soul. As Donald Hudler, who helped build the Saturn automobile into an emotionally rich brand, remarked in a speech: "When you talk about price you lose the opportunity to talk about yourself and build a brand."[13]

The St. Paul Saints illustrate the emotional content of a strong brand. To most of their fans, the Saints are far more than just a professional baseball team. Brand meaning extends beyond sports, baseball, or wins and losses. To many, the Saints mean affordable fun for the family and for the St. Paul community. The Saints are part of the town's culture, a spirited community citizen, a maverick organization with a heart, an organization whose top management greets fans as they enter the ballpark, a team that plays baseball in an outdoor stadium (unlike the Minnesota Twins who play in a domed stadium), a team with a blind radio announcer, a team that in 1997 signed the first female pitcher, Ila Borders, ever to pitch on a regular basis for a professional men's baseball team.

The core of the Saints' presented brand is its basic value: "Fun is good." From sumo wrestling to fans racing around the bases in various contests, mini events occur during breaks in the game action. The Saints not only have a pig as the team mascot, they hold an annual contest for elementary school children to name the pig. In 1997, the pig was "Hamlet;" in 1998, "The Great Hambino." One thousand school children participated in the 1998 name-the-pig contest, with the winner receiving a free night at the ballpark with 10 friends in the "party boat" (an actual boat in the stadium that fans can rent and sit in to view the game). Food, beverages, and Saints tee-shirts and hats also are part of the winner's bounty.

The Saints hold a "Dead of Winter Tailgate Party Recipe Contest" in their parking lot to raise funds for a nonprofit community organization. An RBI Club ("Reading Books is Fun") attracted one thousand fourth- and fifth-grade students in 1998 to participate in a reading program. On "Gardening Day," children plant flowers in the "Reading Tree" area of the stadium. On another day children and players paint murals on the stadium fence. The team holds a charity golf tournament.

The Saints care, and the community knows it; caring is integral to its brand. The St. Paul Saints connect emotionally with their fans and the fans with each other. "Going to a Saints game is like going to your high school reunion," explains General Manager Bill Fanning. "You may not know the people sitting next to you when the game begins, but they are old friends by the time it ends." The St. Paul Saints epitomize every branding principle discussed thus far: the company dares to be different, clearly defines its reason for being, and connects emotionally. For these and other reasons, the St. Paul Saints may be the best known minor-league baseball team in America.

INTERNALIZE THE BRAND

Service performers are a powerful medium for building brand meaning and equity. Their actions with customers transform brand vision to brand reality—for better or worse. Service providers make or break a brand, for the customers' actual experiences with the service always prevail in defining the brand for them. With their on-the-job performances, service providers turn a marketer-articulated brand into a customer-experienced brand.

Negative customer experiences are difficult for a company to overcome in its branding efforts, no matter how effective its marketing communications. Superior customer experiences are difficult for competitors to imitate, no matter how effective *their* marketing communications. As Tom Peters writes, "It seems that you can knock off everything . . . except awesome service."[14] Building the brand *through* service providers requires "internalizing the brand."

> Internalizing the brand involves explaining and selling the brand to employees. It involves sharing with employees the research and strategy behind the presented brand. It involves creative communication of the brand to employees. It involves training employees in brand-strengthening behaviors. It involves rewarding and celebrating employees whose actions support the brand. Most of all, internalizing the brand involves *involving* employees in the care and nurturing of the brand. Employees will not feel part of nor act out the brand unless they understand it and believe in it. Marketers need to verbalize and visualize the brand for em-

ployees, so that employees will verbalize and visualize the brand for customers. Brand internalization must be an ongoing process, just as brand building is an ongoing process with customers.[15]

Enterprise Rent-A-Car and Midwest Express are among the sample companies that specifically consider employees to be a key audience for all of their advertising. They view advertising as a primary means for motivating and educating employees, as well they should given research that clearly shows employees are influenced by their company's advertising.[16]

Enterprise Rent-A-Car first advertised on national television in 1989. The company has honed a consistent presentation of the brand in television advertising: a customer in an auto repair shop phoning Enterprise for a rental car, the theme line "We'll pick you up," the signature "cloaked" car, the distinctive white-on-green *E* logo. The message is clear and brand awareness high. From 1989 to 1997, aided brand awareness for Enterprise Rent-A-Car increased fourfold.

The impetus to advertise was not increasing brand awareness, however. It was to build employee pride in the company. In 1989, company founder Jack Taylor asked his son Andy a decisive question: "You know, Andy, how would we feel if a rental car company half our size came on television and promoted the [car] replacement service?" The seed for the company's inaugural national advertising effort was planted with this simple question. "Our advertising has had a fabulous impact on our employees," comments Andy Taylor. "Our existing employees are proud and prospective employees are impressed when they see that company advertising on *60 Minutes* or a National Football League game."

Midwest Express shares Enterprise Rent-A-Car's philosophy of internalizing the brand through advertising. Says Brenda Skelton, senior vice president of marketing and customer service for Midwest Express, "Our employees are the most important audience for our marketing efforts. It is easy to market when we just have to generate customer trial. Our employees keep the customers coming back. Our national reputation has grown mainly through our reputation for service."

Chick-fil-A invests significant resources to help independent store operators cultivate the Chick-fil-A brand in their local markets. The company organizes brand marketing teams to work with operators in specific markets where it is opening many freestanding stores. The teams consist of marketing, advertising, and public relations specialists from the company's headquarters staff and the marketing firms with which it works. The process begins each year with market-specific brand-equity research for Chick-fil-A and its principal competitors. They hold workshops in individual markets to present the research and discuss its branding implications. The team then works with operators to develop brand-building strategies for their markets based on the research.

Chick-fil-A views the local store operator as the primary brand marketer; the role of the brand marketing team and headquarters staff is to help the operator and market operator teams become more effective. Accomplishing this role involves educating the store operators about brand marketing. The operators can withhold marketing funds or ignore the brand marketing team's advice if they so choose. Internalizing the brand through education, market-specific research, customized advising, and tracking each market's performance is critical. Chick-fil-A's Steve Robinson explains:

> Brand building requires that we educate the operators on why—or they won't do it. This is why we have put more marketing talent in the field. We don't demand. We don't prescribe. We try to persuade by showing how they and Chick-fil-A will benefit. We have to do our homework, do the market research, show the operators why, and ultimately, show results. We cannot use marketing to drive the business unless we are willing to engage operators in the process.

Adds Chick-fil-A consultant Ken Bernhardt, "A key marketing step at Chick-fil-A has been getting the operators to take ownership of building the brand. The cows give the brand a distinct personality across markets, and the operators are strengthening the brand in their local markets. It is a powerful one-two punch."

From Dial-A-Mattress to the St. Paul Saints, the companies studied for this book benefit enormously from brand equity—the marketing advantage that accrues from the combination of brand awareness and brand meaning. The sample firms cultivate their brands by consciously pursuing distinctiveness in communicating the service and in the service itself, by using branding to define their "reason for being," by connecting emotionally with customers, and by internalizing the brand for service providers so that they are more likely to externalize it for customers.

Midwest Express Airlines, Enterprise Rent-A-Car, and the other companies *are* their own brands. This is a reality of creating value for customers primarily through service: the company becomes the brand. Marketing communications help build the brand, but nothing is more powerful than the customers' actual experiences with the service. Being served freshly baked chocolate chip cookies as you relax in a comfortable leather seat on a Midwest Express jet defines brand meaning and builds brand equity more powerfully than any advertisement.

11

GENEROSITY

Ukrop's, the perennial food market share leader in Richmond, Virginia, donates 10 percent of its pretax profits to the community. Another 20 percent of pretax profits goes to associates in quarterly bonuses. Ten percent is allocated for long-term profit sharing, 10 percent for shareholder dividends, and 50 percent is invested directly into the business.

The Ukrop family, who own the business, could retain a much larger portion of the profits—but they don't. Ukrop family members don't even participate in the associate bonus program. Through its Golden Gift Program, Ukrop's donates up to 2 percent of a customer's expenditures in the store during a 10-week period to a charity the customer selects. Ukrop's has donated more than $7 million to more than 5,000 charities over the lifetime of the program.

Ukrop's never misses an opportunity to reward associates for their contributions to the company's success, to recognize associates' special days (weddings, birthdays, births, graduations) with cards and checks or gifts, and to encourage associates' involvement in the community and charitable activities. Ukrop's conducts two blood drives each year at all of its locations and is a leading contributor to United Way, both directly and through its associates. "We try to increase our associates' awareness of opportunities to give," explains company president and CEO Bob Ukrop. "If we don't make them aware, who will?"

Sharing has been a Ukrop's preoccupation from the start. In the

1930s and 1940s, company founders Joe and Jacquelin Ukrop gave charitable organizations a 10 percent discount on groceries. When American soldiers were away during World War II, the Ukrops frequently would close their store on Wednesdays so Joe and his employees could help shorthanded farmers tend to their crops.[1]

Joe and Jacquelin's sons, Jim (who is chairman) and Bob (president and CEO), have continued the tradition of helping the community financially and personally. The brothers are active in the economic development of the Richmond metropolitan area. Jim chaired the Richmond Chamber of Commerce and Bob chaired Richmond's Retail Merchants Association's Economic Development Council. Both are on the boards of civic, charitable, and educational institutions. Both teach Sunday school. "All of this goes back to my parents," says Bob Ukrop. "We grew up giving to the church every Sunday. It's just the way we grew up." Adds Jim Ukrop: "You want this world to be a better place. It won't happen unless concerned people become a little more involved."[2]

Making the community a better place is a core value of Ukrop's and the other companies studied for this book. It is not uncommon, of course, for companies to donate money and otherwise invest in the communities where they operate. What is uncommon is the *centrality* and *depth* of this commitment in the sample companies. These companies are more than civic-minded, more than charitable, more than responsible. The term *generosity* describes them best.

Charlotte Beers, chairman emeritus of Ogilvy & Mather Worldwide, once wrote: "Generosity is the great secret weapon of success in business."[3] The sample companies resoundingly prove her point. An important finding of the research for this book is the unequivocal role generosity plays in sustaining the economic success of service companies. Generosity is not only an outcome of success, it is a critical input. This finding is supported by a comprehensive analysis of companies in the S&P 500 by professors Sandra Waddock and Samuel Graves. The researchers used a weighted eight-factor index of corporate social performance to analyze the relationship between a company's social and financial performance. They conclude that strong corporate social and financial performance are mutually reinforcing; each contributes to the other in a "virtuous circle."[4]

Why does generosity pay off for labor-intensive service companies? The answer is that generosity wins hearts. Winning people's hearts makes an essential difference in businesses where human beings create value for human beings. As discussed earlier, most service employees have considerable discretion in the degree of effort they put into their service; they are, in effect, "volunteer" workers. Generosity motivates people at work to give their best efforts. *The central lesson of this book is that humane values power great service companies; generosity continuously reinforces and enriches these humane values. When the product is a performance, winning the hearts of the performers helps companies win the hearts of their customers.*

A company's generosity reaches customers not only through motivated service performance but also through the fairness of its policies and practices (see Chapter 7) and its community investments. Ukrop's customers experience generous service in the store and observe a generous corporate citizen in the community. Generosity not only inspires employees, it also inspires customers, earning their trust and commanding their loyalty. Great service companies compete most effectively for customers with their character. As Charlotte Beers writes, "You cannot win the hearts of customers unless you have a heart yourself."[5]

One of retailing's stars today is LensCrafters, a fast-growing, thriving optical chain that sells a new pair of glasses every three seconds. LensCrafters' success is a shining example of the powerful role that generosity can play in building a business. Through "Give the Gift of Sight," LensCrafters Inc. and the LensCrafters Foundation, in conjunction with Lions Club International and other charitable groups, provides free optical services and glasses to needy people in North America and around the world. The company's goal is to give the gift of sight to one million needy people, especially children, by 2003. As of year-end 1997, the company had helped 567,000 poor people see better.

Give the Gift of Sight includes the collecting, cleaning, repairing, and classifying of used eyeglasses for distribution by LensCrafters' optometrists and opticians to needy people in developing countries. (The distribution of used glasses is discouraged in the United States.) Host Lions Clubs help plan the missions and operate the clinics. Individuals receive eye exams and are given glasses that fit their prescriptions exactly or as closely as possible. Give the Gift of Sight missions have gone to Costa Rica, Panama, Kenya, Mexico, Albania, Chile, Bolivia, Philippines, Tanzania, Morocco, and Peru.

All LensCrafters stores in North America donate eye exams and new eyeglasses to needy people on "Hometown Day," the first Wednesday in December each year. Affiliated doctors donate their time to examine recipients, store associates dispense new eyeglasses, and Lions Clubs and other local groups identify needy people and transport them to the stores. Frame and lens vendors donate products for Hometown Day.

The LensCrafters Foundation also reaches out to inner cities, Indian reservations, disaster areas, and rural communities with its Vision Van—an eyecare facility on wheels. The Vision Van is a 40-foot vehicle that includes two exam lanes, a lens lab, and eyeglass dispensary. Through 1997, the Vision Van program had reached 23,000 children. LensCrafters added a second Vision Van in 1998.

In 1997 alone, the Give the Gift of Sight programs reached 235,000 needy people. Two million pairs of used glasses were collected. Frank Baynham, executive vice president and chief administrative officer of LensCrafters, captures the impact of Give the Gift of Sight on employees:

> Our associates' commitment to the company has intensified as they have personally experienced giving the gift of sight to someone in need. As our Vision Van pulls into an impoverished area and our associates provide new glasses to children who can then see their world in sharp detail for the first time, our associates are deeply moved. They better understand the expression 'It is greater to give than to receive.' At LensCrafters, the Gift of Sight has given us entree to our associates' hearts.

STRATEGIC GENEROSITY

Frances Hesselbein, president and CEO of the Drucker Foundation, relates a story the Reverend Martin Luther King, Jr. liked to tell: Centuries ago, two travelers were on a dangerous road and spotted a man needing help. The first traveler asked, "What will happen to me if I stop to help?" The second traveler asked, "What will happen to him if I do not stop?" Peter Drucker adds to the story that the second traveler, the Good Samaritan, went back the next day to check on the man. The Samaritan was focused on results.[6]

Dr. King's story, with Drucker's addition, speaks to the importance of strategic generosity: caring for the person on the dangerous road but also caring about the results beyond the moment.

Generosity must know limits. It must have boundaries. A company cannot donate time or money to every worthy cause; it cannot allow its good intentions to become ineffective behaviors because it lacks focus. To be most effective, generosity must be purposeful, channeled, integrated into a company's culture and strategy, and results-oriented. Professor James Austin makes the point well:

> Strategic engagement requires focus. Doing everything would be as nonsensical in the social arena as it is in the marketplace. Priorities should be set, resources focused, and synergies captured. A company should delineate those social needs areas that are most important to its communities and those that have the best fit with the corporation's interests and competencies.[7]

The sample companies are strategic in their generosity. They not only are extraordinarily generous, they are effectively generous. Rather than giving for the sake of giving, they invest with a plan in mind, with a long-term goal. Rather than spreading their resources thinly in numerous initiatives, they concentrate their resources to have a powerful impact and make a meaningful difference. Rather than investing time, energy, and money outside the mainstream of their business, they invest in concert with the business's overall purpose and strategy. Thus, generous acts not only benefit society, they benefit the company too, creating a stronger company and enabling more generous acts in the future.

USAA pays the tuition for its employees to attend college. It will pay for one undergraduate degree and one graduate degree per employee. It provides college classrooms in its headquarters, dedicated areas for doing homework, and on-site college advisors. USAA's annual multimillion-dollar investment to send employees to college clearly benefits society. However, it also benefits USAA in its quest to be an employer of choice that attracts talented people who are adept in using technology to deliver service.

Ukrop's donated $500,000 to establish the Ukrop's Center for Culinary Education at a local Richmond community college. The campus also houses Ukrop's Culinary Institute, which educates company employees in the art and science of food preparation and awards college credit. The gift benefits the Richmond community, the college, and Ukrop's. It perfectly fits Ukrop's emphasis on service excellence. As Bob Ukrop states: "The shopper doesn't just come for products any more. They come for knowledge."[8]

The St. Paul Saints give fans their money's worth—and then some. The Saints sell out every home game by effectively coupling their core value—"fun is good"—with economic value. The Saints make a conscious effort to hold down prices and pack their market offer with nonstop entertainment. Each home game has a promotional theme that offers something extra—"General Mills presents Trix T-shirt night"; "Minnesota State Lottery presents Opening Weekend Fireworks"; "Tombstone Pizza Baseball Glove Giveaway"; "Lamperts presents Seat Cushion Giveaway. A fan(ny) favorite." The team's mascot, a pig, appears between innings, as do sumo wrestlers and other practitioners of on-field fun. The public address announcer orchestrates the collective mood with wit and music. And the Saints play a baseball game. Fans experience a generous total product, which evokes their devotion.

Underscoring Chick-fil-A's remarkable success are outstanding products and outstanding people. Generosity propels the company's ability to attract and retain outstanding people. Each year Chick-fil-A awards $1,000 college scholarships to selected students working part-time in its restaurants. The scholarship program was started in 1973 by company founder Truett Cathy to encourage young employees to further their education. Between 1973 and 1997, the company awarded nearly $13 million in $1,000 scholarships. No other American company of Chick-fil-A's size donates as much money for employee scholarships, according to the Council for Aid to Education.

To commemorate reaching $10 million in scholarships in 1994, the company commissioned art students to design a sculpture reflecting the goals of its scholarship program. The 23-foot sculpture entitled "Climb with Care and Confidence" depicts people lending hands to help others climb an archway constructed of books. It is located in Atlanta on Peachtree Street at Woodruff Park. The scholarship program is a magnet for college-bound high school students looking for parttime work. The program melds Truett Cathy's philanthropic commitment to helping young people with the operators' needs to effectively staff their stores.

The operators who benefit directly from the college scholarship program also benefit from Chick-fil-A's unique "operator deal," described in Chapter 8. Chick-fil-A puts up the capital but splits net operating profits equally with the operators. It is a generous arrangement that helps the company attract and retain excellent people to operate the restaurants. Chick-fil-A's restaurant management turnover rate of approximately 6 percent is one of the lowest in the industry.

The company also attracts exceptional people to work in its Atlanta headquarters and one of its methods is a free lunch. The next time someone claims "there is no free lunch," respectfully disagree and tell the person about Chick-fil-A headquarters, which includes a full cafeteria that serves employees a free lunch. When the company was small, Truett Cathy would bring the headquarters staff food from his Dwarf House® restaurant. Chick-fil-A is no longer small, but Truett Cathy has never stopped serving a free lunch.

To help Public Broadcasting System member stations raise funds, Special Expeditions donated its 80-passenger MS *Polaris*, crew, and staff for a 10-day expedition to the Galapagos Islands in December 1998. As part of public television's annual auctions to raise funds, supporters in selected markets were given the opportunity to bid on a cabin for two for this trip. Actor Alan Alda, host of the PBS Scientific American Frontiers series, joined the voyage and filmed an episode for his series. Company founder Sven-Olof Lindblad served as the expedition leader.

By teaming up with PBS, Special Expeditions furthered its mission of promoting environmental and cultural appreciation. Yes, Special Expeditions gave up more than $300,000 in revenue had it sold this trip, but it gained added momentum for its cause—on-air brand exposure to an audience matching its own target market and access to prospective customers through promotional mailings to station member lists and actual bidders for the trip. Special Expeditions could easily have spent $300,000 on more advertising; instead, it invested the monies in PBS, which shares the company's commitment to environmental education and has access to television viewers. "We share a similar audience with PBS," says Sandra Levy, manager of strategic alliances and promotions for Special Expeditions. "We hope we can turn some viewers into travelers."

PBS supporters responded positively to the trip offer, frequently bidding more than list price. The winning bid in Boston generated $15,500 for a cabin that normally would sell for under $7,000. The winning New Orleans bidder paid $11,000 for a $7,284 cabin. The PBS corporate support office received dozens of calls from viewers who either were unsuccessful bidders or were away during their local PBS station auction. They wanted to know where the next auction would occur. An Indiana resident was the winning bidder for the Dayton, Ohio, station, a Pennsylvania resident the winning bidder for Albany, New York.

GIVING OF SELF

Observing others give has less impact than giving of self. Working for a generous company builds pride in the company. Personal generosity builds pride in oneself. Voluntary self-giving is the purest service experience an individual can have. Making a difference in the lives of others through charitable acts enhances self-esteem, self-confidence, and leadership skills, all critical to job performance in service work.

Giving of oneself off the job transfers to giving of oneself on-the-job. Serving people in need outside the boundaries of a commercial transaction can intensely energize service within the boundaries. The following story from the LensCrafters store in Towson, Maryland, illustrates this dynamic. The experience described occurred during Hometown Day, December 3, 1997. In reading the story, consider the impact on the employees beyond that particular day:

> Our most memorable Hometown Day story is about a student we never even met! We were almost finished delivering exams and free glasses to about 20 students from a local school when the teacher asked if we could repair a student's glasses whose mother would not let her participate in

Hometown Day. When we opened the envelope containing her glasses, we found a frame with lenses but no temples. The girl had taken twist ties and looped them through the hinges, then connected string to the ties which she wore around her head. The teacher told us she had worn them to school everyday, despite her classmates' cruel jokes.

We were moved by this girl's situation and determined to replace her glasses. When we discovered the prescription in her existing glasses was -8.25, -4.5, we all cried. Then the teacher cried because she was so moved by our reaction. We chose a beautiful frame and made the new glasses, which her teacher delivered. Although we did not see the girl's face when she received them, we had the satisfaction of knowing Gift of Sight had made an incredible difference in her life.[9]

Personal Generosity at USAA

USAA encourages the personal involvement of employees in community service through USAA Volunteer Corps, USAA Community Educational Programs, Christmas Cheer, and United Way.

The Volunteer Corps matches current and retired USAA employees with community nonprofit agencies that need additional workers. In 1998, more than 6,000 USAA volunteers contributed some 220,000 hours of personal time to more than 350 community organizations. USAA volunteers helped a local children's hospital raise funds, befriended and aided abused children, assisted crisis hotline counselors, supplied food and clothing for the needy, and contributed computer expertise to community service organizations.

Through the Christmas Cheer program, USAA employees bring food, clothing, furniture, blankets, and gift baskets to low-income families, nursing homes, children's homes, shelters for battered women, and other community agencies. In 1997, more than 90 percent of 18,000 USAA employees across the country participated in the Christmas Cheer program.

Through USAA's Community Educational Programs, volunteers travel to local elementary, middle, and high schools to assist students in their studies, befriend students, and encourage them to stay in school. Volunteers can select the specific program that best fits their time and interests: general mentoring, independent study mentoring, math tutoring, teaching junior achievement classes, being a pen pal. First implemented in the San Antonio Independent School District in San Antonio, Texas, the Community Educational Programs now have been implemented by USAA's regional offices.

In 1997, 68 percent of USAA's employee population contributed $3.8 million to United Way. USAA provided an additional $2 million in matching corporate funds, for a total contribution of $5.8 million. Although USAA accounts for less than 2 percent of San Antonio's work force, the company contributed one out of six dollars to San Antonio's United Way chapter in 1997.

Personal Generosity at Charles Schwab Corporation

In 1997, the Charles Schwab Corporation Foundation supported the work of more than 1,500 local and national nonprofit organizations through corporate contributions, in-kind donations of used computer equipment and printing services, employee volunteerism, and matching gifts.

Schwab encourages the personal involvement of employees in charitable causes through both A.S.S.E.T.S. (Assisting Society through Schwab Employee Teamwork and Service) and its matching gift program. Established in 1995, A.S.S.E.T.S. facilitates employee volunteerism by linking employee interests, community needs, and company community action priorities in areas such as K–12 education, health care, AIDS, literacy, counseling, services to minority groups, seniors, youth, disabled people, the homeless, arts, and culture. Full-time staff and regional A.S.S.E.T.S. committees manage the program and place employees in volunteer activities that fit their interests. Schwab's goal is to formally involve 50 percent of its employees nationwide in community outreach activities. In 1997, about 25 percent participated in company-sponsored outreach activities.

Schwab enjoys a special partnership with a number of nonprofit organizations. Among these partnerships in San Francisco are:

• *Raphael House*, San Francisco's first shelter for homeless families. Raphael House offers families private living quarters, three meals a day, job skills training, recovery programs, and educational tutorials for parents and children. Schwab provides employee volunteers, funding, printing services, and special events.

• *William R. DeAvila Elementary School*, a low-income neighborhood school that Schwab supports with cash contributions, in-kind donations, and employee volunteers. Schwab employees secured computers for the school and wired the school so they could be used. Employees mentor and tutor students, and one Schwab volunteer runs the school's chorus and music program.

• *Florence Crittenton Services (FCS)*, which helps pregnant teenagers and teenage parents. Schwab provides volunteers, mentors, funding, and printing services. Schwab employees also sit on the FCS board of directors. Schwab volunteers have hosted teen mothers at Schwab offices for Take Your Daughters to Work Day.

• *Project Open Hand*, an organization that supports people with HIV/AIDS. Schwab volunteers deliver meals to people afflicted with the disease and befriend them.

Schwab recognizes outstanding volunteerism with its annual Community Service Award, presented by the company chairman at the annual shareholders meeting. Significant cash donations are given to the designated nonprofit charities of the winners.

Schwab not only encourages employees to volunteer their time to charitable causes, the company also encourages them to donate their money through the Employee Matching Gift Program. The Schwab Foundation will match employee donations at a ratio of two Schwab dollars for one employee dollar, up to a maximum of $5,000 per employee annually. Employee gifts will be matched to any nonprofit organization that is not religious, political, or athletic in nature. Approximately 50 percent of Schwab's contributions are made through this matching gift program.[10]

Schwab's encouragement of personal generosity was solidified by a pathbreaking event in January 1995. The company devoted one full day of its annual three-day retail leadership conference to building Habitat for Humanity houses, with 580 leadership conference attendees participating. "It was a huge, powerful event," explains Jim Losi, president of The Charles Schwab Foundation. "It brought out the natural generosity in the human heart and fused it with the company's values and a common purpose. That one day changed my life, and it changed the lives of many others."

Generosity permeates the fabric of Charles Schwab Corporation. Less visible to business observers than Schwab's maverick style as a financial services competitor, generosity defines the company just as much. Jim Losi likes to tell the true story of a Schwab security guard who had been on the job for only three weeks. Early one morning Losi found the man in tears. He had just been diagnosed with cancer and needed surgery. Too new an employee to have accumulated sick leave, the man needed the job and didn't know what to do. Losi made one phone call and in a week's time Schwab employees had donated 1,000 hours of their own vacation and sick leave to the guard's account—the equivalent of three months of time off with pay. The guard believes he is alive because of the generosity that defines the people of Charles Schwab Corporation.

STRENGTHENING THE ORGANIZATIONAL COMMUNITY

Company executives who restrict the fruits of business success to an inner circle of senior managers weaken the organization and shorten its life. Sustaining service success requires trust and teamwork throughout the organization; it requires the high discretionary efforts of service providers; it requires ownership attitudes throughout the company; it requires transforming the organization into a community of shared values and common purpose. All of this vitality is sacrificed at the altar of selfishness. As Arie de Geus, author of *The Living Company*, writes: "In organizations in which benefits accrue to only a few people, all others are outsiders, not members."[11]

The hard truth is: *selfish companies cannot serve*. The emotional commitment necessary for effectively serving customers day after day after day cannot survive an organization of haves and have nots, insiders and outsiders, important people and unimportant people.

Great service companies are great at saying thank you to the people who do the hard work. They recognize the feats of the group—not just the feats of individuals—reinforcing and celebrating a sense of community and encouraging continued commitment. Generosity within an organization helps secure its future.

Every single employee of Dana Commercial Credit—about 550 people at the time—received 25 shares of stock one week after the company was selected for the 1996 Malcolm Baldrige National Quality Award. One DCC employee had been on the job for only two weeks but still was included. Upon hearing the news she cried, telling associates that her previous employer of 17 years had given her only turkeys.

Charles Schwab Corporation celebrated a terrific fiscal year in 1996 by giving every employee 20 shares of stock plus a cash award to pay the taxes on the stock. These gifts were in addition to a holiday bonus and annual bonuses that paid at the maximum rate.

Midwest Express Airlines' Tim Hoeksema insisted that one million dollars in stock be set aside for employees when the company went public in 1995. Every full- and part-time employee was included in the stock grant. Hoeksema wanted to align the interests of employees and shareholders and reward the employees who built a company that could attract public money. He also wanted to strengthen the sense of community within the company. "I wanted to promote the feeling: 'I am Midwest Express,'" explains Hoeksema.

In April 1998, Custom Research Inc. took every employee—125 people—to London, England. The group trip recognized the company's meeting an aggressive profit goal in 1997. The group toured London, went to the theater, and made side trips to other English cities. Custom Research closed its offices for a Friday and Monday to accommodate the trip. The company paid all of the trip expenses. "This was our way of sharing with people who helped us achieve an ambitious goal," explains CRI co-founder Jeff Pope. "The trip had a tremendous team-building effect within our company. It is money well spent. I'll do it every time."

Custom Research's first company-sponsored trip was in 1985. The company had an unexpectedly good year in 1985 and the steering committee wanted to recognize the employees. New York City, the site of a CRI branch office, was the destination for "a long weekend." All full-time and some part-time employees—105 people—enjoyed a boat tour past the Statue of Liberty, a night at the theater, and other activities. The trip was so successful that CRI set the next profit goal and offered San Francisco as the prize. The company achieved the goal in 1990 and the entire staff visited San Francisco, the site of CRI's other branch office. The company then set the next milestone and destination: DisneyWorld. It reached the goal in 1992 and took more than 100 people to DisneyWorld. "Judy [Corson] and I always have talked about making a bigger pie," comments Jeff Pope. "We believe that if you make the pie as big as possible and share it with others, you end up with more than if you tried to keep a small pie just for yourself."

CREATING SOCIAL PROFIT

Chapter 2 introduced the concept of social profit, for it is a core value in the sample companies. Social profit represents the net benefits to society from a company's actions beyond the marketing of goods and services and the creation of employment opportunities. Companies deploy human and other resources to market goods and services to create economic wealth. This orchestration of resources in pursuit of wealth creation is highly beneficial to society. Indeed, no society can function in its absence. But this is the pursuit of economic profit, not social profit. Social profits are net gains in the quality of life beyond the availability of goods and services for sale and the financial resources to buy them.

The creation of social profits is deeply enmeshed in the cultures of the sample companies. Making money is not enough. These companies cherish the opportunity to positively influence the broader community. Creating economic profit is a noble goal—and a necessary one if resources are to be available for social profits. But wealth creation alone is too small a pursuit. It fails to fully unleash the human spirit in organizations, to fully tap into the natural generosity of the human heart about which Jim Losi of Charles Schwab speaks. By generously sharing with society their talents, their leadership, and their money, excellent companies make a bigger, more meaningful difference in the quality of life; win the hearts of employees, customers, and other stakeholders; and become even more excellent companies.

Investing in Tomorrow's Adults

Truett Cathy, founder and chairman of Chick-fil-A, established the WinShape Centre Foundation in 1984 to help children in need. Created to help "shape winners," the foundation supports WinShape Foster Care, Camp WinShape, and the WinShape Centre Scholarship Program. WinShape foster care homes accommodate up to 12 children with two full-time foster parents. Children are encouraged by their foster parents and by the foundation to consider their foster home to be their permanent home, to return for visits after they leave to be on their own. In 1998, there were 11 such homes; Cathy's goal is to add at least one new foster care home annually. Chick-fil-A sponsors a Ladies Professional Golf Association tournament to help raise funds for the foster care program, the Chick-fil-A Charity Championship.

Cathy and his foundation enjoy a special relationship with Berry College, a liberal arts school in Rome, Georgia. The site of the first foster care home, the Berry College campus also is the site of WinShape's summer camp program, a series of two-week camping sessions that serve more than 1,500 boys and girls each year. Camp activities include rock climbing, a ropes course, archery, backpacking, and canoeing.

WinShape's scholarship program at Berry College is a cooperative work-study program offering four-year scholarship funding of up to $16,000 to incoming freshmen. The scholarships are jointly funded by the WinShape Foundation and Berry College. Through 1997, more than 480 Berry College scholarships had been awarded to students from across the nation. These scholarships are in addition to Chick-fil-A's restaurant employee scholarship program discussed earlier in this chapter.

Truett Cathy believes in investing in tomorrow's adults. Deeply committed to the concept of social profit, Cathy quotes this Chinese proverb in his book *It's Easier To Succeed Than To Fail*: "If we plant for days, we plant flowers; if we plant for years, we plant trees, but if we plant for eternity, we plant ideas and ideals into the lives of others."[12]

Kids at Sea

Special Expeditions has developed a program with The High School for Environmental Studies in New York City through which it takes at least 12 tenth-graders each year on voyages in Alaska or Baja California. "Kids at Sea" endeavors to attract students who are not necessarily achieving in school but who have academic potential. The students selected for the trip have not had access to an educational voyage and are not likely candidates for such an experience were it not for this program.

Competition among the students for the trips is keen. Chosen by a teacher selection committee, the students undergo a detailed application and interview process. Those who take the trips share their experiences with fellow students in classroom and assembly presentations. A willingness to share the experiences with others is a selection criterion.

The student travelers, from the inner city of New York, are exposed to a physical and social environment that is very different from the world they know. Although one of the naturalists on board is assigned as a mentor, many of the passengers and crew also befriend the youngsters. They are exposed to many different potential role models. Just as the student travelers are expected to share their experiences when they return to school, so are they expected to do so on board the ship—and each one prepares a five-minute presentation to staff, crew, and passengers on the last day. A trip highlight is learning to drive the Zodiac landing craft. States Tom O'Brien, Special Expeditions' director of environmental affairs, "Learning to drive the Zodiacs is huge for these kids. Most of them have never been near the water before. These kids go back to school and they want to be a ship captain, an engineer." Adds Jeff Cole, who manages "Kids at Sea" for the school, "The opportunity for students to have first-hand exposure to nature, to work alongside positive, encouraging role models, and to drive a Zodiac or to snorkel can be a life-changing event—whether the student realizes it at that precise moment or not."[13]

Special Expeditions, which frequently operates its trips at full capacity, forgoes revenue with Kids at Sea. Is Kids at Sea a sound business proposition? Tom O'Brien strongly believes that it is: "Our passengers receive a valuable added benefit. They see the kids' eyes being opened, and it opens their eyes, too. The kids energize the passengers and, because their presence affirms the purpose and mission of our company, they energize the staff and crew also."

Like Chick-fil-A and the other sample companies, Special Expeditions seeks to create social profit. Social profit is not a peripheral matter or a tangential concern; it is embedded in the company's "reason for being." Gregory Jenkins, a Kids at Sea participant, eloquently captures the force of social profit: "My voyage to Alaska changed my life. I became a traveler, a naturalist, a crew member, a hiker, a passenger, and, most of all, an inspired person."[14]

Generosity is a success sustainer in labor-intensive service companies. The social commitments and sharing of resources that many businesspeople would consider a peripheral matter are in fact central to the ongoing success of the companies studied for this book. Strip away the work of the WinShape Foundation from Chick-fil-A and you have a different company. Eliminate USAA's Volunteer Corps and Charles Schwab Corporation's A.S.S.E.T.S. and you have different companies. Sell all the cabins on the ship rather than give some away to "Kids at Sea" or the Public Broadcasting System, and you still have a fine company in Special Expeditions but not the same company.

Humane values define all great service companies for they are the only values that sustain high levels of employee discretionary effort in serving customers. Generosity embodies and strengthens humane values. Generosity inspires employees and customers. It truly is a service company's "secret weapon."

12

LESSONS FROM
WORLD-CLASS SERVICE
COMPANIES

All companies are service companies to the degree that they create
value for customers through performances. Hotels, airlines, and
baseball teams are pure service companies in that they create value
largely or exclusively through performances. Manufacturers and goods
retailers are hybrid organizations in that they create customer value
with a goods-services combination.

Miller SQA is a manufacturer of office furniture that differentiates
itself with service. Remove Miller SQA's value-creating service innovations ranging from collaborative selling through a laptop computer
to a two-day order-to-shipping option and the company becomes just
another office furniture manufacturer. But Miller SQA is hardly just
another competitor. The company stands apart in its industry as a
pathbreaking innovator that is achieving robust sales and profit
growth. For "manufacturer" Miller SQA, service excellence is making
a critical difference.

Virtually all goods retailers add value to their market offers through
services. Textbooks commonly refer to supermarkets as "self-service"
stores, even though America's most successful food retailers all are
stellar service providers. The Ukrop's story told in this book illustrates
the pivotal role of quality service in the food-retailing sector. Eliminate Ukrop's customer-friendly store atmosphere, valued customer

membership program, meal idea centers, in-store restaurants, made-to-order takeout foods, catering service, nutrition hotline, and a host of other services and Ukrop's becomes a very different—and much less appealing—company to customers. Facing greater competition than at any time in more than 60 years of operations, Ukrop's remains the market-share leader in Richmond, Virginia, by a large margin. The company owes its success to the combination of superior merchandising *and* servicing.

Because all companies are service companies, all are in the business of marketing promises. Until a service is delivered, it is a promise of performance. It is difficult for customers to evaluate most services prior to purchase because services are intangible. Customers usually purchase a service before experiencing it. To fly Midwest Express, passengers must first buy a ticket. To stay in the Paper Valley Hotel, guests must first check in—and agree to pay. Service customers must trust the company to keep its promise. Nothing is more important to a service company's future than to instill confidence in customers that it can and will keep its promises; the customers' confidence is a service company's most precious asset. Service companies that lose their customers' confidence lose control of their future.

Sustaining service success is difficult because it requires sustaining customers' confidence. Labor-intensive service companies are especially vulnerable to losing the customers' confidence because they must rely on people to create customer value. As these firms expand and add services, facilities, and employees, quality control becomes more problematic. As a business becomes older and bigger, more complex, and more spread out, the qualities that initially made it special to both customers and employees can easily be lost. Bureaucracy replaces boldness. Turfism replaces teamwork. Formality replaces informality. Price-cutting replaces innovation. Rule-book management replaces inspired leadership.

The more labor-intensive the service, the greater the challenge of success sustainability. Keeping the human engine going at a high level day after day, week after week, month after month, year after year is more difficult than keeping the inanimate engine going. When the product is a labor-intensive performance, the skills, knowledge, commitment, and creativity of the performers figure prominently in the customers' perception of value.

One Fundamental Question

The research for this book explored one fundamental question: How do excellent service companies keep the human engine going to sustain their excellence? How do they retain their sharpness, their boldness, their civility, their service soul? So many service companies never surpass mediocrity and others regress to average or below over time. Yet some service firms keep getting better. How do they do it? How do great service companies *stay* great?

I studied 14 service companies that have achieved sustained success to answer my question. I purposely selected a diverse company sample that includes a professional baseball team, an airline, a marketing research company, a quick-service restaurant chain, an automobile insurance and financial services association, a hotel firm, an office furniture manufacturer, a car rental chain, a firm that sells mattresses over the telephone, a retailer of storage and organization products, a leasing company, an expedition travel company, a food retailer, and a securities brokerage and financial services firm.

These companies create value for customers through labor-intensive service operations, and they have achieved sustained customer acceptance and financial success. Through year-end 1997, the sample companies collectively had operated profitably for 402 out of 407 total years. The average age of the companies as of 1999 is 31 years.

I studied these companies closely. I visited each company for interviews and observations, examined considerable background material, personally experienced the companies' services whenever possible, and conducted numerous follow-up telephone interviews. In all, I interviewed more than 250 people from the 14 companies.

These companies are remarkable organizations that would compete effectively with any competitor in the world. The core strength of this study lies in the sample. Through due diligence but also good fortune, the companies selected for the sample proved to be excellent choices.

The opportunity to study them as a group reveals how great service companies stay great.

This book identifies, describes, and illustrates the underlying drivers of sustainable success in labor-intensive service businesses. The first chapter models nine success drivers (Exhibit 1–1), and subsequent chapters discuss in depth each element of the model. The most exciting finding of the research is that the drivers of sustainable service success are common across the different businesses. The success sustainability model presented in this book perfectly fits all 14 companies. I am confident that this model accurately represents what a world-class service company looks like. I am equally confident that sustainable success has little or nothing to do with company size or industry growth rates.[1] A small company in a stagnant industry can indeed achieve sustainable success while larger companies in growth industries falter.

The sample companies teach important lessons about the true meaning of success, how to achieve it, and how to sustain it. What follows is a brief overview of the most salient of these lessons organized by the elements of the success sustainability model.

Values-Driven Leadership

Humane organizational values sustain human excellence. Sustaining service success requires humane organizational values that inspire and guide service providers, that bring their artistry and passion for serving and creativity to full flower, that nourish their energy and commitment, that give them a high quality of life on the job, not just off the job. Ideals, principles, and philosophy at the center of the enterprise that celebrate human potential are most likely to stimulate that potential, to nurture and grow it, to sustain it. People are an essential part of the product in labor-intensive service companies; organizational values that enable people at work to realize their full potential as individuals and as members of the organizational community create "product strength" for customers. The core *values* of the sample companies—excellence, innovation, joy, teamwork, respect, integrity, and social profit—generate compelling *value* inside and outside these companies.

Strong values depend on strong leaders. The most effective service leaders cherish, teach, model, and reinforce humane organizational values. Values-driven leaders articulate the company's "reason for being," define the meaning of organizational success, live the company's values in their daily behavior, cultivate the leadership qualities of others in the organization, assert core values during difficult times, continuously challenge the status quo, and encourage employees' hearts with caring, involvement, participation, opportunity, fairness, and recognition.

Values-driven leadership must permeate the organization. Leadership that comes only from the top of a labor-intensive service organization is insufficient to sustain the core values that guide service providers and inspire high discretionary effort. Except in the smallest of organizations, service providers report to middle managers rather than top managers. Inspired leadership at the point of service delivery is critical. Great service companies lead from the middle of their organizations, not just from the top. They leverage the power of values-driven *middle-leaders,* in addition to values-driven *senior leaders.*

Stable leadership stabilizes values. Sustaining service success requires senior leadership stability. It is no coincidence that the majority of sample companies still have their original CEOs as this book goes to press. Humane values require organizational trust, and building trust takes time. The work of values-driven leaders is never finished; it is an ongoing process, a continuous journey. Leadership changes can introduce values uncertainty into an organization, especially if the new leader comes from outside the company. One reason the sample companies follow promotion-from-within policies is to preserve their core values. Insiders' values are known.

Values-driven leadership propels all other success sustainers. Values-driven leadership actuates sustainable service success. Clear, compelling values that promote human achievement offer pathways to a company's transforming decisions. Strong values open certain doors and close others. Values such as excellence, innovation, joy, and social profit clarify objectives and motivate accomplishment. How does an organization acquire these values? Leaders who view their infusion and cultivation in the organization as a primary responsibility bring them.

Great service companies have a soul that underlies their strategies and day-to-day operations. The company's soul—its value system—is its foundational center, its inner core. America's schools—from its grammar schools to its collegiate schools of business—would contribute more to excellent organizational practices if they devoted more attention to exploring the powers and mysteries of humane values and organizational soul. Sustaining successful human enterprise derives from humane values and inspired leadership. It is that simple and that complex.

Strategic Focus

Constancy of purpose leads customer value creation. A clear value system paves the way to clear strategy. Sustainable service success requires a core strategy—a definition of the business—that focuses organizational attention, guides business design decisions, channels execution, and galvanizes the human spirit. Excellent service companies define their business in strikingly clear terms. They know how they want to create value for customers, they know their "reason for being," and they stay focused on this central purpose. Focusing facilitates excellence. Strategically, less is more. The sample companies have chosen core strategies that reflect their values and fulfill underserved market needs; and they pursue these strategies with unrestrained exuberance. Strategic commitment shows through to customers.

High purpose motivates. People at work need a mission that resonates with their own value systems and energizes their efforts. A meaningful mission is critically important to sustaining high discretionary service efforts in labor-intensive service companies. A clear mission guides; a clear mission of high purpose guides *and* motivates. Special Expeditions exists to "inspire travelers." The St. Paul Saints believe "fun is good." Midwest Express offers "the best care in the air." The Container Store "betters customers' lives by giving them more time and space." These and the other sample companies benefit enormously from core strategies that touch the human spirit. As Peter Senge told a Drucker Foundation conference audience: "Mission instills the passion and patience for the long journey."[2]

Strategic focus inspires innovation. Effective strategy involves knowing what to change and what not to change. The answer lies with the customer. An effective core strategy focuses on serving an enduring customer need. The core strategy changes rarely, if at all. Conversely, supporting substrategies and execution—the market offer—are in constant motion as the company seeks performance improvement and superiority over competitors. Strategic focus is the ally of innovation because it guides action and because it is customer based. True innovation comes from focusing on the customer rather than the competitor.

Executional Excellence

A well-executed strategy diminishes opportunity for competitors. A customer does not experience a strategy; a customer experiences the execution of the strategy—that is, the "total product." Unexecuted strategy spells failure. Great service companies not only have focused strategies, they also focus on execution. Strategy cannot be hidden, and success invites imitation. The only option is to outperform competitors. A poorly executed strategy clears a path for competitors to succeed with imitation.

The sample companies have brilliant core strategies. Midwest Express's strategy of providing a first-class air-travel experience at coach prices commands a frequent traveler's attention. Buying a mattress can be a stressful, time-consuming experience for customers, but Dial-A-Mattress's strategy removes much of the stress and saves most of the time. The Container Store helps people get organized—a nearly universal need. But brilliant strategy is like a red cape to a bull: competitors find it irresistible. To sustain their success, excellent service companies continually raise their service delivery standards in pursuit of performance-based competitive differentiation. Many of the approaches discussed in this book are integral to the pursuit of executional excellence, including service providers well-prepared to go onstage, carefully managed evidence, flexible service systems, active listening systems, and structured improvement processes.

Attracting great people is the first rule of execution. Great service companies attract great people to perform the service. It is a simple idea. It is a powerful idea. And it is—for most companies—an elusive idea. The companies studied for this book, however, put this idea into practice. Cora Griffith, Jennifer Grassano, Craig Hall, Joanne Peratis-Weber, Bud Lehnhausen, Jody Beaulieu, and dozens of other service providers introduced in these pages are real people. And they are exceptional—in their skills, their competence, and their commitment to service excellence and to their company. When a product is performance based, the quality of the performer greatly influences the customers' total product experience.

The sample companies do not just recruit employees, they compete for talent. But talent alone is insufficient. These companies seek people who not only are talented enough for a career at the firm but who hold the right values. The sample firms hire only people whose own personal values will support and sustain organizational values. This is one of the study's most important lessons: *humane values power excellent service companies, and these companies insist on hiring people with these values to stay excellent.* By attracting exceptional people with the right values, the companies rarely need to go outside the organization to fill executive positions. They promote from within instead, reflecting and preserving their core values in so doing.

The sample companies' strong value systems help them to attract and retain talented people who share these values. These companies are employers of choice in an era of low unemployment in America. They compete for the best people, but so do the best people compete for positions in these firms. Chick-fil-A receives 9,000 applications a year for about 80 store operator openings. Many more people want to work for USAA and Midwest Express and Custom Research than the number of available openings. Historically, the American Dream has been defined extrinsically: "What do I possess?" Increasingly, it is being defined intrinsically: "What do I feel?"[3] Values compatibility on the job creates a quality of work life that talented employees seek.

Control of Destiny

Pursue success on your own terms. Freedom to act is as important to a company's success as it is to an individual employee's success. Excellent service companies preserve their freedom to act; they chart their own course and pursue it with minimal distraction and interference.

The companies featured in this book not only have brilliant strategies, they are pursuing these strategies *unfettered*. They fiercely resist allowing outsiders to dictate the direction and the operations of the business. Leading the business is the leaders' mandate—and not the privilege of competitors, lenders, institutional shareholders, unions, or anyone else.

Great service companies control their destiny by:

- Continually raising the bar of excellence and generating competitive differentiation and customer loyalty as a result
- Expanding and growing within their capabilities
- Staying focused on what targeted customers truly value and giving it to them through perpetual innovation and investment
- Acting like a private company regardless of whether they actually are or not, e.g., investing for long-term strength in the business, serving all stakeholder groups rather than favoring the interests of large shareholders, and prizing the creation of social profit in addition to economic profit
- Controlling processes that directly affect customers' perceptions of quality and value

Control of destiny is an attitude, a mindset. The senior leaders of the sample companies believe in what their companies stand for, believe in the contribution their companies are making, believe in the future. Outside interference is unwelcome. Distraction from the mission is unacceptable. If the company succeeds, the success will be on the company's terms; if the company fails, at least it will be its own failure. Sustaining service success means sustaining control of the business.

Trust-Based Relationships

Sustaining service success requires trust. Service companies sustain their success by offering an appealing service and delivering on their promise. Labor-intensive service companies live on their ability to sell performances delivered by human beings. Holding this fragile arrangement together is trust. Service companies cannot function for very long without trust. Customers trust companies to keep their promises, as do employees and business partners. Promises kept strengthen commitment; promises broken weaken commitment.

Trust is confidence that the other party can and will keep its explicit and implicit promises. Trust comes from perceptions of past performance, from an assessment of the other party's competence (ability to keep the promise) and fairness (willingness to keep the promise). Services and jobs are inherently intangible, intangibility creates uncertainty, and trust reduces uncertainty. Trust is important to any organization, but in no organization is it more important than in labor-intensive service companies.

A service company's future is measured by the strength of its relationships. Relationships are important to companies because they are the link to the future—tomorrow's customers, tomorrow's employees, tomorrow's business partners. Mutual commitment is the essence of a relationship. The stronger the commitment, the stronger the relationship. Relationships are the company.

Trust is the foundation of mutual commitment and relationships. Not only must the customer trust the company, the company must trust the customer. Not only must the employee trust the company, the company must trust the employee. Not only must the business partner trust the company, the company must trust the business partner. Trust binds the parties together in a complex and turbulent market environment; trust generates loyalty because when people find trust, they are reluctant to relinquish it.

The companies studied for this book all are high-trust companies. Trust is one of their most powerful competitive weapons, for it forges the deeply felt stakeholder relationships at the heart of their sustained success. Relationship commitment can exist at various levels. The highest level of relationship commitment is "ownership"—a bond so intensely felt by customers, employees, and business partners that they feel the company belongs to them. Great service companies operate at the "ownership" level with stakeholders to a much greater degree than most companies. Strong relationships are cherished not only by the company but also by the stakeholders. Trust is the centerpiece of this state of affairs.

Investment in Employee Success

Investing in the performer contributes to the performance. Excellent service companies invest in their employees' success. They compete for talented people with compatible values and then continually invest in their service skills and knowledge and their sense of inclusion in the organization. Top service companies create their own success by first creating successful employees.

Superior serving is more than enabling technology and intelligent service system design, although both are exceedingly important. Superior serving also is human artistry and attitude and spontaneous decision making and physical effort and mental energy. It is skills and knowledge and judgment. It is commitment, caring, and confidence. Companies reap the benefits of superior serving by investing in the servers.

So many service companies are miserly investors in employees' serving capabilities. They lack confidence in the quality of people they are hiring, or superior service is not viewed as a salient competitive issue, or profit margins are falling and such investments are considered unaffordable, or employee turnover rates are so high that any employee investments are seen as a waste. In any case, the performer is unequipped to perform. It is a common failing that opens the market to companies like the ones studied in this research. These firms take the opposite approach. They invest with great conviction in the preparedness and willingness of people to serve. It is not a difficult decision. If you believe performance quality is the key to your company's future, if you believe strong employee relationships enable performance quality, if you believe you are hiring great people, why wouldn't you invest in their on-the-job success?

Through initial and ongoing employee skill and knowledge development, through generously sharing company information with employees, through a belief in employees to make their own good service decisions, through offering employees a financial stake in the company's success, through the creation of a trust-based organizational community, the sample companies sustain their success. Investing in their employees' success helps ensure the company's success.

Acting Small

In services, acting small is big. Because services are performances, because these performances often are delivered by human beings, and because customers interact with these human servers, the opportunity to personalize and customize the service experience for customers is significant. Rote behaviors in a manufacturing plant assembly line are not part of the customers' experience. Rote behaviors in a service factory—in an airplane, hotel, or supermarket—are part of the customers' experience.

Excellent service companies—even if they are large—find ways to act small with customers. They find ways to leverage the "build-to-order" potential of a service, to tailor it to the preferences and personality of the individual customer. They find ways to mold the service to the moment; to ease the customer's burden if a problem occurs; to act quickly, responsively, freely and personally; to make customers feel a little bit special. Acting small means "purposely treating customers personally."[4]

Excellent service firms also strive to make the organization feel small for employees. Just as customers may feel lost or helpless or ignored when dealing with a company, so may employees have these feelings. Humane organizational values such as joy, teamwork, and respect; a shared vision of high purpose; and an emphasis on organizational trust, "relationship employees," and employee ownership attitudes all contribute to an intimate, collaborative work environment that encourages human excellence.

Bill Cooney, USAA's deputy CEO for property and casualty insurance, continually asks, "Is it easy for customers to do business with us, and is it easy for us to do business with ourselves?" These questions capture the essence of acting small. USAA is a multibillion-dollar business with more than three million customers and more than 18,000 employees, but Bill Cooney insists that it behave like a small organization that is quick, responsive, seamless, flexible, and caring. And why not? A big service company that can minimize bureaucracy, fend off rigidity, and maintain its service soul will make more money and have more fun. Small companies that act small and big chains that don't act like chains claim a decided advantage in services markets.

High touch and high tech are mutually supportive. Information technology supports a company's efforts to act small. Combining the powers of technology and personal service enables a company to take advantage of the special virtues of each. Technology can do some things better than people; people can do some things better than technology. Wisely used, technology can make people far more effective in the service role. Top service companies serve customers situationally—with technology-driven speed, precision, and customizing in some situations; with personalized bonding and expertise in other situations; and with a balanced blend of technology and personal service in still other situations. Technology and personal service are mutually supportive, interconnected keys to acting small.[5] This is why companies such as USAA, Custom Research, and Charles Schwab Corporation deliver services not just through teams but through high-tech teams.

Brand Cultivation

Branding the company means performing the service. Strong brands are critical to service companies because they increase customers' trust of the invisible. Strong brands enable service customers to better understand what they are buying and reduce their sense of risk. A service brand tells the essential, capsulized story of a service: what it is and why it matters. The purpose of the brand not only is to define the service but also to differentiate it, to establish a distinct personality, to connect customer and company emotionally.

The sample companies illustrate the reality of service branding: first, branding the service means branding the company; and second, branding the company well means performing the service well. Midwest Express Airlines *is* its own brand. Enterprise Rent-A-Car *is* its own brand. Chick-fil-A *is* its own brand. The Container Store sells branded products but customers first must select The Container Store brand. The brand becomes the customer experience. When customers' service experiences with a company differ from the company's advertising message, customers believe their experiences rather than the advertising.

When a performance creates most or all customer value, the source of the performance becomes the primary brand, and the quality of the performance disproportionately determines brand meaning and brand equity. The companies studied for this book understand the performance-based nature of service branding; they build their brands with image-reinforcing performance rather than with image alone.

Generosity

Generosity drives service success. It is common to think of corporate generosity as a success outcome; a company creates wealth and shares it. However, the high-performance service companies in this study teach a different lesson. Generosity not only is an outcome of success, it is a critical input.

Uncommon generosity is a primary reason the 14 sample companies are so successful. Generosity drives success in these companies because it embodies and reinforces the humane organizational values that inspire extra-effort service performance. Uncommon generosity also commands customers' attention and respect and earns their trust and loyalty.

Service companies with a big "heart" become better at service because of it. Caring, giving people—the kind of people who make the best servers—want to be part of a company with heart. Once on the job they are energized by the company's contribution to the quality of life both inside and outside the organization.

Smart business in a service business makes life better. Performance-selling companies must win the hearts of the performers to win the hearts of their customers. Selfish companies cannot serve. Greed provides no basis to create anything special—or lasting.

The companies studied for this book teach significant lessons about services management, about leadership, about sustainable business success, and about life. These companies are not without their challenges and setbacks. They are not problem-free. But they truly are special organizations that bring the best out of people and contribute a high net return to society. They are successful, very successful, in financial terms and in human terms. And they are getting better as they age and grow. Their futures are not assured—they never can be—but they appear promising indeed.

The success sustainability model presented in this book is not easily implemented. It requires extraordinary leadership, commitment, and determination. Rule-book management is easier than values-driven leadership. Commanding human beings is easier than inspiring them.

Pursuing economic gain is a more conventional goal than simultaneously pursuing economic and social profit. But values-driven leadership, human inspiration, and social profit make a service company great—and sustain the human engine of service.

Service companies need not die young. But many will continue to do so until we effectively communicate the message that service businesses must make life better for people on and off the job. Great service companies are *humane* communities that *humanely* serve customers and the broader communities in which they live. Everyone benefits from the existence of a great company—customers, employees, vendors, investors, cities, nations. This is why a great company lives for a long time.

NOTES

Chapter 1. Sustaining Success in Service Companies

1. Gregory J. Gilligan, "Ukrop's Increases Market Share—Supermarket Chain Continues Dominance of Richmond Area in Survey," *Richmond Times-Dispatch*, June 11, 1997, pp. C1 and C4.
2. Robert Levering and Milton Moskowitz, *The 100 Best Companies to Work for in America* (New York: Currency Doubleday, 1993).
3. "Dial 'A' for Aggravation," *Business Week*, March 11, 1996, p. 34.
4. Arie de Geus, *The Living Company: Habits for Survival in a Turbulent Business Environment* (Boston: Harvard Business School Press, 1997).
5. Arie de Geus, "The Living Company," *Harvard Business Review*, March-April 1997, p. 52.
6. Quoted in Julia Vitullo-Martin, "How a Hot Business Keeps Its Sizzle," *Wall Street Journal*, March 24, 1997, p. A18.

Chapter 2. Success-Sustaining Values

1. James M. Kouzes and Barry Z. Posner, *Credibility—How Leaders Gain and Lose It, Why People Demand It* (San Francisco: Jossey-Bass Publishers, 1993), pp. 121–22.
2. See Robert Waterman, *The Renewal Factor* (New York: Bantam Books, 1987), Chapter 7.
3. Herb Kelleher, "A Culture of Commitment," *Leader to Leader*, Spring 1997, p. 22.
4. As quoted in Kouzes and Posner, p. 124.
5. Edwin McDowell, "Quality Service with Wings—Midwest Express Prospers by Pampering Passengers," *New York Times*, September 23, 1997, p. 10.
6. Peter F. Drucker, "My Life as a Knowledge Worker," *Inc.*, February 1997, p. 78.
7. "Beginnings," 1996 USAA *Annual Progress Report*.
8. Leonard L. Berry, *On Great Service: A Framework for Action* (New York: Free Press, 1995), p. 109.

Chapter 3. Leading with Values

1. James M. Kouzes and Barry Z. Posner, *The Leadership Challenge* (San Francisco: Jossey-Bass Publishers, 1995), p. 13.
2. Peter F. Drucker, "Leadership: More Doing Than Dash," *Wall Street Journal*, January 6, 1988, Section 1, p. 14.
3. Leonard L. Berry, *On Great Service: A Framework for Action* (New York: Free Press, 1995), pp. 16–17.
4. Noel M. Tichy, "The Mark of a Winner," *Leader to Leader*, Fall 1997, pp. 25, 28.
5. From a speech at the Center for Retailing Studies Fall Retailing Symposium, Dallas, Texas, October 23, 1997.
6. Kouzes and Posner, p. 13.
7. Dick Bergstrom's quote is drawn from Steve Prestegard, "The Hotel Brothers," *Marketplace*, January 7, 1997, p. 22.
8. See "Blueprints for Business" and "The Speed of Natural Light," *Business Week*, November 3, 1997, pp. 113–16 and p. 128, respectively.

Chapter 4. Strategic Focus

1. Based in part on Napoleon Barragan, *How to Get Rich with a 1-800 Number* (New York: Regan Books), 1997, pp. 1–7.
2. James C. Collins and Jerry I. Porras, "Building Your Company's Vision," *Harvard Business Review*, September-October, 1996, p. 66.
3. Theodore Levitt, "Marketing Myopia," *Harvard Business Review*, July-August, 1960, pp. 45–56.
4. Michael E. Porter, "What is Strategy?" *Harvard Business Review*, November-December 1996, pp. 68–69.
5. Porter, pp. 70, 76.
6. Porter, pp. 61–78.
7. Leonard L. Berry, Kathleen Seiders, and Larry G. Gresham, "For Love and Money: The Common Traits of Successful Retailers," *Organizational Dynamics*, Autumn 1997, p. 13.
8. *The Economy at Light Speed—Technology and Growth in the Information Age—and Beyond*, Federal Reserve Bank of Dallas Annual Report, 1996, pp. 9–10 and Exhibit B.
9. Leonard L. Berry, "Leading for the Long Term," *Leader to Leader*, Fall 1997, p. 33.
10. David S. Pottruck, "Charles Schwab: Maverick Retailer," *Arthur Andersen Retailing Issues Letter*, March 1997, p. 4.
11. Pottruck, p. 4.
12. As quoted in "Charles Schwab Corp.—E-trader," *Forbes*, July 7, 1997, p. 246.

Chapter 5. Executional Excellence

1. Linda L. Price, Eric J. Arnould, and Patrick Tierney, "Going to Extremes: Managing Service Encounters and Assessing Provider Performance," *Journal of Marketing*, April 1995, pp. 83–97.

2. Price, Arnould, and Tierney, p. 87.
3. Ron Zemke, "World-Class Customer Service," *Boardroom Reports*, December 15, 1992, p. 1.
4. Lewis P. Carbone and Stephan H. Haeckel, "Engineering Customer Experiences," *Marketing Management*, Winter 1994, pp. 9–19.
5. As quoted in Thomas Teal, "Service Comes First: An Interview with USAA's Robert F. McDermott," *Harvard Business Review*, September-October 1989, p. 126.
6. Leonard L. Berry and A. Parasuraman, "Listening to the Customer—The Concept of a Service Quality Information System," *Sloan Management Review*, Spring 1997, p. 66.
7. As quoted in the Dana Commercial Credit 1996 Annual Report, p. 13.
8. As quoted in "Bergstrom Hotels: A Case Study in Continuous Improvement," *Quality Management*, September 10, 1996, p. 6. Also see Deborah Breiter, Stephen A. Tyink, and Susan Corey-Tuckwell, "Bergstrom Hotels: A Case Study in Quality," *International Journal of Contemporary Hospitality Management*, Number 6, 1995, pp. 14–18.

Chapter 6. Control of Destiny

1. Bonnie Schwartz, "Ready, Set, Go!," *I.D. Magazine*, March/April 1997, p. 88.
2. See John Huey, "In Search of Roberto's Secret Formula," *Fortune*, December 29, 1997, pp. 230–34; David Greising, "What Other CEOs Can Learn from Goizueta," *Business Week*, November 3, 1997, p. 38; and William J. Holstein, "Drink Coke, and Be Nice," *U.S. News & World Report*, June 9, 1997, p. 50.

Chapter 7. Trust-Based Relationships

1. John A. Czepiel, "Service Encounters and Service Relationships: Implications for Research," *Journal of Business Research*, Vol. 20, 1990, pp. 13–21.
2. For an overview of managerial research findings, see Leonard L. Berry, A. Parasuraman, and Valarie A. Zeithaml, "Improving Service Quality in America: Lessons Learned," *Academy of Management Executive*, Vol. 8, No. 2, 1994, pp. 32–45.
3. J. Brock Smith and Donald W. Barclay, "The Effects of Organizational Differences and Trust on the Effectiveness of Selling Partner Relationships," *Journal of Marketing*, January 1997, pp. 3–21.
4. Christine Moorman, Rohit Deshpande, and Gerald Zaltman, "Factors Affecting Trust in Market Research Relationships," *Journal of Marketing*, January 1993, pp. 81–101.
5. Lawrence A. Crosby, Kenneth R. Evans, and Deborah Cowles, "Relationship Quality in Services Selling: An Interpersonal Influence Perspective," *Journal of Marketing*, July 1990, pp. 68–81.
6. Patricia M. Doney and Joseph P. Cannon, "An Examination of the Nature of Trust in Buyer-Seller Relationships," *Journal of Marketing*, April 1997, pp. 35–51.
7. Susan M. Keaveney, "Customer Switching Behavior in Service Industries: An Exploratory Study," *Journal of Marketing*, April 1995, pp. 71–82.

8. Leonard L. Berry, *On Great Service: A Framework for Action* (New York: Free Press, 1995), pp. 80–81.

9. The interpersonal treatment of individuals in a justice context sometimes is presented as the separate category of Interactional Justice. See, for example, R. J. Bies and J. S. Moag, "Interactional Justice: Communication Criteria of Fairness," in R. J. Lewicki et al. [Eds.], *Research on Negotiation in Organizations* (Greenwich, CT: JAI Press, 1986).

10. This paragraph and the two preceding paragraphs are based on Kathleen Seiders and Leonard L. Berry, "Service Fairness: What It Is and Why It Matters," *Academy of Management Executive*, May 1998, pp. 8–20.

11. See Helen Axel, *HR Executive Review: Implementing the New Employment Compact*, Vol. 4, No. 4, 1997.

12. Robert M. Morgan and Shelby D. Hunt, "The Commitment-Trust Theory of Relationship Marketing," *Journal of Marketing*, July 1994, p. 23.

13. Moorman, Deshpande, and Zaltman, p. 82.

14. Julian B. Rotter, "A New Scale for the Measurement of Interpersonal Trust," *Journal of Personality*, Vol. 35, No. 4, 1967, p. 651.

15. See Valarie A. Zeithaml, Leonard L. Berry, and A. Parasuraman, "The Nature and Determinants of Customer Expectations of Service," *Journal of the Academy of Marketing Science*, Vol. 21, No. 1, 1993, pp. 1–12, or Leonard L. Berry and A. Parasuraman, *Marketing Services: Competing Through Quality* (New York: Free Press, 1991), Chapter 4.

16. Leonard A. Schlesinger and James L. Heskett, "Breaking the Cycle of Failure in Service," *Sloan Management Review*, Spring 1991, pp. 17–28; also see James L. Heskett, W. Earl Sasser, Jr., and Leonard A. Schlesinger, *The Service Profit Chain* (New York: Free Press, 1997).

17. See Arlie Hochschild, *The Managed Heart: The Commercialization of Human Feeling* (Berkeley: University of California Press, 1983) and Benjamin Schneider and David E. Bowen, *Winning the Service Game* (Boston: Harvard Business School Press, 1995).

18. Sandra L. Robinson, "Trust and Breach of the Psychological Contract," *Administrative Science Quarterly*, Vol. 41, 1996, pp. 574–99. This study is summarized in Charley Braun, "Organizational Infidelity: How Violations of Trust Affect the Employee-Employer Relationship," *Academy of Management Executive*, Vol. 11, No. 4, 1997, pp. 94–95.

19. See Nirmalya Kumar, "The Power of Trust in Manufacturer-Retailer Relationships," *Harvard Business Review*, November-December 1996, p. 97.

20. Kumar, pp. 95, 97.

21. This research is summarized in John T. Landry, "Supply Chain Management— The Value of Trust," *Harvard Business Review*, January-February 1998, pp. 18–19.

22. Barnes, James G, "The Issues of Establishing Relationships with Customers in Service Companies: When Are Relationships Feasible and What Form Should They Take?" Paper presented at Frontiers in Services Conference, American Marketing Association and Vanderbilt University Center for Services Marketing, October 1994.

23. Morgan and Hunt, pp. 20–38.

24. Feargal Quinn, "Becoming a Customer-Driven Organization: Three Key Questions," *Managing Service Quality*, Vol. 6, No. 6, 1996, p. 6.

25. Leonard L. Berry, "Relationship Marketing of Services: Growing Interest, Emerging Perspectives," *Journal of the Academy of Marketing Science*, Vol. 23, No. 4, 1995, p. 237.

26. Kevin P. Gwinner, Dwayne D. Gremler, and Mary Jo Bitner, "Relational Benefits in Service Industries: The Customer's Perspective," *Journal of the Academy of Marketing Science*, Spring 1998, pp. 101–14.

27. Richard G. Barlow, "Relationship Marketing: The Ultimate in Customer Services," *Retail Control*, March 1992, p. 29.

28. Don Jackson, "The Seven Deadly Sins of Financial Services Marketing . . . and the Road to Redemption," *Direct Marketing*, March 1993, pp. 43–45, 79.

29. Czepiel, pp. 13–21.

30. See Leonard L. Berry, "Retailers with a Future," *Marketing Management*, Spring 1996, pp. 39–46.

31. Frederick F. Reichheld and W. Earl Sasser, Jr., "Zero Defections: Quality Comes to Services," *Harvard Business Review*, September-October 1990, pp. 105–111.

32. As discussed in Susan Fournier, Susan Dobscha, and David Glen Mick, "Preventing the Premature Death of Relationship Marketing," *Harvard Business Review*, January-February 1998, p. 48.

33. Don Peppers and Martha Rogers, *The One to One Future* (New York: Currency Doubleday, 1993), p. 141.

34. Berry, "Relationship Marketing of Services: Growing Interest, Emerging Perspectives," p. 238.

35. The concepts of dedication-based and constraint-based relationships are developed in Neeli Bendapudi and Leonard L. Berry, "Customers' Motivations for Maintaining Relationships with Service Providers," *Journal of Retailing*, Vol. 73, No. 1, 1997, pp. 15–37. This section is based on a part of this article.

36. Morgan and Hunt, pp. 25–26.

37. Scott M. Stanley and Howard J. Markman, "Assessing Commitments in Personal Relationships," *Journal of Marriage and the Family*, August 1992, pp. 595–608.

38. Richard Cross and Janet Smith, *Customer Bonding* (Chicago: NTC Business Books, 1995).

Chapter 8. Investment in Employee Success

1. The material on Cora Griffith is drawn from personal interviews with her, observation, and the article, "Sincerely, Cora" published by *Fox Magazine* in its 1996 Holiday Issue.

2. Leonard L. Berry, *On Great Service: A Framework for Action* (New York: Free Press, 1995), pp. 194–95.

3. See Ellyn A. McColgan, "How Fidelity Invests in Service Professionals," *Harvard Business Review*, January-February 1997, pp. 137–43.

4. As quoted in Gina Imperato, "Dirty Business, Bright Ideas," *Fast Company*, February-March 1997, p. 89.

5. Leonard L. Berry, "Leading for the Long Term," *Leader to Leader*, Fall 1997, p. 36.
6. "Key to Success: People, People, People," *Fortune*, October 27, 1997, p. 232.

Chapter 9. Acting Small

1. Howard Schultz, *Pour Your Heart Into It* (New York: Hyperion, 1997), pp. 275–76.
2. For some fascinating case studies of companies beyond the sample that illustrate this point, see: Rob Walker, "Back to the Farm," *Fast Company*, February-March 1997, pp. 112–22 (about Rosenbluth International); Richard Teitelbaum, "The Wal-Mart of Wall Street," *Fortune*, October 13, 1997, pp. 128–30 (about Edward Jones); and Alan M. Webber and Heath Row, "Do You Organize Around Customers?" *Fast Company*, October-November 1997, p. 136 (about People-Soft, Inc.).

Chapter 10. Brand Cultivation

1. Lynn O'Dell, "The Inside Story," *Los Angeles Times*, Orange County, Section N, June 1, 1996, pp. 1–2.
2. See Leonard L. Berry and A. Parasuraman, *Marketing Services: Competing Through Quality* (New York: Free Press, 1991), Chapter 7.
3. Howard Schultz, *Pour Your Heart Into It* (New York: Hyperion, 1997), p. 247.
4. Leonard L. Berry, "Branding the Store," *Arthur Andersen Retailing Issues Letter*, September 1997, p. 1.
5. Kevin Lane Keller, "Conceptualizing, Measuring, and Managing Customer-Based Brand Equity," *Journal of Marketing*, January 1993, p. 2.
6. Stephen King, as quoted in David A. Aaker, *Managing Brand Equity: Capitalizing on the Value of a Brand Name* (New York: Free Press, 1991), p. 1.
7. Tom Peters, *The Circle of Innovation* (New York: Alfred A. Knopf, 1997), p. 300.
8. See Seth Gordon, "Permission Marketing," *Fast Company*, April-May 1998, pp. 198–212.
9. As quoted in Roger Thurow, "A Sports Icon Regains Its Footing by Using the Moves of the Past," *Wall Street Journal*, January 21, 1998, p. A8. This example is based on this article.
10. "What Great Brands Do," an interview of Scott Bedbury by Alan M. Webber, *Fast Company*, August-September 1997, pp. 96–100.
11. Charlotte Beers, "Building Brands Worthy of Devotion," *Leader to Leader*, Winter 1998, p. 39.
12. Howard Schultz, p. 248.
13. Donald W. Hudler, "Leadership with Enthusiasm," a speech at Texas A&M University's Center for Retailing Studies Fall Symposium, Dallas, Texas, October 17, 1996.
14. Tom Peters, p. 457.
15. Berry and Parasuraman, p. 129.
16. See Mary C. Gilly and Mary Wolfinbarger, "Advertising's Internal Audience," *Journal of Marketing*, January 1998, pp. 69–88.

Chapter 11. Generosity

1. Ron Hawkins, "Family Mixes Morals, Marketplace," *Potomac News*, August 2, 1997, p. A1.
2. Bill Lohmann, "Big Brothers—Business, Civic Pursuits Make the Ukrops Richmond's Valued Customers," *Richmond Times-Dispatch*, August 14, 1994, p. G2.
3. Charlotte Beers, "Where Great Minds Become Good Friends," *Advertising Age*, August 4, 1997, p. 20.
4. Sandra A. Waddock and Samuel B. Graves, "The Corporate Social Performance—Financial Performance Link," *Strategic Management Journal*, 1997, pp. 303–19.
5. Charlotte Beers, "Building Brands Worthy of Devotion," *Leader to Leader*, Winter 1998, p. 40.
6. Frances Hesselbein, "A Traveler Along the Road," *Leader to Leader*, Spring 1998, p. 6.
7. James E. Austin, "The Invisible Side of Leadership," *Leader to Leader*, Spring 1998, p. 44.
8. Gregory J. Gilligan, "Ukrop's Donates $500,000 to J. Sargeant Reynolds," *Richmond Times-Dispatch*, p. C7.
9. This story was selected as a winner in LensCrafters' Hometown Day Most Inspiring Story contest for 1997. It was submitted by Valarie Smith of Store 576 in Towson, Maryland.
10. Much of the information in this section on Charles Schwab Corporation is based on a 1998 report written by Lita Benton, manager, community relations, Charles Schwab & Co., Inc.
11. Arie de Gues, "The Living Company," *Harvard Business Review*, March-April 1997, p. 57.
12. S. Truett Cathy, *It's Easier to Succeed Than to Fail* (Nashville: Oliver Nelson, 1989), p. 181.
13. Memorandum from Jeff Cole of Friends of The High School for Environmental Studies to Tom O'Brien of Special Expeditions, September 5, 1996.
14. Quoted in *A World of Possibilities*, a Special Expeditions booklet, p. 20.

Chapter 12. Lessons from World-Class Service Companies

1. Other research supports this assertion. See Jeffrey Pfeffer, "The Real Keys to High Performance," *Leader to Leader*, Spring 1998, pp. 23–29.
2. As quoted in Frances Hesselbein, "A Traveler Along the Road," *Leader to Leader*, Spring 1998, p. 7.
3. See Shannon Dortch, "Kaleidoscope: Boomer Dreams," *American Demographics*, January 1997, p. 27.
4. Leonard L. Berry and A. Parasuraman, *Marketing Services: Competing Through Quality* (New York: Free Press, 1991), p. 181.
5. Leonard L. Berry, *On Great Service: A Framework for Action* (New York: Free Press, 1995), pp. 154–55.

INTERVIEWEES AND
OTHER CONTRIBUTORS

Bergstrom Hotels

Lisa Barry
Richard Batley
Dick Bergstrom
John Bergstrom
Patrick Berndt
Ellen Brown
Robert Dove, Jr.
Gloria Erickson
Tamara Erickson
Cora Griffith

Jean Kasper
David Krumplitsch
Keith Martin
Pat Molash
Mitch Morrison
Dean Murzello
Pam Padilla
Anthony Reese
Shirley Rohloff
Daniel Schetter

Michelle Schewe
Scott Schwandt
Mary Ellen Scieszinski
Gerald Smith
Marc Snyder
Shirley Tesch
Stephen Tyink
Eike Van Horn
Paula Walters
Ben Weyenberg

The Charles Schwab Corporation

Lita Benton
Joan Joyner
Holly Kane
Jim Losi

Susanne Lyons
Nancy Mitchell
David Pottruck
Eric Salz

Elizabeth Sawi
Eileen Schloss
Leonard Short III
Mark Thompson

Chick-fil-A, Inc.

Kenneth Bernhardt
(consultant)
Dan Cathy
Dwayne Craig
Todd Grubbs

Craig Hall
Wayne Hoover
Ed Howie
Linda McEntire
Craig Perry

Steven Robinson
Tim Tassopoulos
Huie H. Woods

The Container Store

Barbara Anderson
Elizabeth Barrett
Garrett Boone
Amy Carovillano
Nancy Donley
Peggy Doughty
Daren Fagan
Elaine Fuqua
Heidi Gingerich

Keath Hance
Diane Higgins
Mike Hoover
Natalie Levy
Karla Marie
Melani Meyer
Cindy Moore
John Mullen
Fernando Ramos

Danielle Raska
Melissa Reiff
Kip Tindell
Sharon Tindell
Sheila Tranguch
Jon Wavra
Marty Williams

Custom Research Inc.

Helen Ballhorn
Judy Corson
Janice Elsesser
Lisa Gudding
Patricia Hughes

Kaia Kegley
Diane Kokal
Rhonda Lind
Carolyn MacLeod
Laura Olson

Stephanie Parent
Jeffrey Pope
Christine Sharratt
Eileen Taylor
Jeanne Wichterman

Dana Commercial Credit

Tricia Akins
John Barry
James Beckham
Rodney Filcek
J. Stephen Gagne
Michael Gannon

Donna Marie Lilly
Gina Lumia
Laura Moore
Bruce Mullkoff
Robert Piernik
Barney Schoenfeld

Edward Shultz
Michael Springer
Steve Taylor
Jan Torley
Berk Washburn

Dial-A-Mattress

Luis Barragan
Napoleon Barragan
Jay Borofsky
Phildelis Cooper-Snell

Kathleen Desmond
Camellia Fleischman
Jennifer Grassano
Maureen Renneberg

Louise Siracusano
Michael S. Stern
Joe Vicens

Enterprise Rent-A-Car

Scott Bailey
Christy Conrad
Daniel Gass
Russell Hamilton
Rob Hibbard

Dick Janicki
Jeff Klein
Callaway Ludington
Scott MacDonald
Vicky Meehan

Joanne Peratis-Weber
Nathan Pickle
Mary Schmitz
Andrew Taylor
Monica Thompson

Midwest Express Airlines

Julie Ardell	Timothy Hoeksema	Sandra Opdahl
Randy Beres	Marie Johnson	Jo-Ann Parrino
Timothy Biondo	Patty Keepman	Lauri Phillips
Mary Blundell	Dory Klein	Mike Rabbitt
Frank Brenner	Kenneth Krueger	Jim Reichart
Denise Dembosky	Debbie Kujawa	Julie Zeikm Ruetz
Michael Desmond	Amy Jasniewski	Jill Schuetz
Beverly Donaldson	Michael Jilot	Jerry Scott
Carrie Ehley	Michelle Libesch	Brenda Skelton
Michael Filippell	James David Marks	Carol Skornicka
LouAnn Gifford	Steve Mathwig	Kristine Steck
Debbie Hanson	Tamara McClelland	Daniel Sweeney
Lauree Garcia Hart	Scott Milligan	Sonya Wilborn

Miller SQA

Deb Abraham	Robert Enders	Dave Mitchell
Douglas Bonzelaar	Del Ensing	Bix Norman
Bill Buhl	Steve Frykholm	Rick Vander Bie
Mabel Casey	Anita Greer	Gary Van Spronsen
Nathan Chandler	Linda Milanowski	Charles Vranian

Special Expeditions

Martin Albert, M.D.	Janet Hollander	Thomas O'Brien
Peter Butz	Bud Lehnhausen	Jill Russell
Pamela Fingleton	Sandra Levy	Jim Wilcox
Frank Gang	Sven-Olof Lindblad	Ross Wilson
Sharon Eva Grainger	William Lopez-Forment	
Margaret Hart	Lee Moll	

St. Paul Saints

Jody Beaulieu	Peter Orme	Dave Wright
Bill Fanning	Mike Veeck	

Ukrop's Super Markets, Inc.

Jim Blackwell	Linda LaFoon	Scott Ukrop
Wade Carmichael	Debbye Mahan	Robert Ukrop
Cheryl George	Kathy Meadows	Mike Waldron
Bill Jackson	Kevin Rosenfeld	Roger Williams
Bob Kelley	Cathy Strobel	Tony Wiseman
Shannon Lacks	Scott Strobel	

USAA

Billy Bowen	Patty Garza	Pam Sanchez
Norma Villarreal Brooks	William James	Gina Santonastaso
Michael Burns	Donna Kirby	Gilbert Santos
Del Chisolm	Eunice McFall	Hal Schade
Edna City	Corrie McHugh	Allison Tomasini
Stacy Conger	Michael Merwarth	John Walmsley
Bill Cooney	Berniece More	Deborah White
Nancy Cuellar	Rudolph Ostovich III	Karen Wolfshohl
Norman Epstein	Susan Poteete	Jo Wynn
Lupe Flores	Paul Ringenbach	

INDEX

ABOUT THE AUTHOR

Leonard L. Berry holds the JCPenney Chair of Retailing Studies, and is Professor of Marketing and Director of the Center for Retailing Studies, at Texas A&M University. A former national president of the American Marketing Association, he is author of *On Great Service* and coauthor of *Marketing Services* and *Delivering Quality Service*. Dr. Berry received the 1996 Career Contributions to Services Marketing Award from the American Marketing Association. He also has twice been recognized with the highest honors Texas A&M bestows on a faculty member: the Distinguished Achievement Award in Teaching (in 1990) and the Distinguished Achievement Award in Research (in 1996). He is a board member of CompUSA, Hastings Entertainment, Lowe's Companies, Inc., and the Council of Better Business Bureaus.